IMAGES
of America

HELOTES

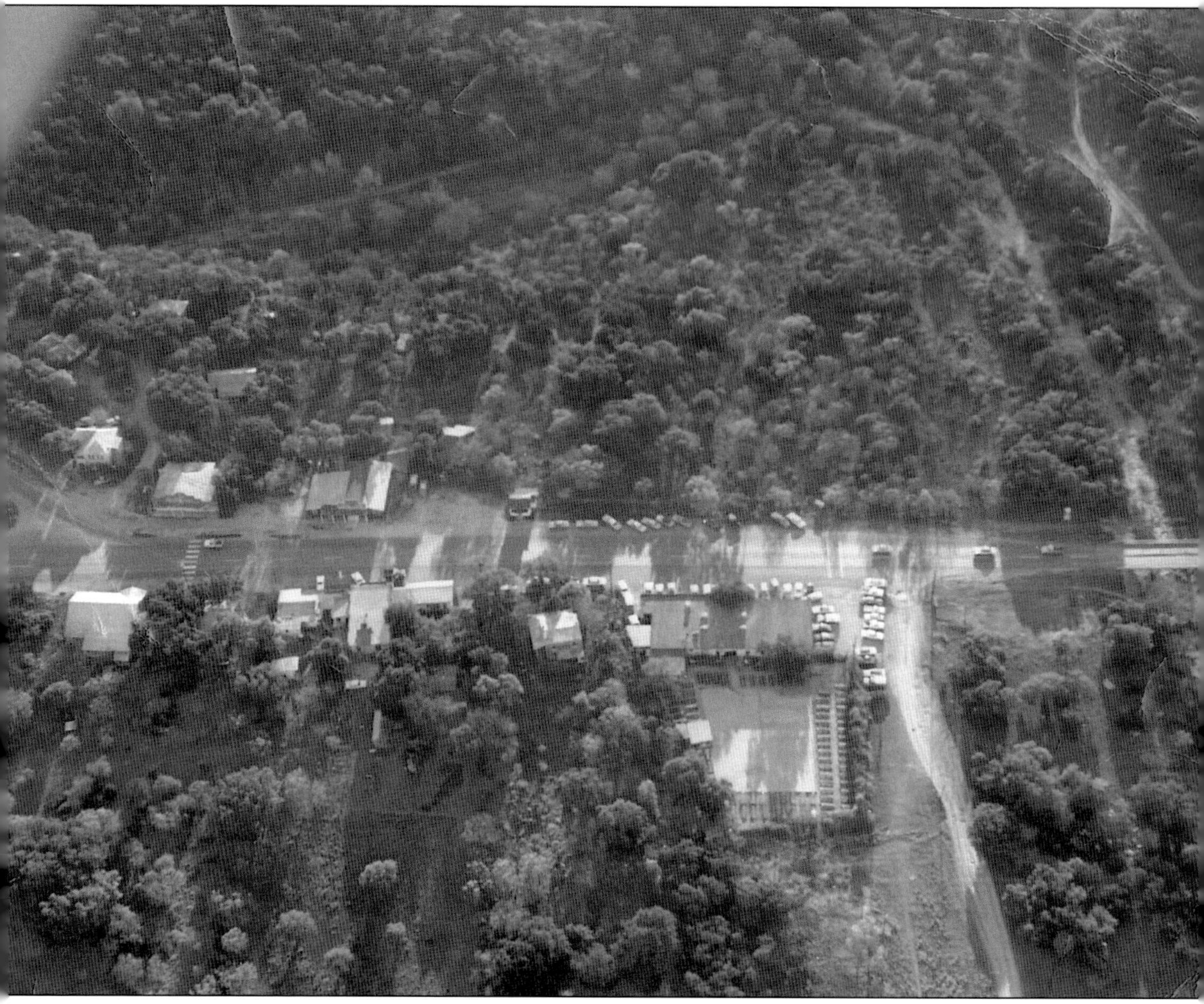

This 1970 aerial photograph of downtown Helotes, now the Old Town Helotes District, shows Bandera Road before the new highway was built in 1974. When the Texas State Highway Department began a campaign to make Bandera Road a four-lane divided highway and move it to the east of downtown Helotes, John T. Floore argued that it would kill downtown businesses—in particular, his own. Ultimately, the new highway, which was constructed behind his famous dance hall and patio, seen in the lower-right portion of the photograph, proved to be a boon. (Courtesy of Byron Faust.)

On the Cover: This photograph of Floore Country Store, which opened in 1946 in downtown Helotes, commemorates the 1949 completion of "the largest patio in the Southwest," as John T. Floore dubbed the big concrete slab attached to the back of his famous dance hall and music venue. A large crowd, including children from Helotes Elementary School, turned out for the event, which was aired on the radio. In 2005, John T. Floore Country Store was honored with a Texas Historic Landmark designation and a listing in the National Register of Historic Places. (Courtesy of John T. Floore Country Store.)

IMAGES
of America

HELOTES

Cynthia Leal Massey

ARCADIA
PUBLISHING

ISBN 978-0-7385-7944-3

Published by Arcadia Publishing
Charleston, South Carolina

Printed in the United States of America

Library of Congress Control Number: 2010928309

For all general information, please contact Arcadia Publishing:
Telephone 843-853-2070
Fax 843-853-0044
E-mail sales@arcadiapublishing.com
For customer service and orders:
Toll-Free 1-888-313-2665

Visit us on the Internet at www.arcadiapublishing.com

This book is dedicated to Shirley A. Owen, president of the Historical Society of Helotes, for 30-plus years of volunteerism, much of it in the pursuit of preserving local and regional history.

Contents

Acknowledgments 6

Introduction 7

1. Early Settlement 9
2. Entrepreneurs 31
3. Schools and Churches 49
4. Recreation and Civic Activities 65
5. Farm and Ranch Life 83
6. Connecting Communities 93
7. John T. Floore Country Store 101
8. Cornyval, Spring Festival 113
9. A City Is Born 121

Historical Society of Helotes 126

Index 127

ACKNOWLEDGMENTS

This book could not have been produced without the cooperation of many individuals and entities. I'd first like to acknowledge the contributions of the late Lucy Perkins Brown, founder and editor of the *Helotes Echo* and cofounder of the Helotes Historical Society, and her husband, the late Charles O. Brown, publisher of the *Helotes Echo*, for donating old issues of the newspaper and its photograph archives to the historical society. The newspapers and photographs covering the 1960s through the end of the 1980s were invaluable resources for this book. I'd also like to thank past historical society boards for their efforts in keeping the archives together in the face of great difficulty.

Helotes is fortunate to have many family historians, names you will see in the courtesy lines after each caption—their contributions are deeply appreciated. I'd like to acknowledge two especially: Fred W. Wendt and Juanita "Janie" Madla provided photograph collections that are not only extensive but also well catalogued and documented. I'd like to acknowledge the help of the following for providing photographs and/or information: Estella Algueseva, Daisy Anderson, Mort Ault, Bill Barker, Jim and Maxine Benke, Mary Jane Blanco, Christine Castro, Walton and Patty Daugherty, Cynthia Elizondo, Pascual Gonzalez, Allison Hyde, Emma Leal, Becky Logan, Jim McKinney, Becca Payne, Tiffany Singleton, Sarah "Vi" Swift, Nora Villarreal, Cheryl Ryder, and Diane Wootton.

Special thanks to the City of Helotes staff for their unflagging courtesy as I located photographs in the city archives, and to city administrator Rick Schroder for allowing the historical society to place its archives in the safekeeping of the town's municipal building pending a permanent home. I'd also like to acknowledge Bexar county clerk Gerry Rickhoff for spearheading the effort to place Bexar County's historical land records online, Spanish archivist Alfred Rodriguez for his courteous support, and the staffs of the San Antonio Public Library Texana/Genealogy Department and the Institute of Texan Cultures for providing a valuable service to historians.

Finally, I'd like to thank my colleagues on the Historical Society of Helotes board of directors for their steadfast support and efforts to keep our town's history alive.

INTRODUCTION

Helotes (pronounced *hel-LO-tes*), a Texas town 20 miles northwest of downtown San Antonio, dates back to the 1850s when the first European and Mexican pioneers settled the area. On Bandera Road, also called Texas State Highway 16, between the towns of Bandera in Bandera County and San Antonio in Bexar (pronounced Bear) County, Helotes became a stagecoach stop in the 1860s. After a post office was established in 1873, the settlement was included on county maps. Home of the famous John T. Floore Country Store dance hall and the annual Cornyval Festival, Helotes is known as a place to "let down yer hair and kick up yer heels." This hill country community, incorporated in 1981, took its name from the ancient creek that meanders through town, most prominently in its Old Town Helotes District.

Helotes comes from the Spanish word *elote*, which means stalk corn or corn on the cob. Although there is no definitive explanation for how the name originated, it is believed that Spanish explorers in the 18th century came upon cornfields along the creek and gave it the name.

The bucolic hill country environs along Helotes Creek were the campgrounds for bands of nomadic tribes that migrated seasonally in search of food and game. Lipan Apaches, Tonkawa, and Comanches roamed the Helotes hills well into the 19th century. Their constant attacks prevented permanent settlement until after Texas became part of the Union in 1845, and the United States established forts along the state's frontier.

Homestead grants given by the state brought settlers of many ethnic backgrounds to Helotes starting in the 1850s; however, a good number of pioneers purchased the land of their choice outright. Dr. George Frederick Marnoch, a Scottish surgeon who immigrated with his family in 1858, purchased almost 1,500 acres, 875 of them in the Helotes settlement, saying the hill country landscape reminded him of Scotland. Although the doctor was the original owner, both the ranch land and family homestead would become more associated with his eldest son, frontier naturalist Gabriel Wilson Marnoch.

German immigrants Carl and Amalie Mueller arrived in 1862 and established a stagecoach stop and inn a few miles southwest of the Marnoch ranch. In 1873, Carl became the town's first postmaster. After his death five years later, his wife took over the position.

In late 1880, Dr. Marnoch's heirs sold 110 acres to Arnold Gugger, son of Swiss immigrants, who had recently married Amalie "Molly" Benke, the daughter of German-Hungarian pioneers. The property, then known as "the Helotes crossing," included the intersection of Bandera Road (now called Old Bandera Road) and Helotes Creek. Well traveled, it was a prime location for commerce. Gugger built his family home, a general store, blacksmith shop, and a saloon, founding downtown Helotes in 1881.

Gugger's property displaced the original center of the Helotes settlement, the Mueller stagecoach stop and post office (now a private residence in Helotes Ranch Acres subdivision). In 1888, Gugger became postmaster, and downtown Helotes became firmly established. Nevertheless, for several decades, the town center, surrounded by large farms and ranches, remained little more than a "cow town," a few buildings on either side of a dusty, packed earth road wide enough to accommodate cattle drives.

Wilbert "Bert" Hileman purchased downtown Helotes in 1908, realizing its potential as a destination for city folks looking for recreation. He built the town's first dance hall in 1913. Called Hileman's Hall [and] Scenic Loop Pool Room, the venture was a rollicking success, setting the stage for the town's reputation as a place for good music and dancing.

Hileman sold the property to the Gottschalck family, who ran a mercantile for three years. By 1919, the land had passed to Kate and James Riggs, who built one of the town's first gas stations and garages, and who began to subdivide and sell off portions of the downtown property. Riggs also brought John T. Floore to town to work at his Red and White Grocery Store in 1942.

Like Hileman, Floore saw potential in the dusty little town of Helotes. A showman and astute businessman, he took note of the crowd on the weekends at the Helotes Inn dance hall (the original Hileman dance hall). By 1946, he had purchased almost 17 acres downtown, erecting Floore Country Store, his legacy to Helotes, and ultimately, to the world of country music. His vision to bring top-rated country musicians to his dance hall was realized in the next few decades, putting Helotes on the world map.

As the town center grew, so did civic and religious organizations. One-room schoolhouses on donated ranch land made way for a consolidated school district in 1950. The two wood-frame churches, Zion Lutheran (dedicated in 1906) and Our Lady of Guadalupe Catholic Church (built in 1908), gave way to more substantial buildings in the 1940s. Joining these established congregations in the 1960s were Baptist, Methodist, and Presbyterian denominations.

In early May 1966, the first Helotes Cornyval was held in downtown Helotes. Sponsored by the Lions Club and spearheaded by Floore, the spring festival was held in downtown Helotes to celebrate the opening of a new permanent post office there. Proceeds from the festival funded local nonprofits and was so popular it became an annual event, with a parade and the Miss Helotes Scholarship Pageant inaugurated the second year.

Cornyval is now held over a four-day period on the first weekend in May at the Helotes Festival Association Cornyval Grounds on Leslie Road, bringing an average of 30,000 people to Helotes over the long weekend. The festival includes a parade, carnival, rodeo, dances, and lots of food, including plenty of roasted corn on the cob.

Helotes remained primarily rural until the late-20th century when the sale of farmland to developers created a housing boom. In 1998, Sandra Day O'Connor High School opened with 1,848 students from Helotes and northwest San Antonio. Two years later, Helotes' population had grown to 4,295—three times its 1990 population. The town's 2010 population estimate is 10,000.

Despite its growth, Helotes retains a unique small town appeal. In 1992, the Texas Historical Commission awarded the town its first historical marker, recognizing it as a historic settlement. An Old Town Helotes revitalization project was completed in 2010, complementing its historic heritage. Renowned as much for its citizens' independent spirit as for its hill country landscape, frontier history, and fun-loving attitude, Helotes is the quintessential Texas town.

One

Early Settlement

In the 1850s, European and Mexican immigrants began arriving in the Helotes area to claim their 160 acres, public domain land offered by the State of Texas to induce pioneers to settle the wild frontier. These homesteaders were farmers, stock raisers, and day laborers, many with wives who listed themselves on early census forms as "Keeper of the House." The Europeans were primarily German immigrants who settled in the southeastern and western parts of Helotes on flat prairie. The Mexicans, descendants of 18th-century Spanish immigrants, moved to the hills in the northeast and northwest. The area was rich in springs and creeks, and wells never failed to reach water. The land lay over cavernous aquifers: the Edwards and Glen Rose/Trinity. The early pioneers lived 20 miles from downtown San Antonio, a full day's journey on horseback. They built homes of wood that no longer exist, others of limestone that stand today. From their arrival until the 1870s, they were under constant threat of raid by Comanches. Several settlers were killed, and thousands of horses and cattle stolen. Nevertheless, the pioneers were not easily intimidated. Their children intermarried, solidifying their ties to the land and to each other. They became the backbone of the settlement and the town that later became Helotes, Texas.

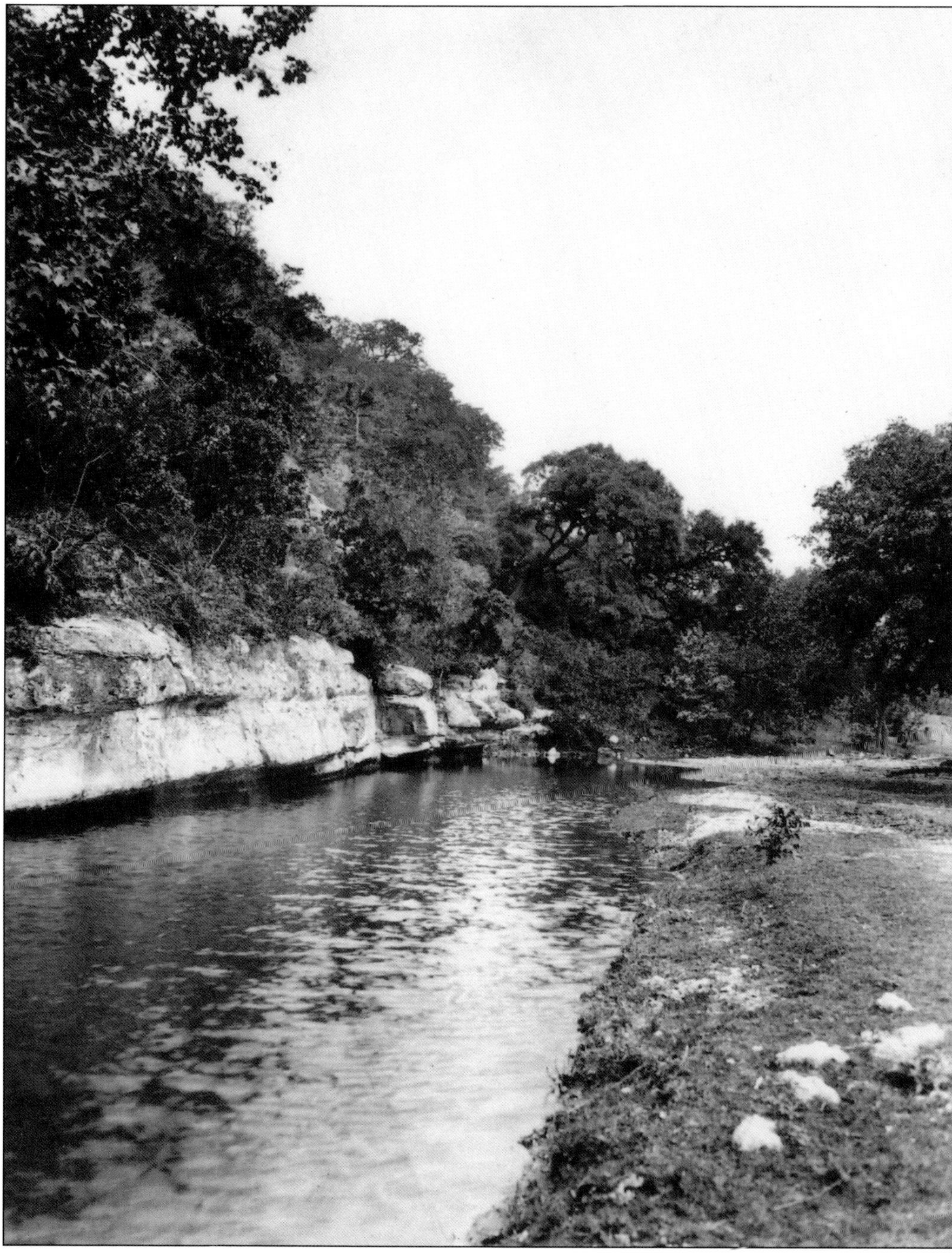

Nineteenth-century pioneers settled in northwest Bexar County on land along Helotes Creek and its tributaries, Los Reyes and Chimenea Creeks. Another tributary, Lee Creek, was named after a family that settled along its banks in the 1860s. This 1925 photograph shows Helotes Creek near its intersection at Bandera Road. Its headwaters are 2 miles north of the town of Grey Forest in northwestern Bexar County, and the creek runs south for 12 miles, through Helotes, to its mouth on Culebra Creek, near the junction of Loop 1604 and Farm Road 471. (Courtesy of Institute of Texan Cultures, Ellen Schultz Quillin Collection.)

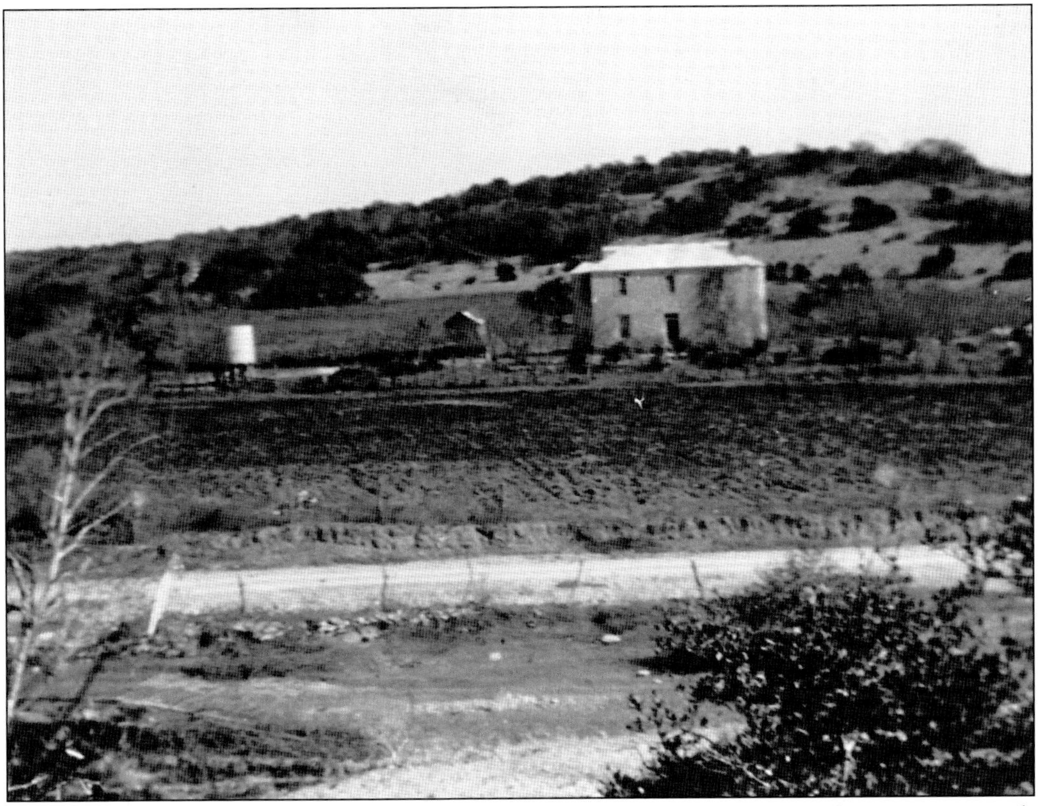

The Marnoch homestead, built in 1859, a half-mile north of the Helotes Creek intersection with Bandera Road, is the oldest residence in Helotes. The house, shown in these early 1900s photographs, was on a 1,500-acre ranch encompassing land that later became the town of Helotes. Dr. George Frederick Marnoch (1802–1870), a licentiate of the Royal College of Surgeons of Edinburgh, Scotland, immigrated with his family to Helotes in 1858 and commissioned San Antonio architect John M. Fries to build the unique home. In 2010, the Marnoch homestead received Texas Historic Landmark designation. (Above and below, courtesy of Greg and Rodenna Biering.)

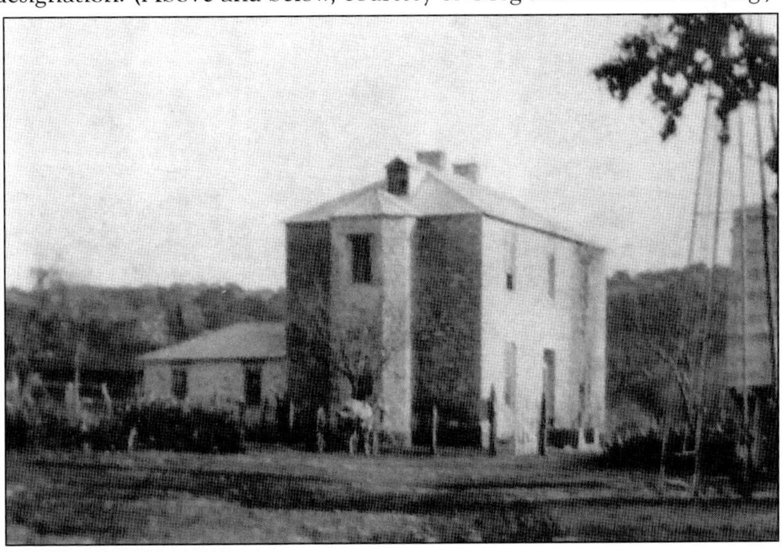

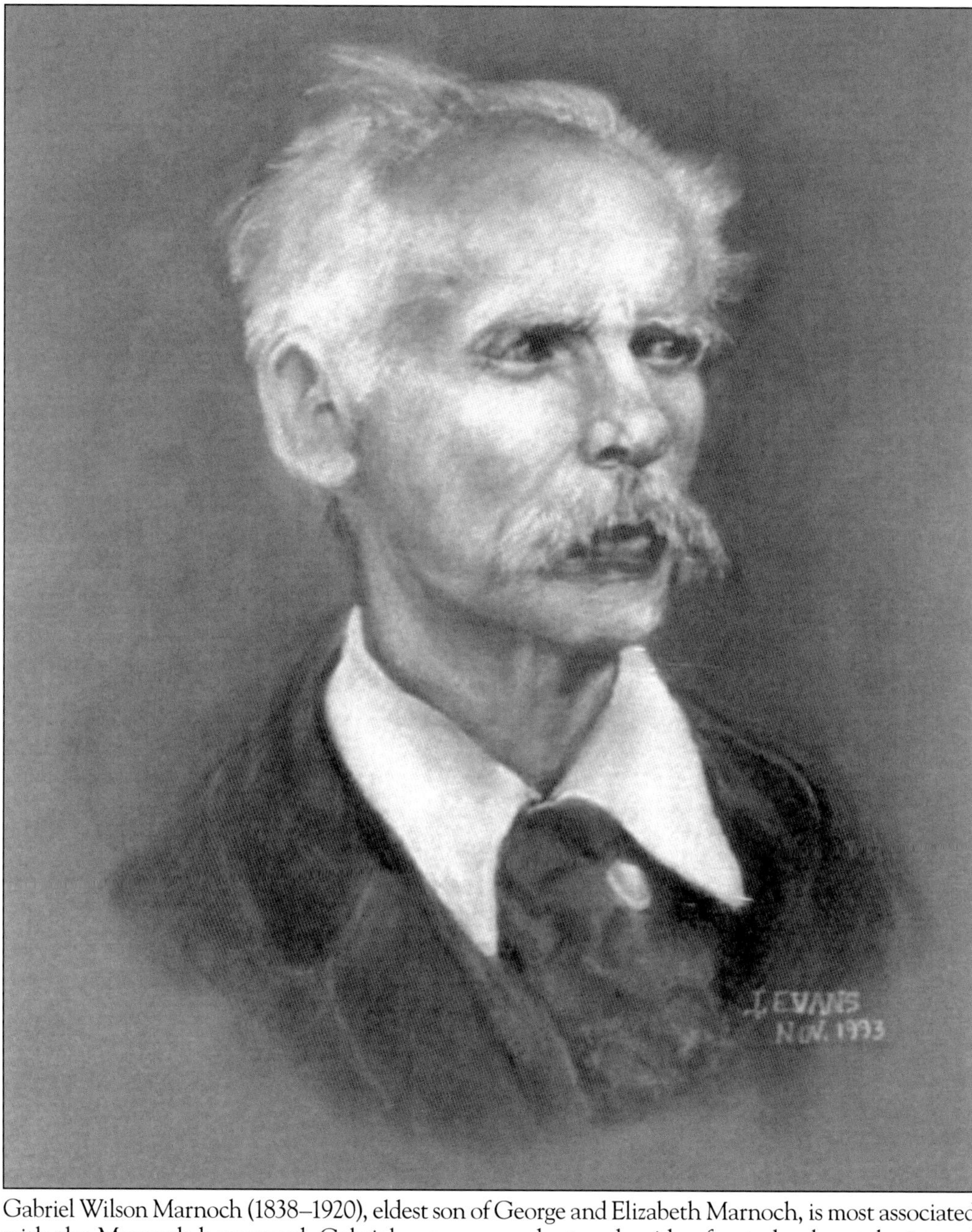

Gabriel Wilson Marnoch (1838–1920), eldest son of George and Elizabeth Marnoch, is most associated with the Marnoch homestead. Gabriel, a correspondent and guide of noted paleontologist and herpetologist Edward Drinker Cope, was a frontier naturalist who discovered two amphibian and two reptile species in the limestone cliffs in the Helotes hills, including the Cliff Chirping Frog, or *Eleutherodactylus (Syrrhophus) marnockii*. Marnoch was also interested in topography, taking geologist Dr. Robert T. Hill to an unusual outcropping in the Helotes hills in 1884. This became known as the Balcones Escarpment, a fault that divides Texas between the lowland and the upland. Marnoch was a Los Reyes School trustee and postmaster of Helotes from 1904 to 1919. He was also a founding member of the Scientific Society of San Antonio, serving as a corresponding member from 1904 until his death on February 4, 1920. (Courtesy of Marie Davis Steinhauer.)

Carmel Treviño (1862–1950) daughter of Helotes rancher Pedro Treviño and Manuela (Torres) Treviño, married Gabriel W. Marnoch in 1882. The couple raised nine children—Alfred, Robert, Gabriel, Charles, Margaret, Lucy, Agnes, Laura, and George—in the Marnoch homestead, which stayed in the family for 88 years. (Courtesy of Greg and Rodenna Biering.)

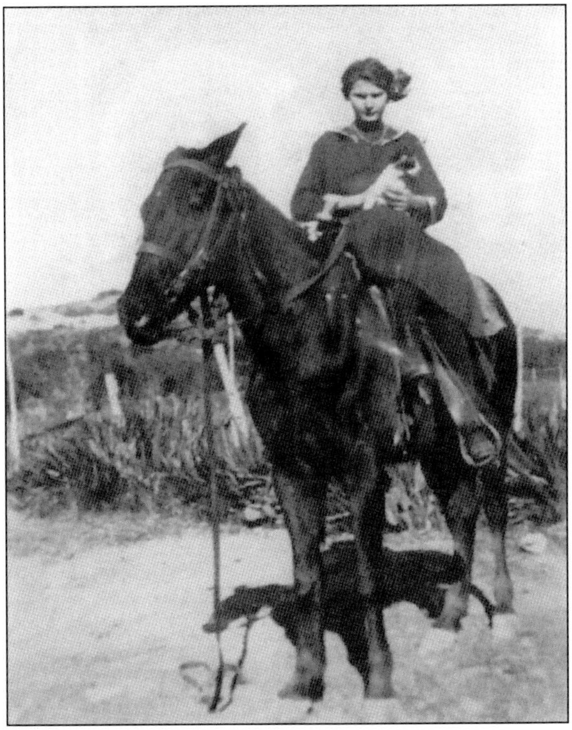

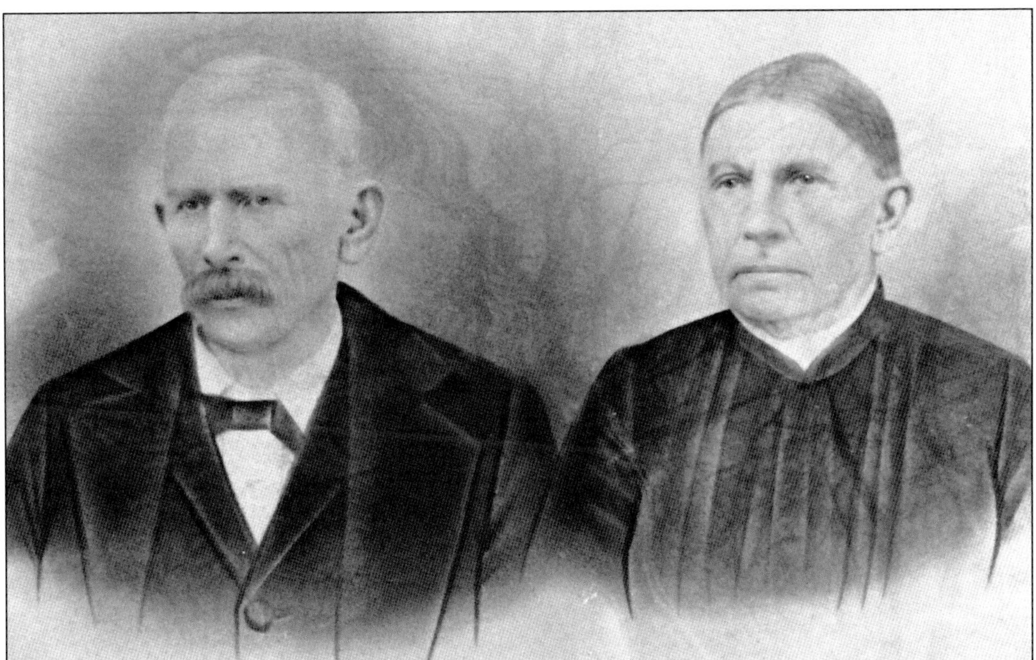

Pedro and Manuela (Torres) Treviño donated land for Helotes's first Catholic Church, built in 1908. After the church burned down, the land along Bandera Road was used for the Catholic cemetery. Family lore says that Gabriel Marnoch, at age 24, accompanied his father to the Treviño homestead and assisted in the delivery of the couple's first child, Carmel, who 20 years later became Marnoch's wife. (Courtesy of Emma Leal.)

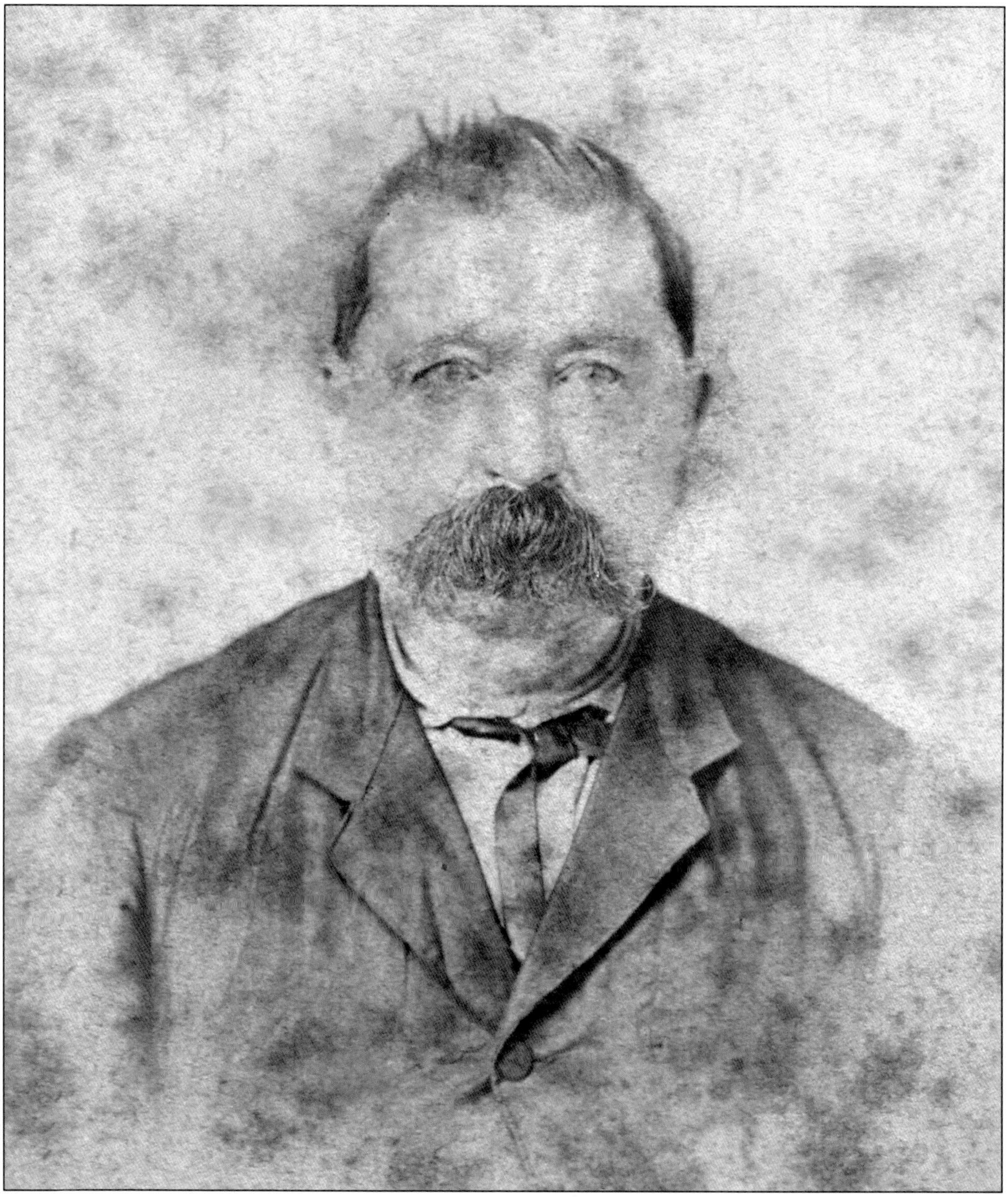

Anton Gugger (1807–1881) was a Bexar County justice of the peace, Precinct 2, which encompassed the Helotes area, from 1869 until 1876; he was also a county road supervisor. The Swiss-born Gugger immigrated with his wife Marie (1819–1911) to New York, where their daughter Mathilda was born. In 1849, the family moved to Texas, living for a while in San Antonio and Leon Springs, where Gugger began a freighting business transporting cotton, lime, and buffalo hides throughout south and central Texas in wagons pulled by ox teams. Three more children—Emma, Ida, and Arnold—were born to the couple. The family moved to Helotes in 1868, where Anton received a 160-acre land grant near present-day Loop 1604 and Braun Road. He started a rock quarry, hauling limestone to San Antonio and San Geronimo, and continued his freighting business until his death. Gugger's wife was a founder of Zion Lutheran Church of Helotes, donating land for the church and cemetery after her husband's death. (Courtesy of Fred W. Wendt.)

By the time Arnold Gugger, shown in this mid-1860s photograph, was eight, he was helping his father Anton transport merchandise throughout south Texas. He continued working in the freighting business until 1880 when he decided to strike out on his own in the mercantile business, detailed in the next chapter. (Courtesy of Fred W. Wendt.)

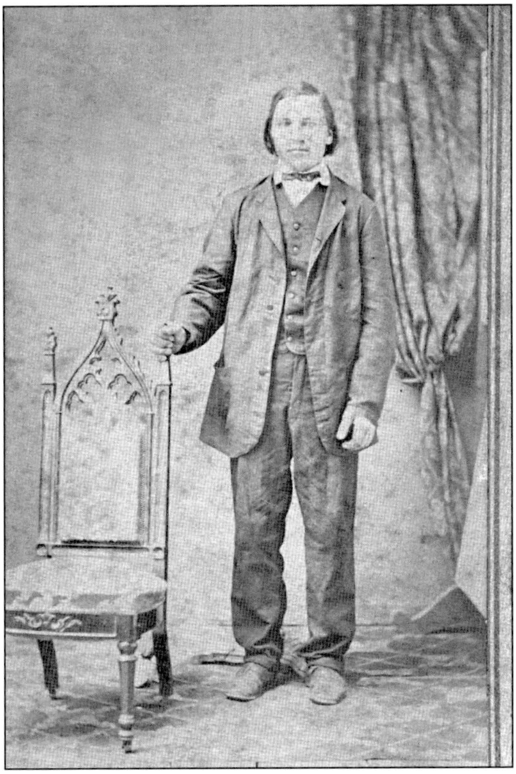

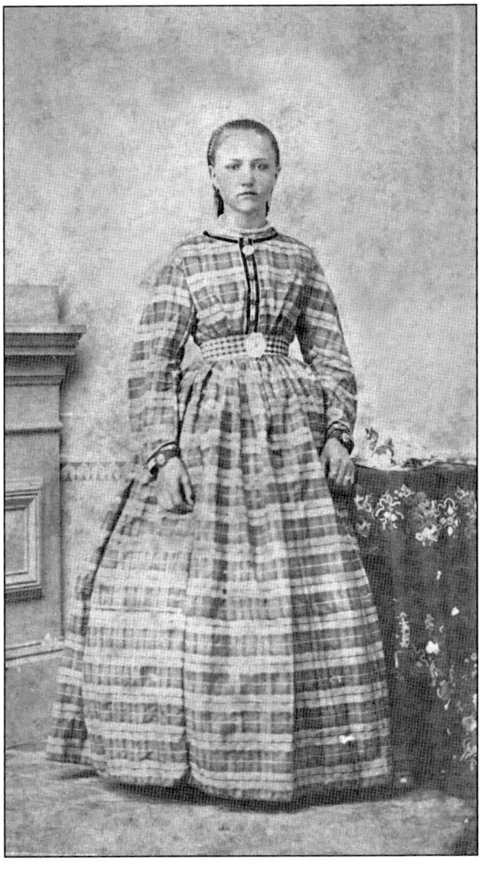

Mathilda Gugger, eldest daughter of Anton and Marie Gugger, married Friedrick Braun in 1866. The Gugger family lived on land adjacent to the Braun family. As was common in rural areas in the 19th century, young men often married the "girl next door." Descendants of Mathilda and Friedrick Braun number in the hundreds, and many still live in Helotes. (Courtesy of Fred W. Wendt.)

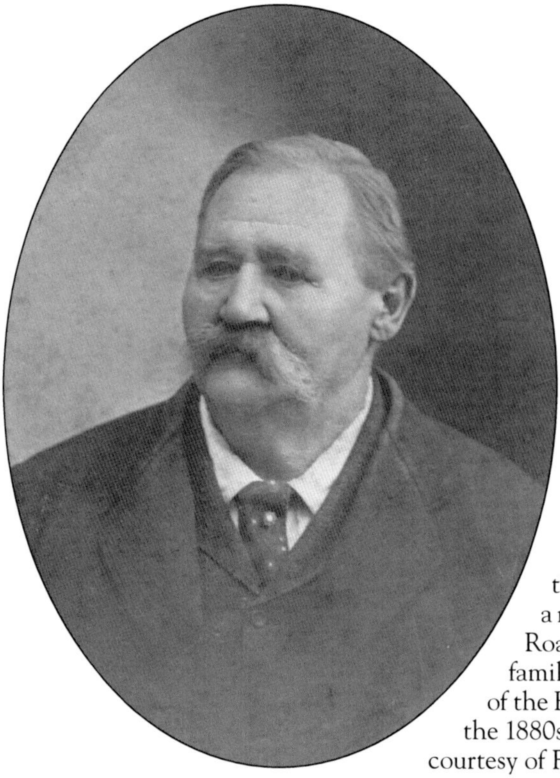

William Boerner (1833–1911), a Bexar County Commissioner from 1888 to 1896, and wife Emma (Gugger) Boerner donated land for Helotes's first public school in 1874. Built of rock near Helotes Creek and present-day Sandra Day O'Connor High School, the building was often referred to as the Boerner School. It was razed in 1902, and a new school was built on the west side of Leslie Road, also on property donated by the Boerner family. Emma opened a store in the southern part of the Helotes settlement, which she operated from the 1880s until her death in 1935. (At left and below, courtesy of Fred W. Wendt.)

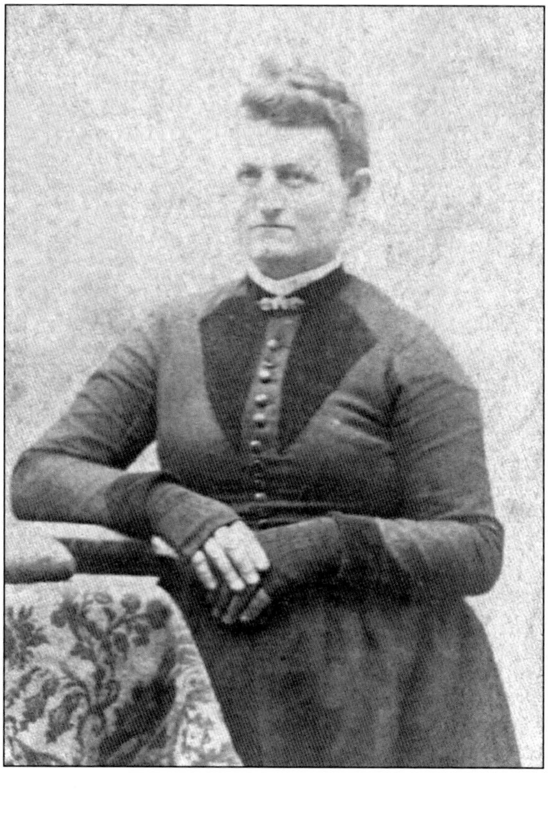

In this photograph taken after the funeral of Carl Mueller, Helotes's first postmaster and proprietor of the town's stagecoach stop, are from left to right, Amalie (Stolz) Mueller (1835–1928), nephew Karl Stolz, and sister Carolina (Stolz) Galm. Gabriel W. Marnoch shot and killed the postmaster on March 18, 1878, over a boundary dispute that turned into allegations of postal improprieties. After two trials and an appeal, the case against Marnoch was dismissed in 1887. (Courtesy of Mildred Galm.)

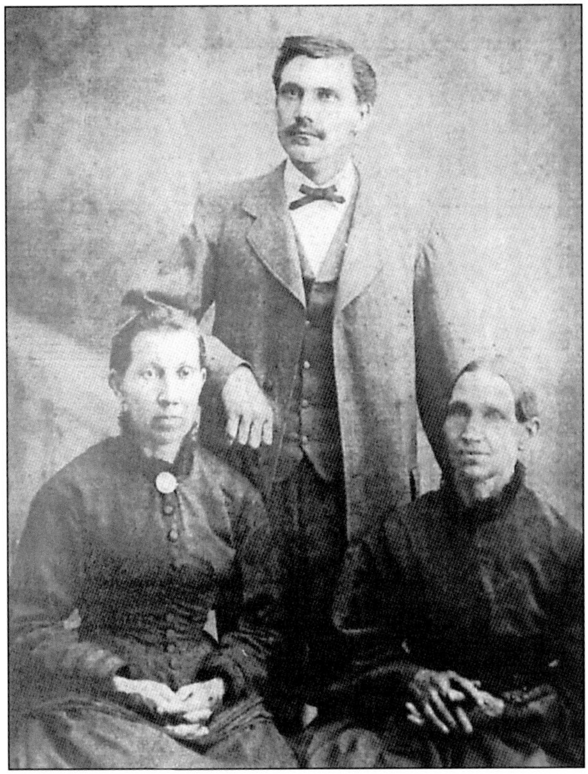

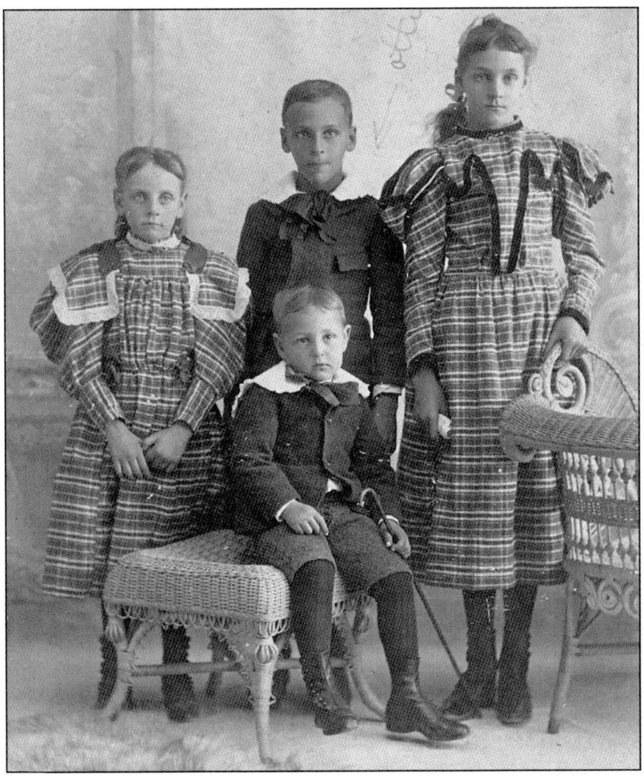

German immigrants Valentine and Carolina Galm moved to Helotes in 1870 with sons Edward, age 14, and Samuel, age 7. Edward married Sophie Bruhn and Samuel married Marie Biering. The four eldest children of Samuel and Marie Galm are shown in this 1896 photograph, (first row) sitting, Otto; left to right, (second row) Emma, Walter, and Amalia. The couple had five more children: Lillian, Henry, John, Fred, and Clarence. (Courtesy of Fred W. Wendt.)

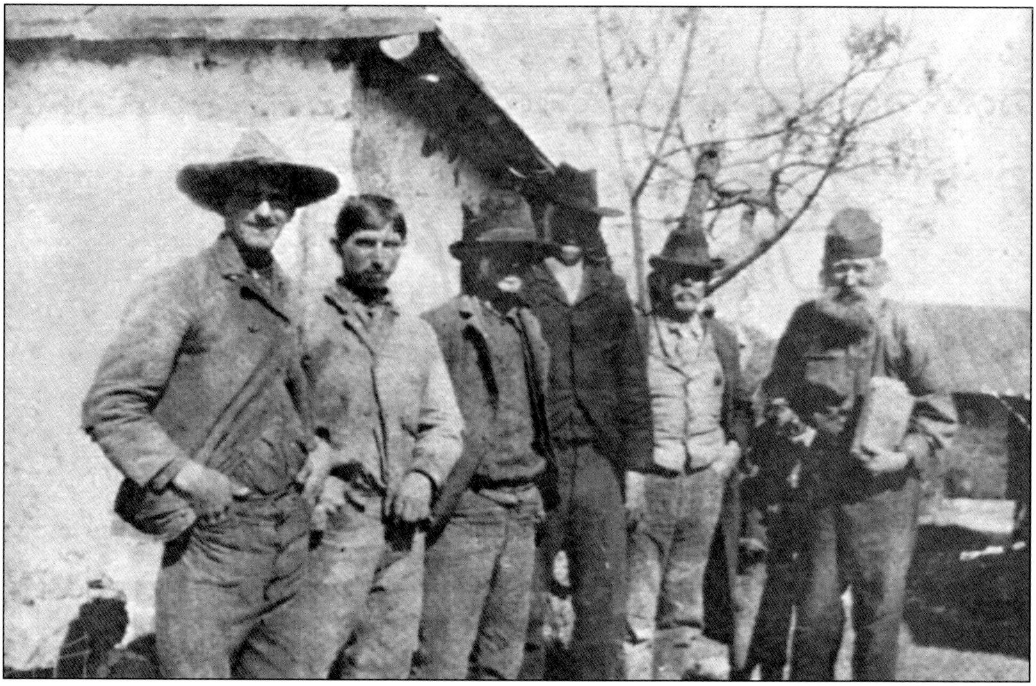

Alexander Benke (1824–1906) immigrated to Texas from Hungary in 1845, settling in Helotes in 1857. Together with his wife, German-born Anna Elise Schmidt, whom Benke married in 1858, he accumulated more than 1,400 acres. Shown in front of a bunkhouse at the Benke Ranch are, left to right, Louis Benke, Adolph Benke, ? Lee, ? Biering, Alexander J. Benke, and Alexander Benke. (Courtesy of Jim Benke.)

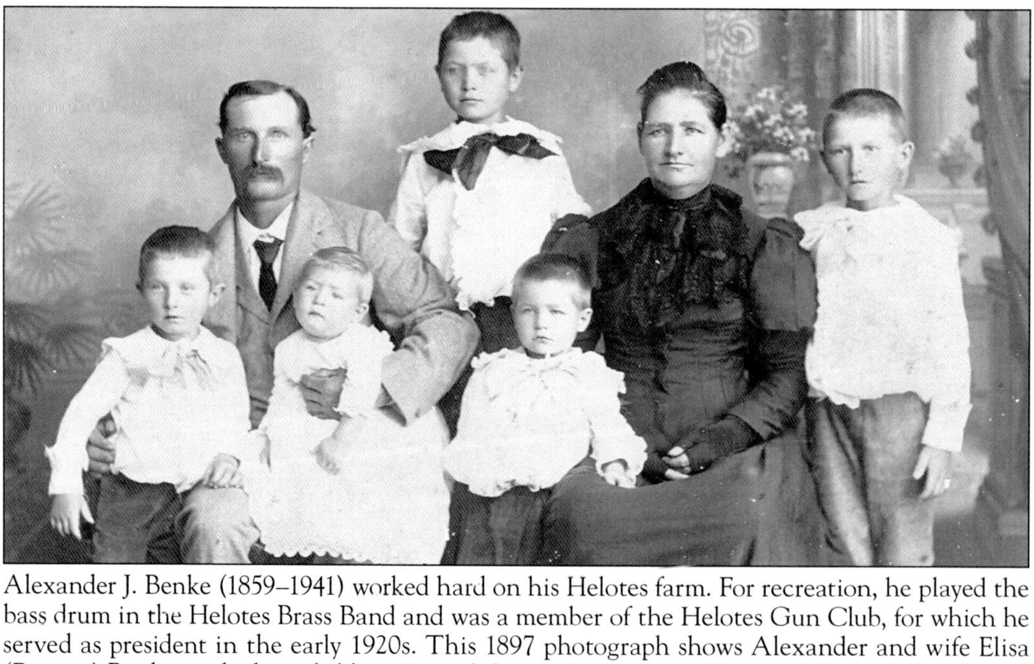

Alexander J. Benke (1859–1941) worked hard on his Helotes farm. For recreation, he played the bass drum in the Helotes Brass Band and was a member of the Helotes Gun Club, for which he served as president in the early 1920s. This 1897 photograph shows Alexander and wife Elisa (Biering) Benke, with their children. From left to right, they are (first row) Samuel, Ralph, and George; (second row) Theodore and Edwin. (Courtesy of Fred W. Wendt.)

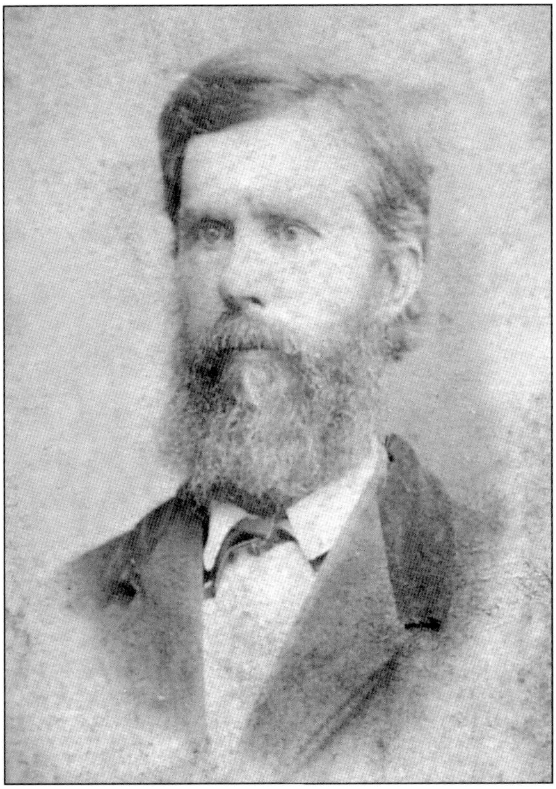

Shelly Augustine Lee (1828–1884), shown in this 1860s photograph, arrived in Texas in the mid-1850s. Born in Loudon, Tennessee, he was a skilled tinsmith. He quickly found a position and a wife, Jesusa María de la Garza (1839–1887), in the photograph below. Jesusa was the daughter of a prominent Spanish family in San Antonio. The couple married January 22, 1859, and by 1862, had moved to the Helotes hills and settled on 160 acres near a stream that would become known as Lee Creek. They had 15 children: Shelly Augustine "Gus," Joseph, Thomas, William, Susan, Evaline, Charles, Melissa, Sarah, Nancy, Ada, Robert, Jessie, Henry, and James. (At right, courtesy of Linda Bloom; below, courtesy of Steven Lee.)

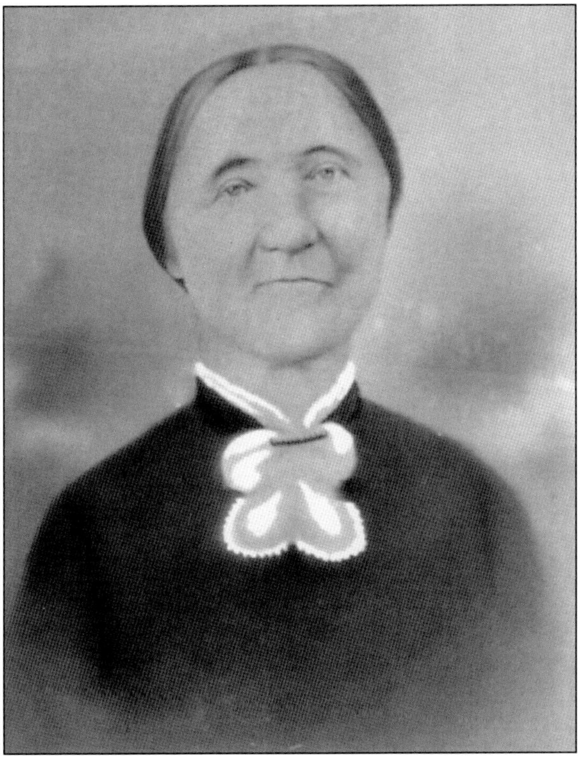

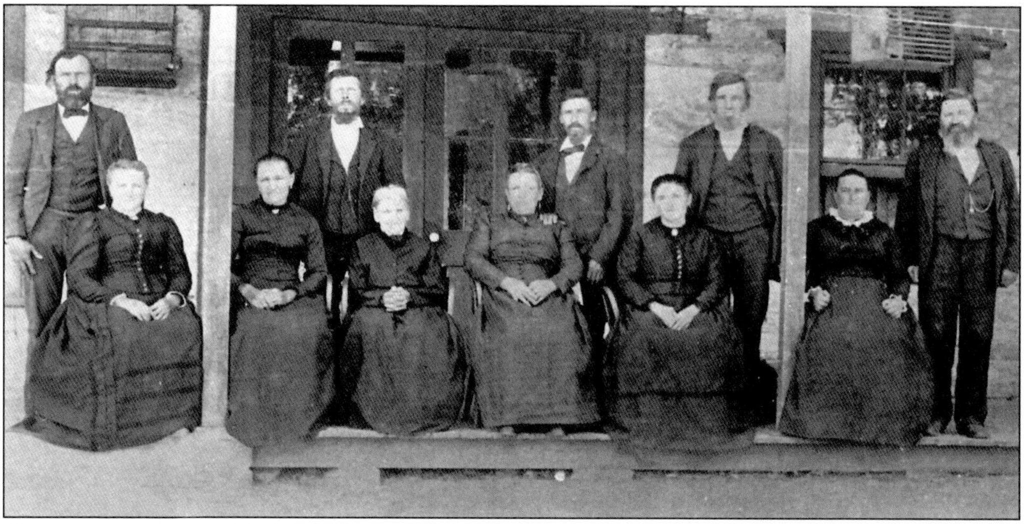

German immigrants Philip and Mara Susanna Braun and their children settled in Helotes in 1862. The family accumulated more than 3,000 acres. Shown in this 1887 photograph taken after Philip's funeral are, left to right, (first row) Susanna (Braun) Gass, Carolina (Braun) Ruempel, Mara Susanna Braun, Kathrina (Steubing) Braun, Carolina (Nickel) Braun, and Mathilda (Gugger) Braun; (second row) Carl Gass, Phillip Ruempel, Charles Braun, Wilhelm Braun, and Friedrick Braun. (Courtesy of Fred W. Wendt.)

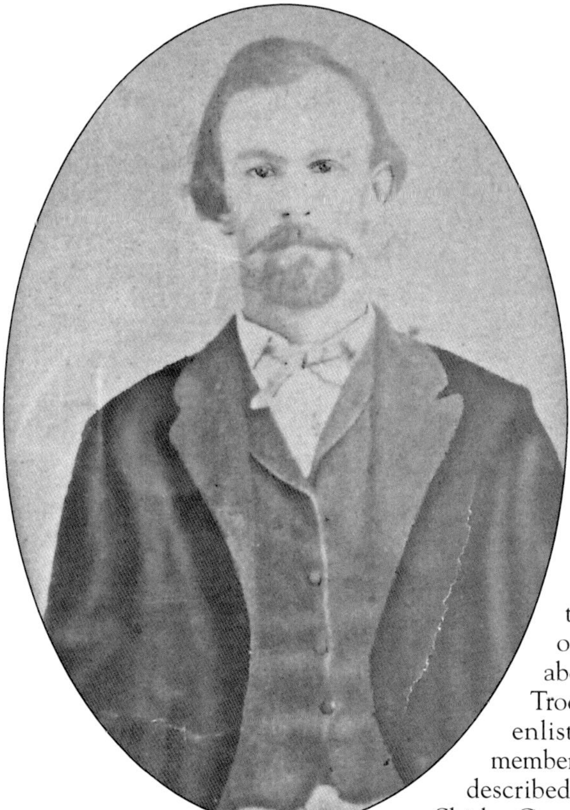

John F. Green, in this late-1860s photograph, raised horses on his Helotes ranch. After continuous raids by Comanches depleted the settlement's stock, Green and several others, including Charles Braun, shown above, joined a Texas Ranger Minute Men Troop. An experienced Indian fighter, Green enlisted as first sergeant. On July 9, 1873, a member of his troop killed him, in what was later described as an accidental shooting. (Courtesy of Shirley Green Sweet.)

Green's death left his wife, Augusta (Specht) Green, a widow with three children. Daughter of the first postmaster of Fredericksburg, Texas, she continued living on her husband's ranch and remarried twice, having two more children and outliving two more husbands. In this 1916 photograph, Augusta is with third husband Julius Ballscheit, whom she married in 1882, and their three grandchildren, Augusta (standing in back), Lillie, and Julius Braun. (Courtesy of Ruth Lampman.)

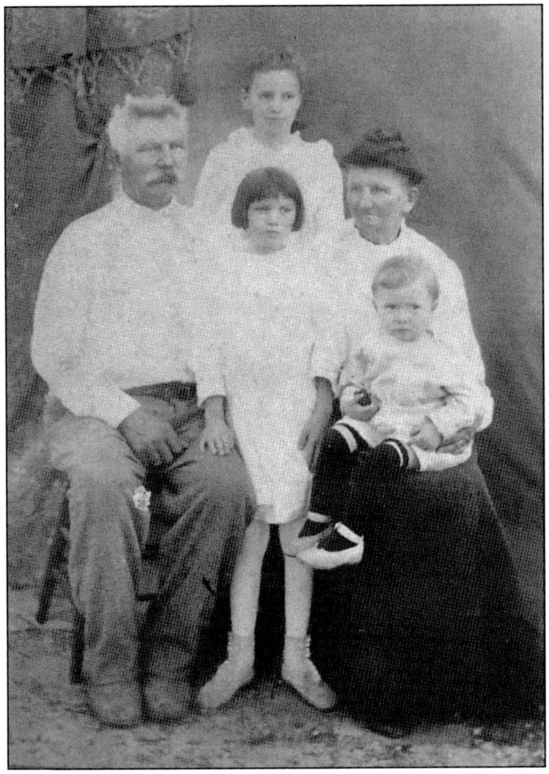

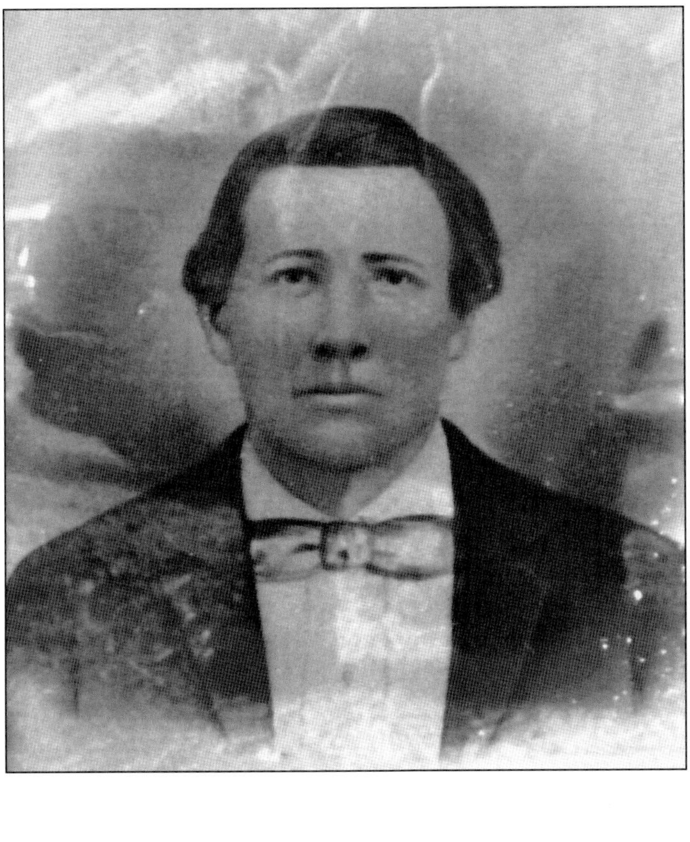

Frederick August Biering (1859–1906) was born in Helotes, the first of six children of German immigrants Friedrich August Biering and Marie Louise (Reis) Biering. By the spring of 1884, the family owned 1,678 acres of ranchland. Frederick married Emilie Hoffmann in 1883, and they had eight children: Henry, Alfred, Charles, Emil, Edward, Lena, Rose, and Fred. Numerous descendants still live in Helotes. (Courtesy of Fred W. Wendt.)

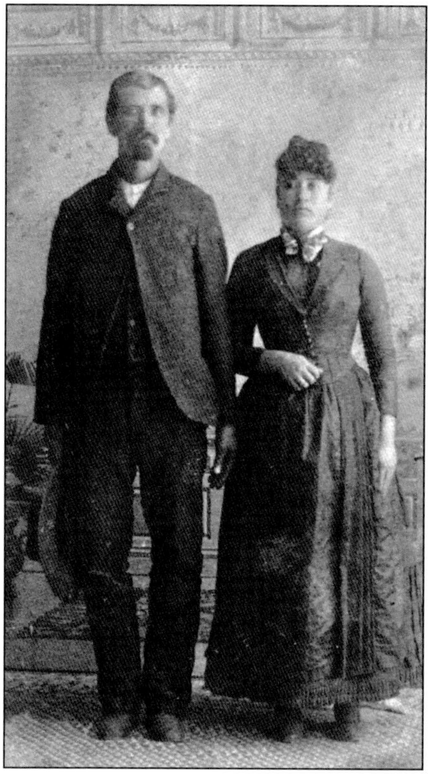

Menchaca Road, off Scenic Loop Road, was named for pioneer Francisco Menchaca and wife Catarina Garza, shown in this photograph taken after their March 26, 1867, wedding. Francisco, who was from Candela, Coahuila, Mexico, worked as a hired hand and night watchman at the Mueller Stagecoach Inn until obtaining an 160-acre homestead property where he farmed and raised livestock. He and Catarina had 13 children. (Courtesy of Juanita "Janie" Madla.)

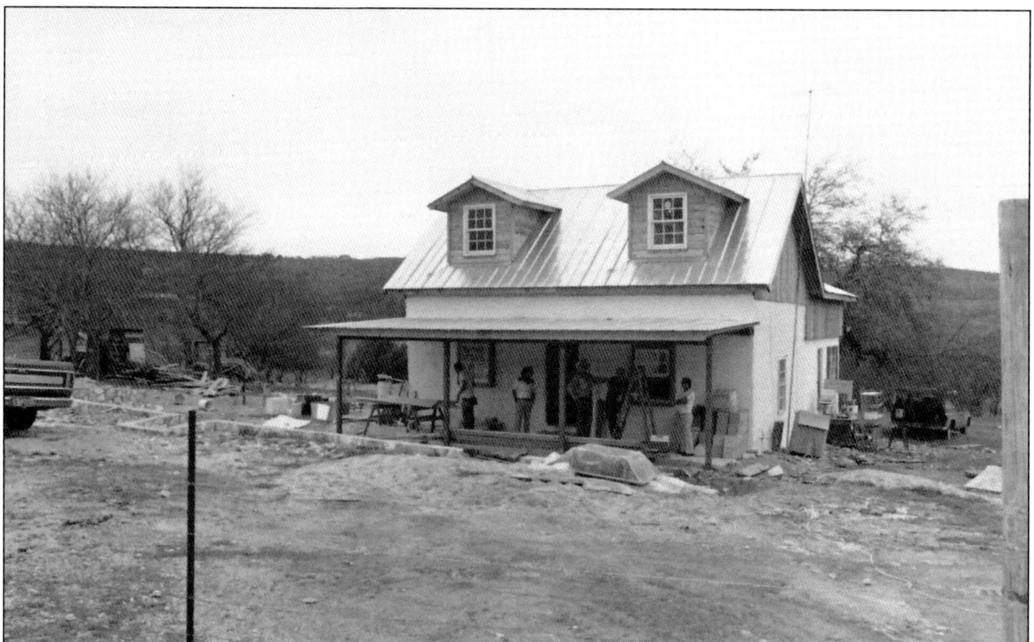

Francisco Menchaca built his family homestead in 1884. The photograph shows the homestead as it was being restored in 1981. Wilbur and Yolanda Algueseva Davis, who had purchased the property, initiated the restoration. Yolanda is a descendant of Helotes pioneers Mathias and Constantina Madla. (Courtesy of Historical Society of Helotes, HSH.)

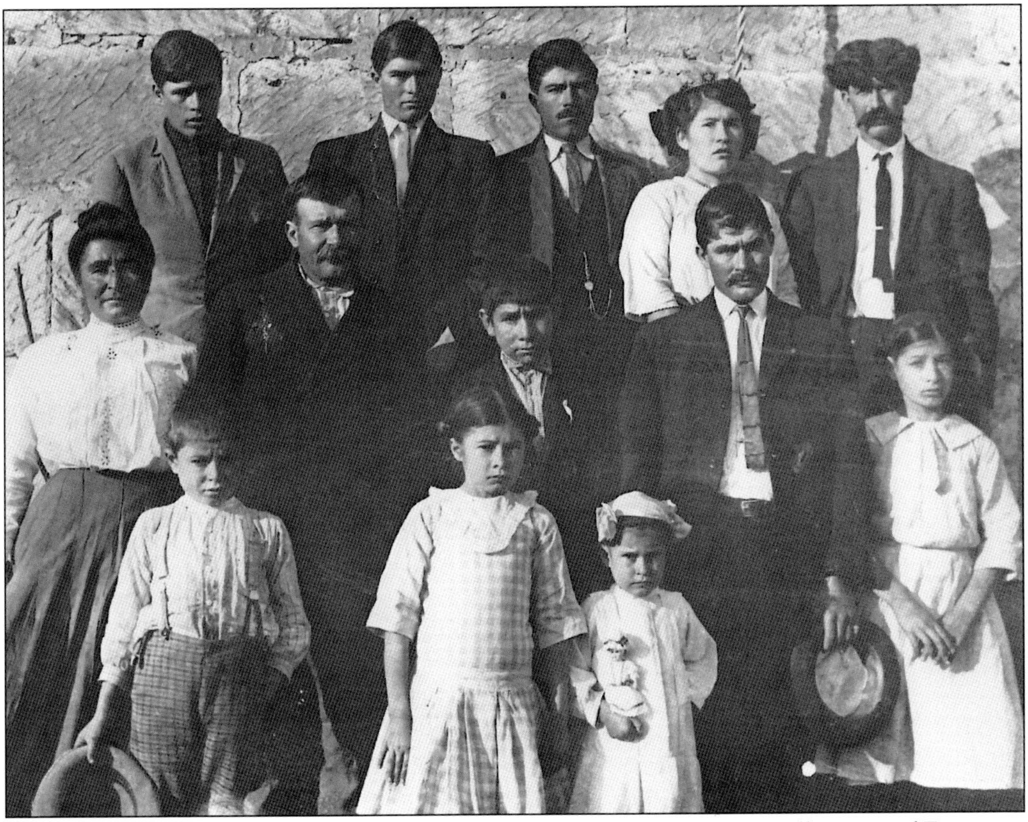

In 1889, Frank Madla, son of Polish pioneers Mathias and Constantina Madla, married Francisca Menchaca, daughter of Francisco and Catarina. Frank acquired more than 1,000 acres that became known as the Madla Ranch. In this 1912 photograph are, left to right, (first row) Frank (father of the late state senator), Concepción, and Eloisa; (second row) Francisca, Frank Sr., Cristobal, Juan, and Mary; (third row) Jesse, Felix, Manuel, Pasquelina, and Pasquelina's husband, Manuel Hernandez. (Courtesy of Juanita "Janie" Madla.)

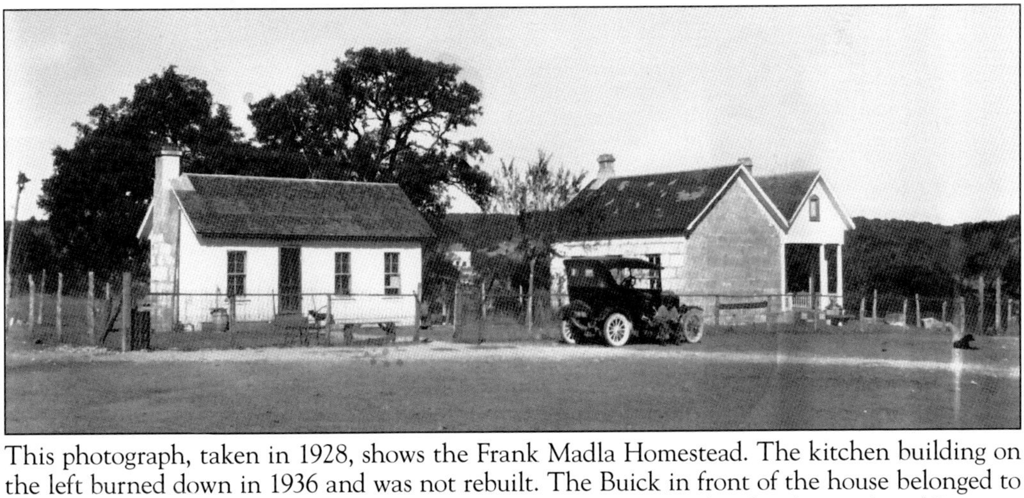

This photograph, taken in 1928, shows the Frank Madla Homestead. The kitchen building on the left burned down in 1936 and was not rebuilt. The Buick in front of the house belonged to Jesse Madla, who is sitting on the running board, along with another family member. (Courtesy of Juanita "Janie" Madla.)

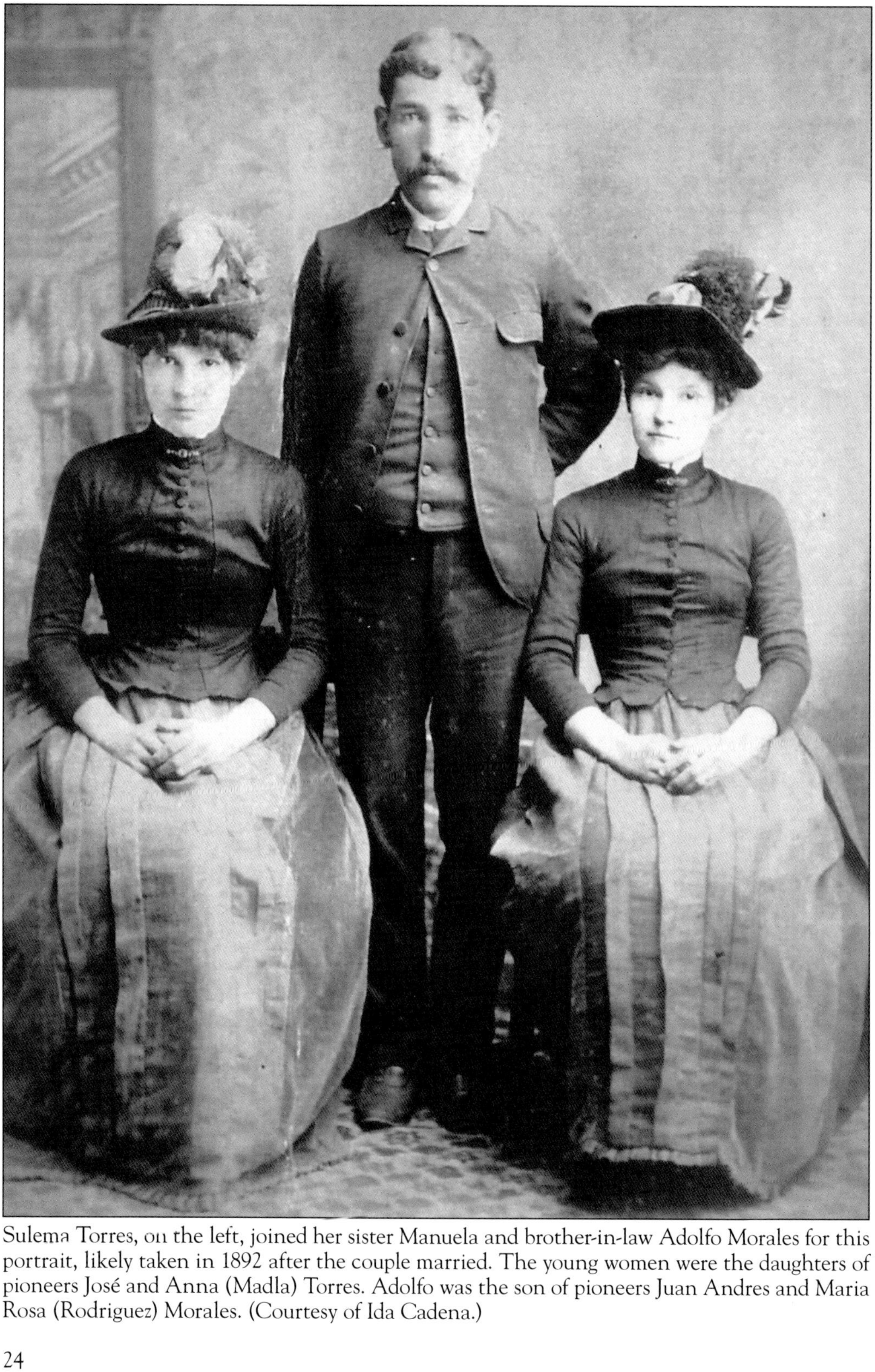

Sulema Torres, on the left, joined her sister Manuela and brother-in-law Adolfo Morales for this portrait, likely taken in 1892 after the couple married. The young women were the daughters of pioneers José and Anna (Madla) Torres. Adolfo was the son of pioneers Juan Andres and Maria Rosa (Rodriguez) Morales. (Courtesy of Ida Cadena.)

Juan Andres Morales (1832–1911) emigrated from Mexico in 1874 with wife, Maria Rosa (Rodriguez) Morales, and six children: Salomé, Mucio, Lorenzo, Adolfo, Miguel, Cornelio, and Cleofas. They arrived in Helotes soon afterwards. He started a family farm on his homestead grant of 160 acres, and soon his children began to accumulate their own properties. By the 1930s, Morales descendants owned more than 500 acres along Bandera Road. (Courtesy of Lawrence Morales.)

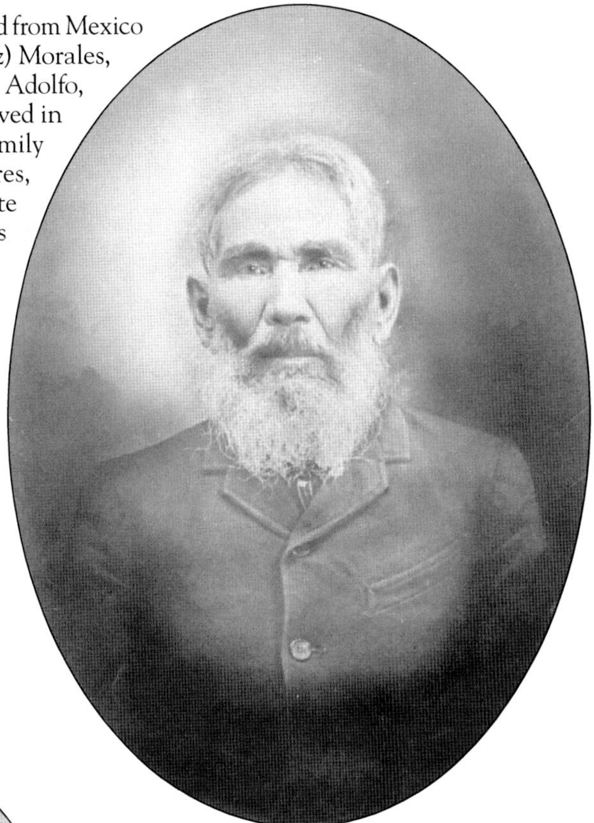

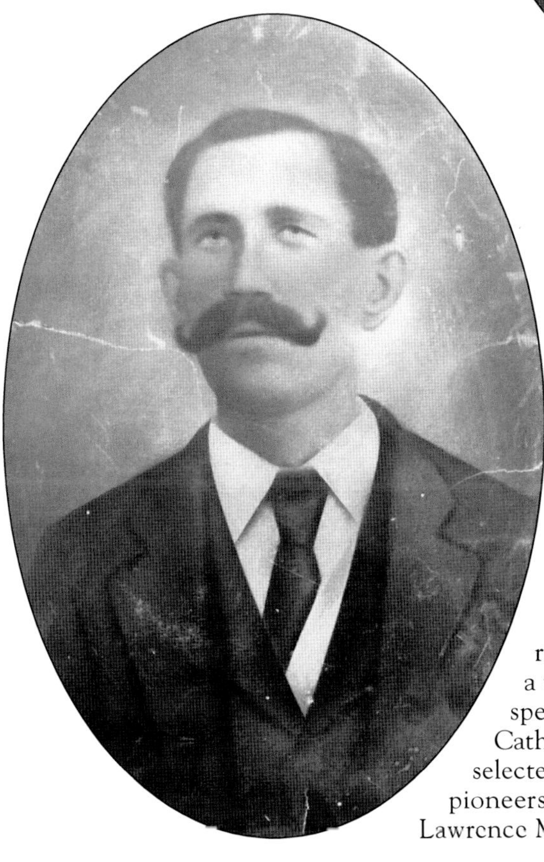

Hispanic neighbors of Lorenzo Morales (1860–1956) often called upon him for help reading and writing documents. He served as a trustee of the Los Reyes School and in 1908 spearheaded the effort to build the town's first Catholic church. A Catholic women's organization selected him for a portrait to represent the Spanish pioneers who settled Bexar County. (Courtesy of Lawrence Morales.)

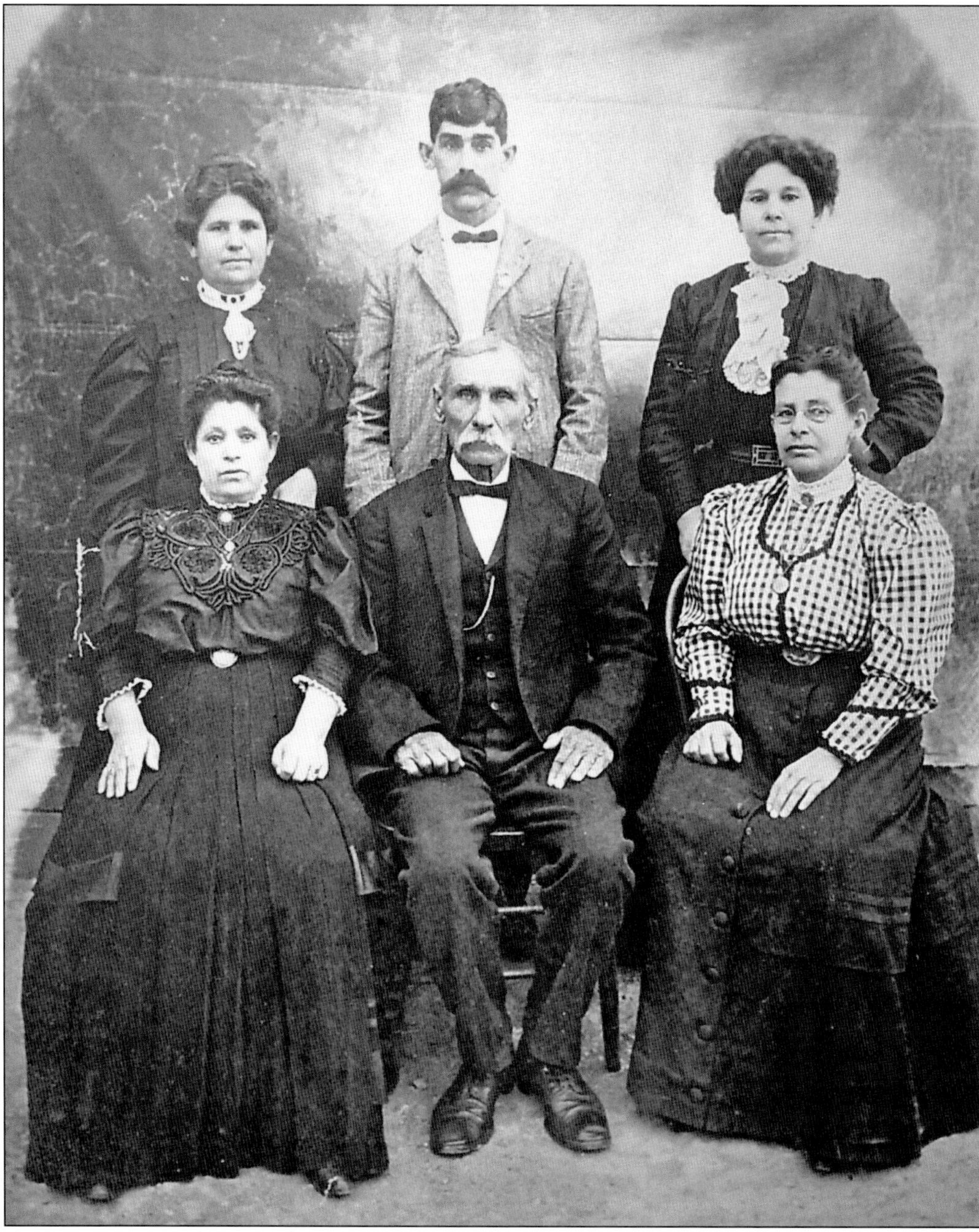

In this 1890s-era photograph are members of the Jesús Martinez family, left to right, (first row) Antonia, Jesús, María de Jesusa; (second row) Ygnacia, Mamerto, Francisca. Three of the sisters married three brothers, sons of Helotes rancher and freighter Máximo Cadena (seen on the next page). Matriarch Rosalia Villarreal Martinez is missing from this family photograph. Comanches killed her February 25, 1871, less than a month after she and her husband, Jesús, settled with their children in Helotes. For several years after the Civil War, Comanche raids intensified—children were kidnapped, livestock stolen, and settlers were killed. In Helotes, several thousand horses and cattle were stolen over several years; Rosalia Martinez was one of the few settlers murdered during a livestock raid. (Courtesy of Pat Castañon.)

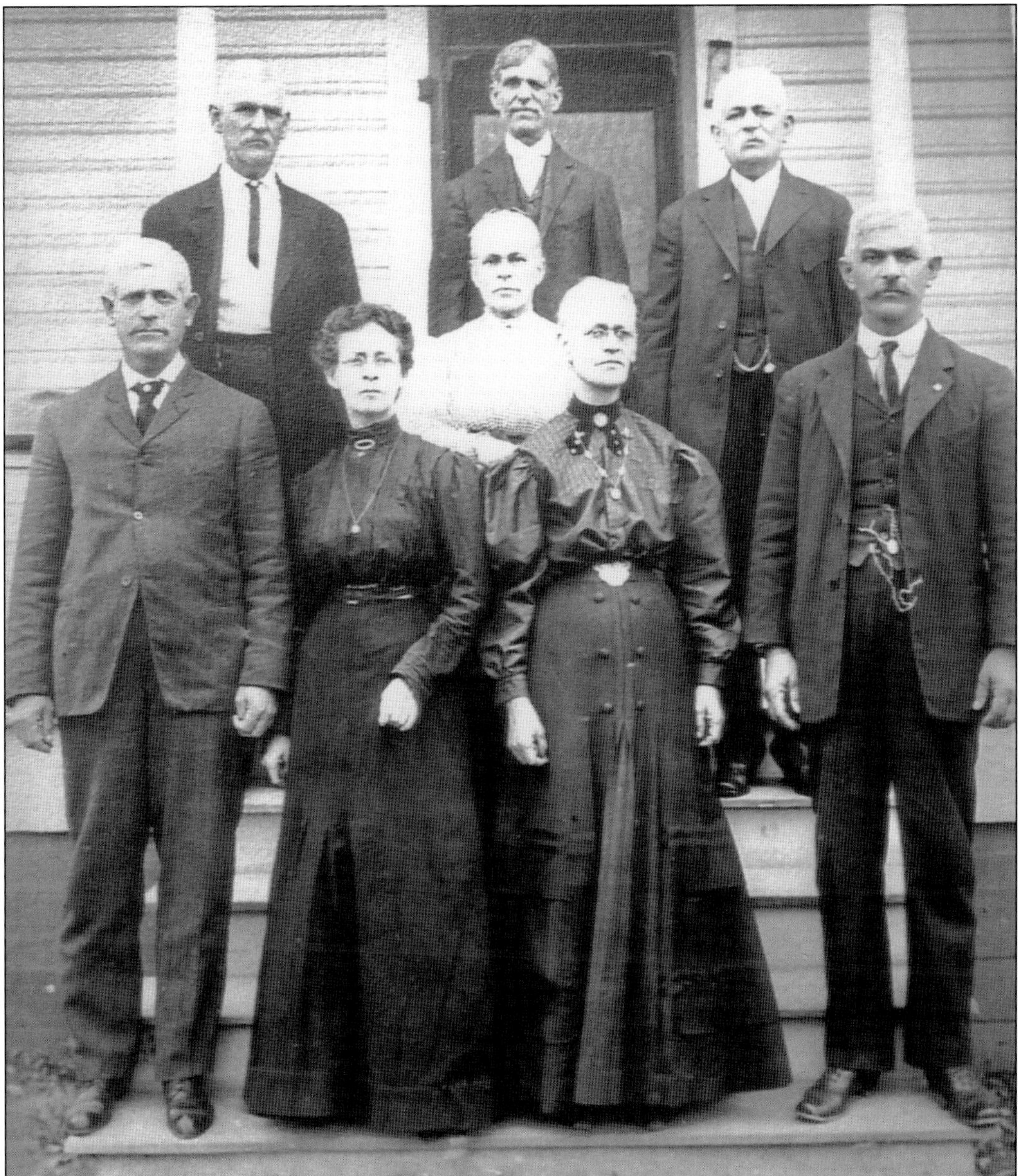

Descendants of Máximo Cadena, freighter and owner of a large cattle ranch in the Helotes settlement near what is today Prue Road, are shown in this 1888 photograph. From left to right, they are (first row) Santiago, who married Ygnacia Martinez; Pomposa, Eulalia, Manuel; (second row) Urbana; (third row) Antonio (who married Francisca Martinez), Jesús, and Celedonio (who married María de Jesusa Martinez). (Courtesy of Pat Castañon.)

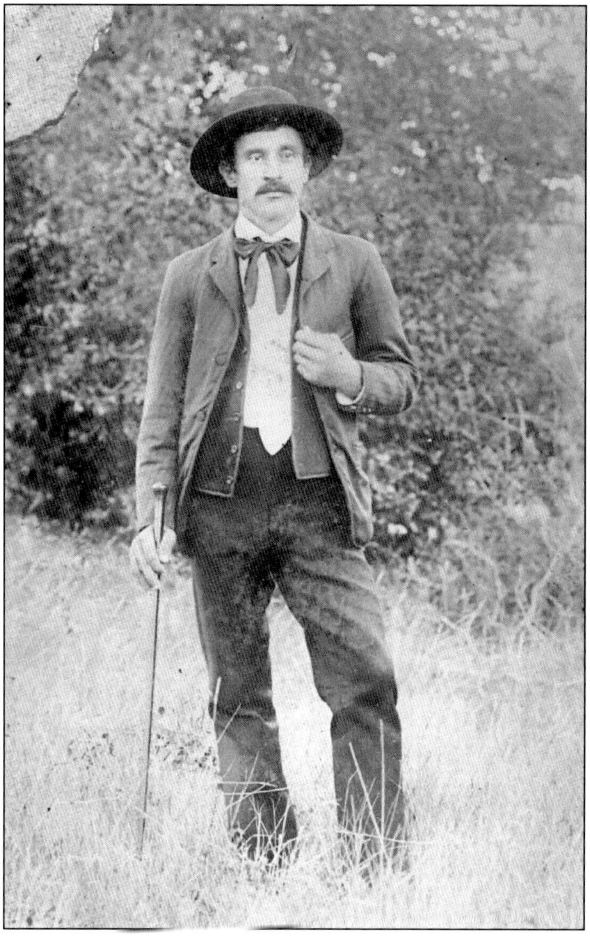

Máximo Martinez (1859–1940), son of Manuel and Teodora (Lazarín) Martinez who moved to Helotes from Nacogdoches during the Civil War, was one of Helotes's early blacksmiths. He shod mules and horses for the cavalry stationed at the U.S. post in Leon Springs. A farmer, he was also a talented violinist and often played at the dance hall in downtown Helotes. He married Jesusa "Susie" Treviño, daughter of Pedro and Manuela Treviño, in 1893, and raised ten children. The Martinez home, shown below, was built near Helotes Creek in 1858 by Miguel Menchaca, a soldier for the Republic of Texas. The Martinez family purchased the land and house, called La Quinta de las Piedras, in 1867, and kept it in the family for the next 94 years. In 1965, it was awarded Texas Historic Landmark status. (Courtesy of Emma Leal.)

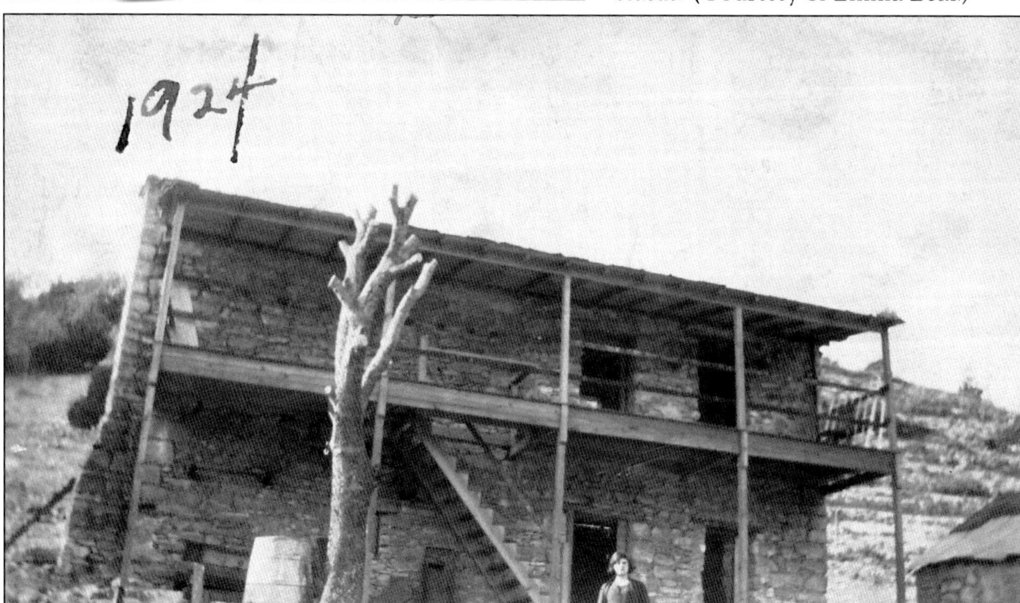

Daughters of Máximo and Jesusa Martinez, Mercedes (standing), and Aurelia, pose with friend Felix Madla in this 1915 photograph. Madla was living in Mexico with several of his brothers when he contracted the Spanish Influenza and died on October 18, 1918, at the age of 23. (Courtesy of Juanita "Janie" Madla.)

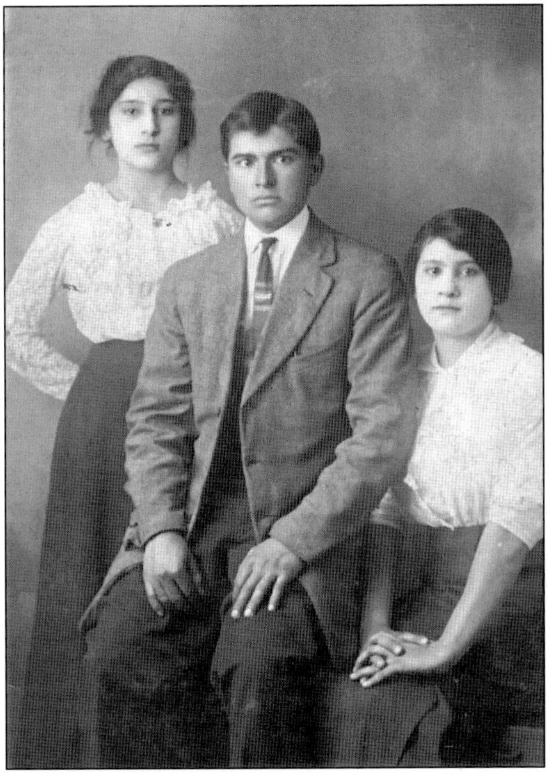

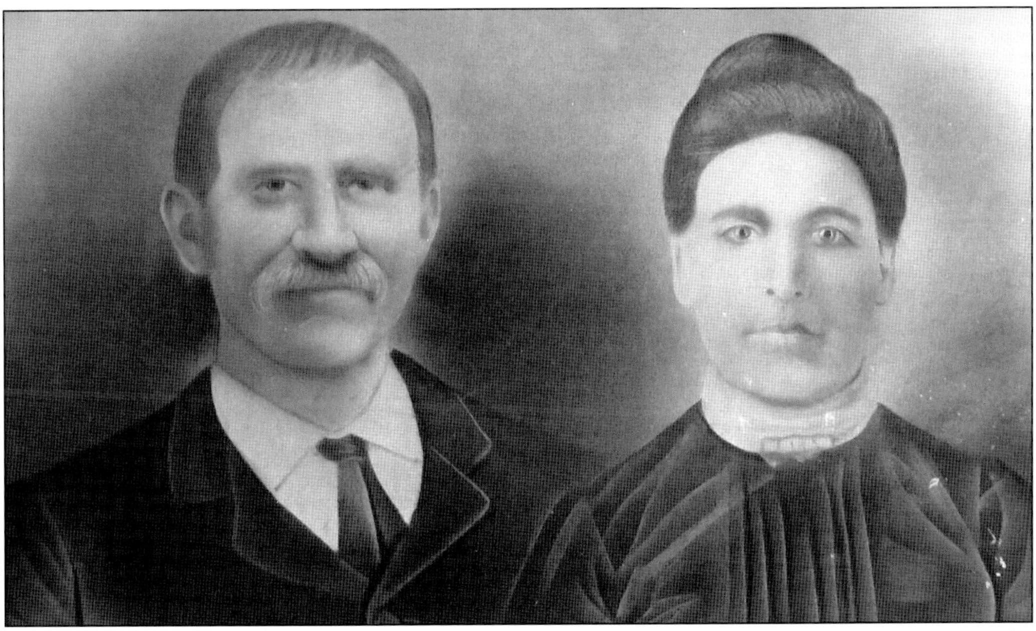

Frank Woller (1862–1925), who participated in the last cattle drive out of San Antonio in the mid-1880s, is shown in this 1888 photograph with wife María Ricarda Cadena, daughter of Helotes pioneers José and Dolores (Valdez) Cadena. Frank was the youngest son of German immigrants Nickolas and Theresia (Dirwimmer) Woller. Frank and María Ricarda had 10 children. (Courtesy of Jeanine Eaves and Fredrick Woller.)

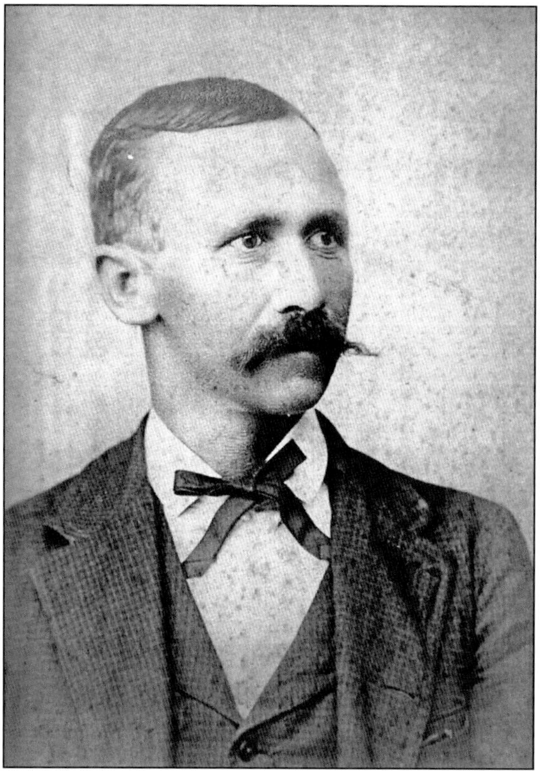

In 1876, Joseph Woller (1858–1928) and his brothers moved onto property near today's Prue and Hausman Roads on land purchased by their father Nickolas. Joseph was 17 when they began farming, growing corn and prairie hay, and raising horses and cattle. After one brother died and another moved away, Joseph and younger brother Frank stayed on the land and became community leaders, helping to build the wood-framed Catholic church in Helotes in 1908. Joseph Woller married Nancy Lee (below) in 1901. She was the daughter of Helotes pioneers Shelly and Jesusa María (de la Garza) Lee. The couple had three children. (At left and below, courtesy of Linda Bloom.)

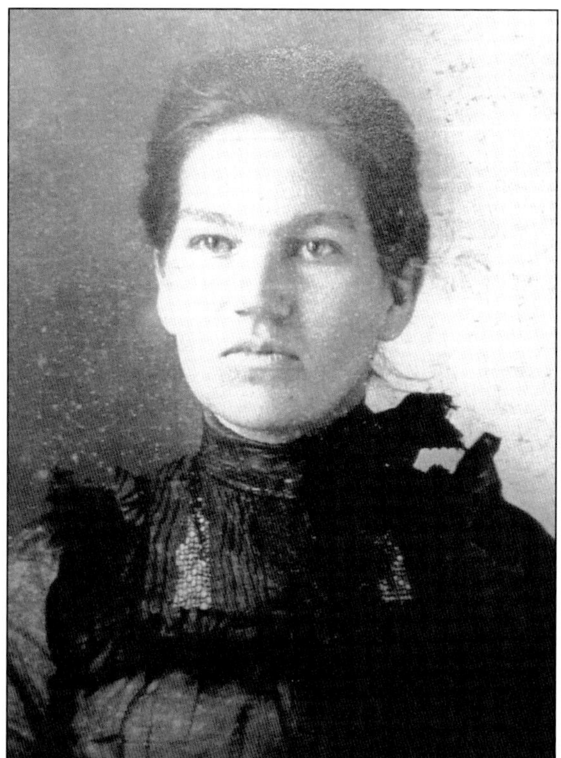

Two

Entrepreneurs

Helotes was a farm and ranching community until well into the mid-20th century. Throughout the farming seasons and during cattle drives, travelers stopped at the intersection of Bandera Road and Helotes Creek to camp before moving on to San Antonio or Bandera to market. Fields offered soft accommodations for overnight stays, and the spring-fed Helotes Creek provided drinking water. Commerce-minded people saw potential in this influx of people and hastened to provide services. Downtown Helotes, at the crucial juncture of Bandera Road and Helotes Creek, began with a general store, blacksmith shop, and saloon. A boardinghouse and dance hall followed. Nevertheless, even after a grocery store and gas station opened for business in the 1930s, downtown remained primarily a stopover rather than a destination. However, as farms began to shrink after the pioneer settlers passed away and their property was divided among their many children, commercial interests increased. During World War II, many Helotes residents worked in San Antonio and nearby government posts to help in the war effort. With a taste of something different from country life, descendants of the early pioneers were enticed by developers offering them goodly sums for their farms, particularly the land along Bandera Road, prime commercial property.

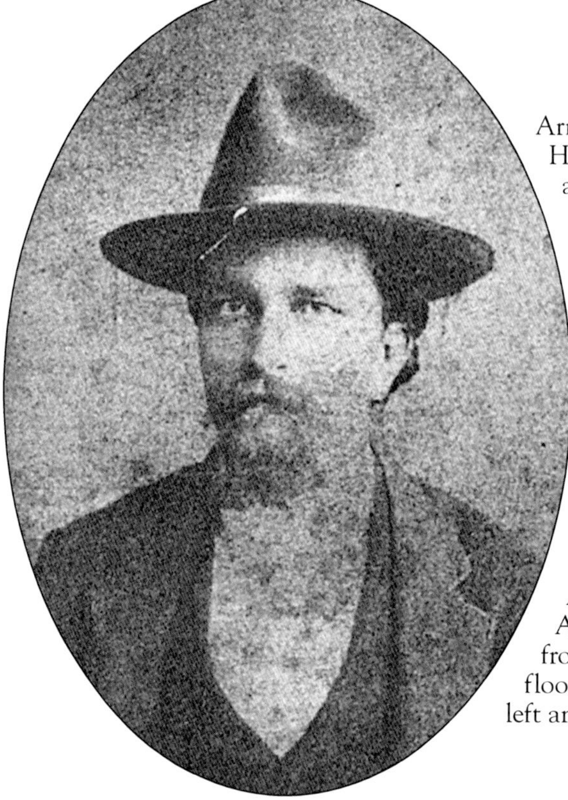

Arnold Gugger (1855–1928) founded downtown Helotes. Having traveled throughout Texas as a freighter with his father, Arnold knew the mercantile business. When he heard that a portion of the Marnoch family land was for sale, he made an offer for 110 acres that included the prime intersection of Bandera Road and Helotes Creek. He purchased the property on December 10, 1880, for $200, and by 1881 he had built a residence for his wife Amalia "Mollie" Benke (1861–1921), seen in the photograph below, and their baby son, Anton. He also built a blacksmith shop, general store, and saloon, the first buildings in downtown Helotes. The couple had five more children: Albertine, Alex, Ella, Amalia, and Pearl. Arnold served as Helotes's third postmaster from 1888 to 1904, reserving a part of the first floor of his homestead for the post office. (At left and below, courtesy of Jim Benke.)

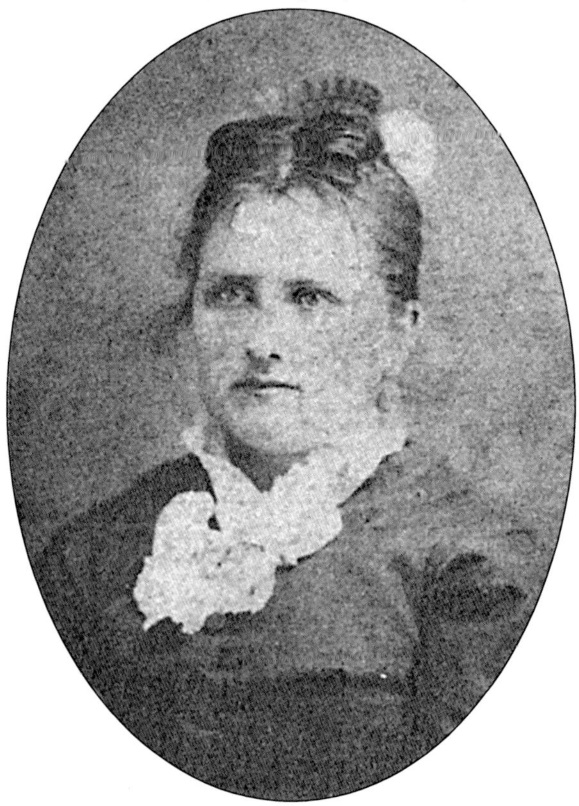

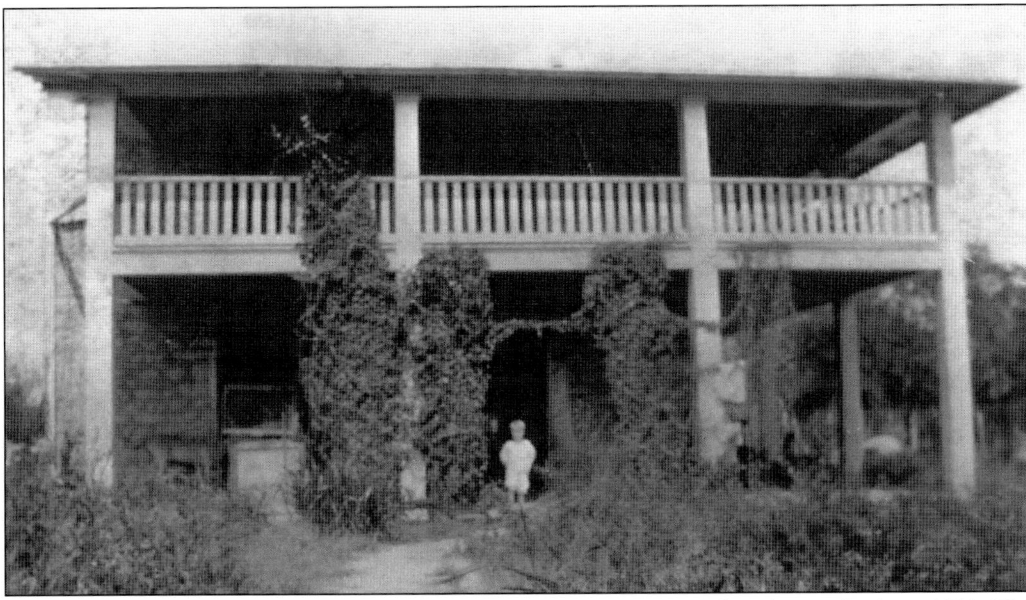

The Gugger homestead, honored in 2008 as a Texas Historic Landmark, was built in 1881. The oldest building in downtown Helotes, it has served as a residence, post office, and business establishment. This is the earliest-known photograph of the homestead, taken about 1914. The child is Otis Hileman, son of the home's second owner. (Courtesy of Kyle Cunningham.)

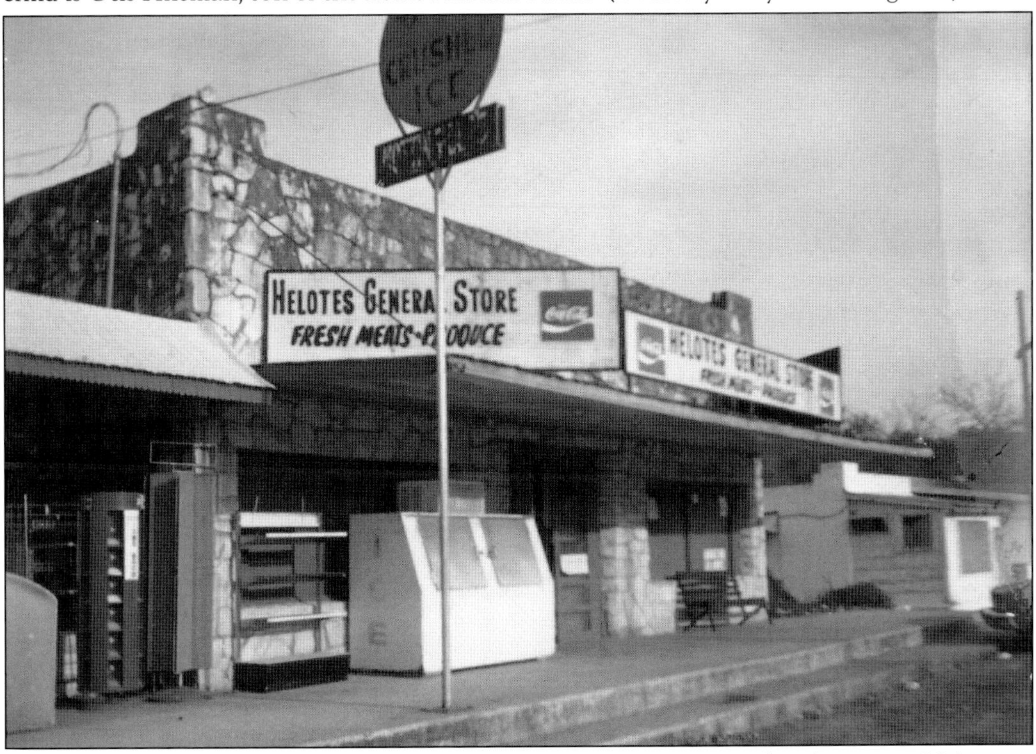

Arnold Gugger built this limestone general store next to his homestead in downtown Helotes in 1881. The building was in continuous operation as a general store run by different families over the years until Corbin and Wanda Terry converted it into a restaurant in 1980. (Courtesy of HSH.)

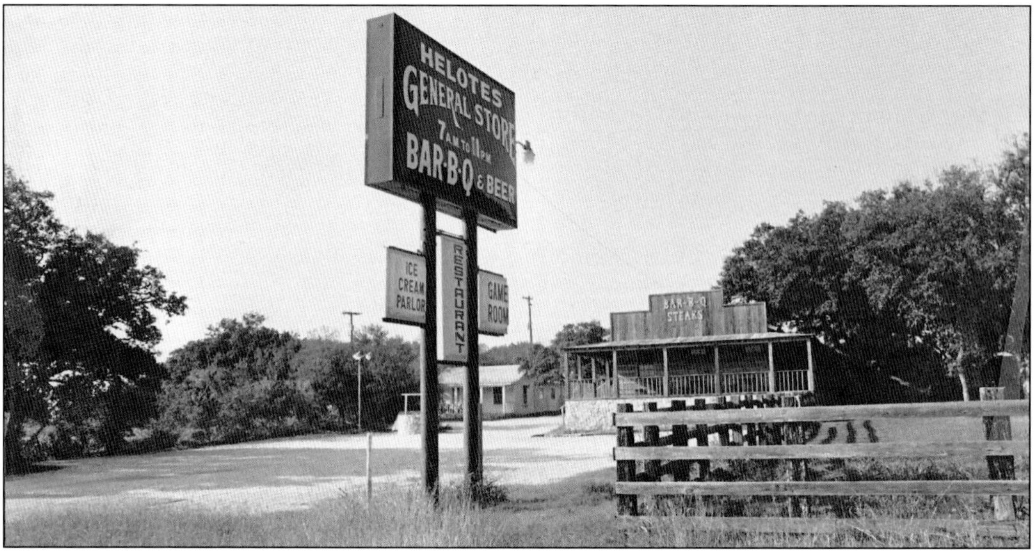

The back of the Helotes General Store is shown in this 1979 photograph, just after well-known restaurateurs Corbin and Wanda Terry purchased the property to house the popular Hickory Hut Restaurant, which operated until 2006. (Courtesy of HSH.)

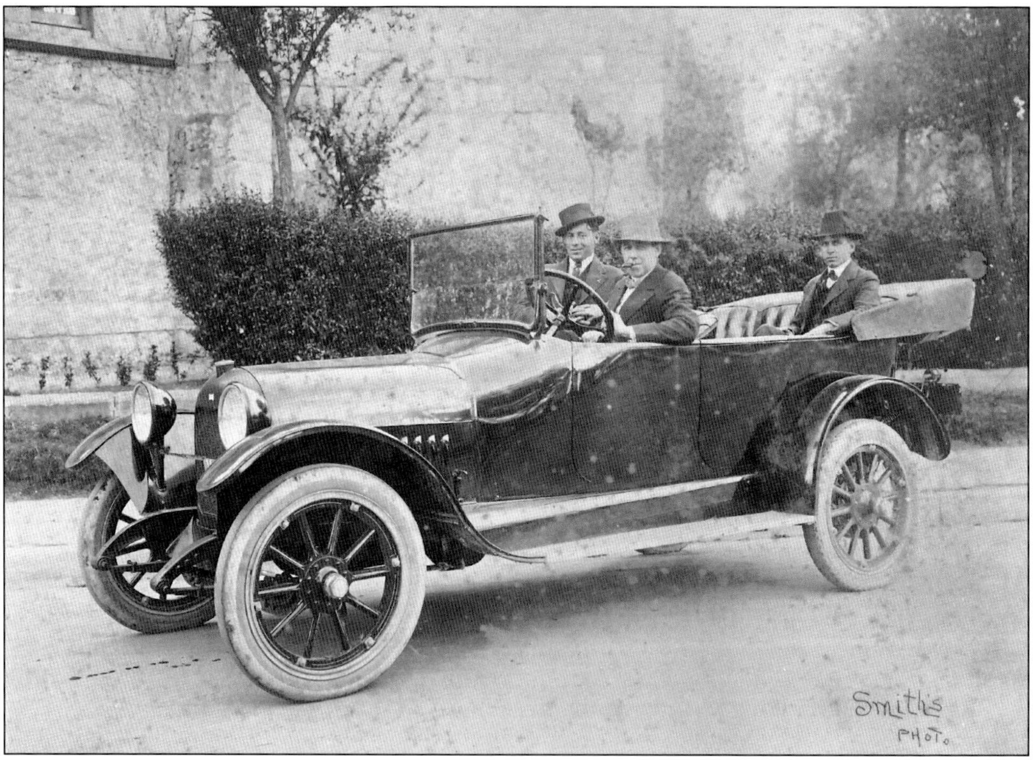

Alex Parrigin (1874–1971), on the far left with business associates in this 1913 photograph taken in San Antonio, came to Helotes in 1906 after Arnold Gugger solicited his help to sell his downtown Helotes property. Parrigin, born in Kentucky, moved to Helotes several years later with wife Bettie and their daughter, Marie. His expertise was in real estate; he sold property at Scenic Loop Playground and developed Helotes Ranch Acres. (Courtesy of HSH.)

Parrigin, Helotes's "senior statesman," received birthday congratulations from Michael Keating at Rudy and Irene's restaurant on November 12, 1969, his 95th birthday. (Courtesy of HSH.)

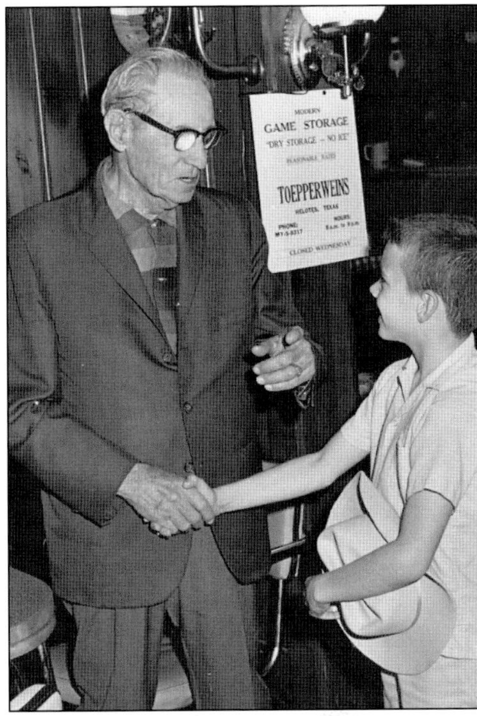

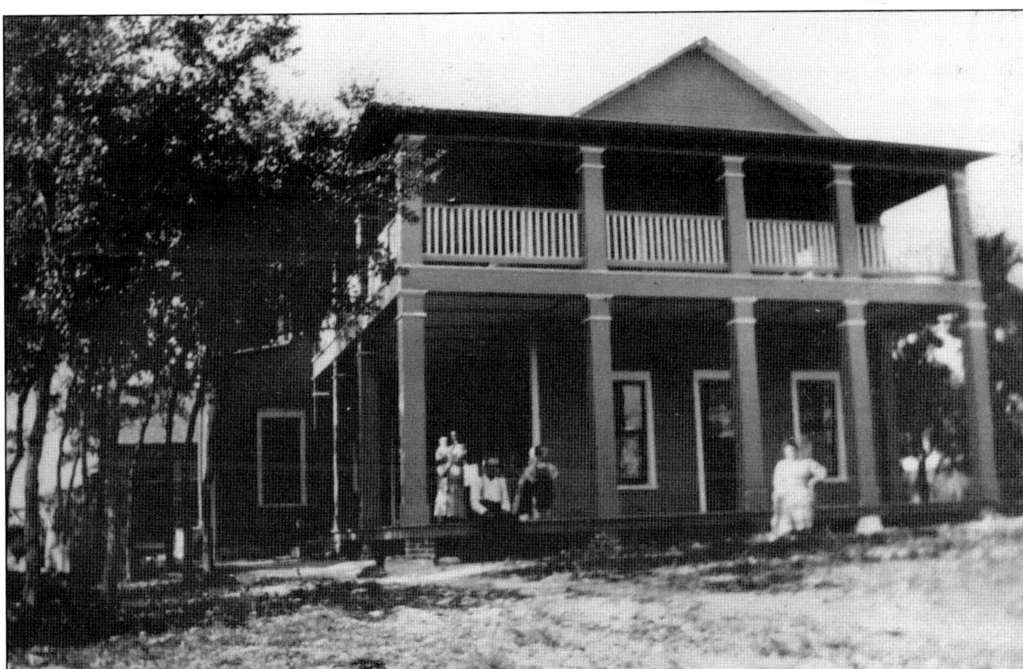

Wilbert S. "Bert" Hileman purchased the Gugger property in 1908. In this photograph, he sits near his wife, Nellie, and two of their children on the porch of the downtown Helotes boardinghouse he built in 1912 for his mother-in-law (far right) to operate. Remodeled by subsequent owners and covered with a limestone facade, the house has been used as an apartment building, a bed and breakfast, a newspaper office, and as home to retail shops. (Courtesy of Kyle Cunningham.)

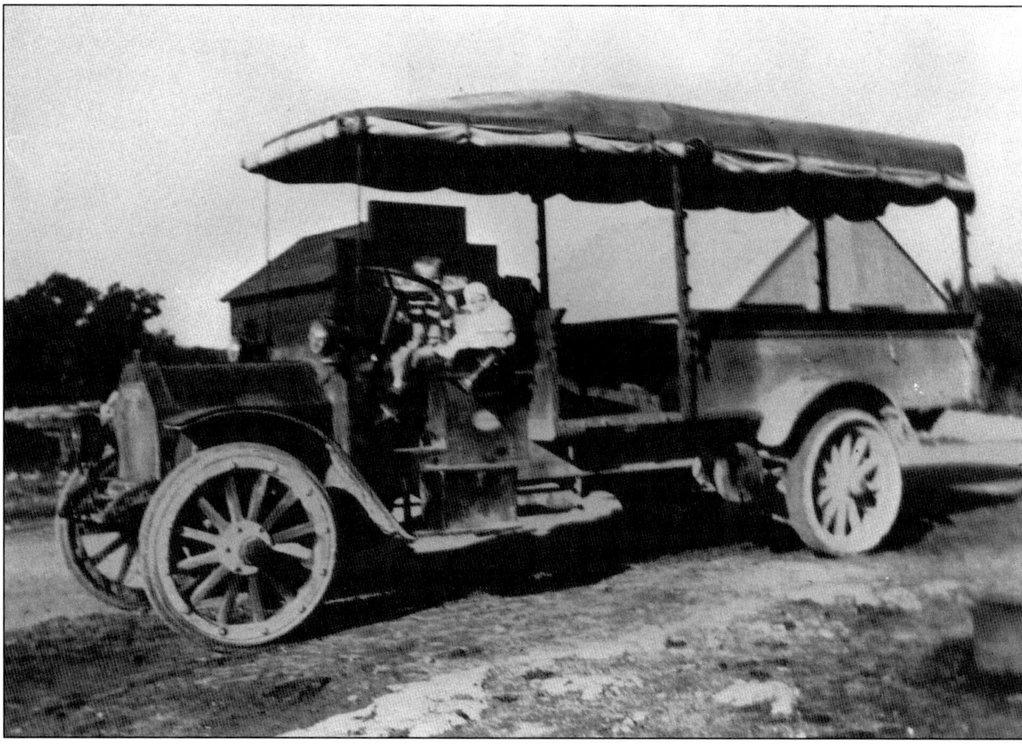

Seen here around 1912, this chain-driven vehicle transported people and merchandise from downtown Helotes to and from Bandera, Texas. Two of Bert Hileman's children are in the cab. (Courtesy of Kyle Cunningham.)

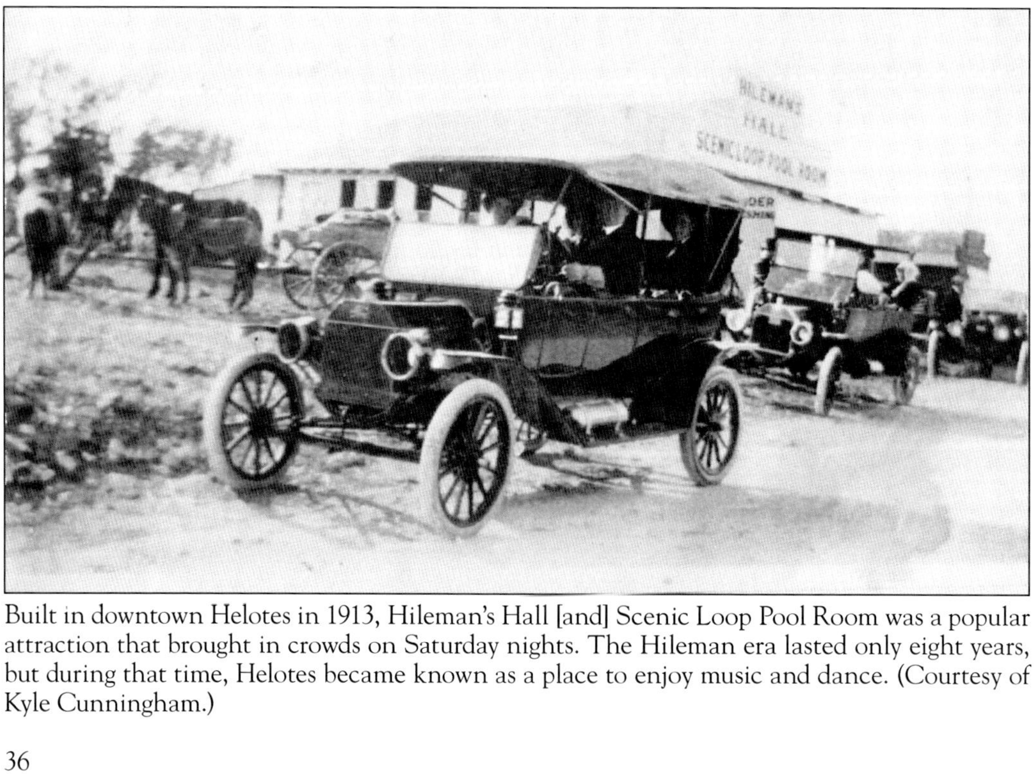

Built in downtown Helotes in 1913, Hileman's Hall [and] Scenic Loop Pool Room was a popular attraction that brought in crowds on Saturday nights. The Hileman era lasted only eight years, but during that time, Helotes became known as a place to enjoy music and dance. (Courtesy of Kyle Cunningham.)

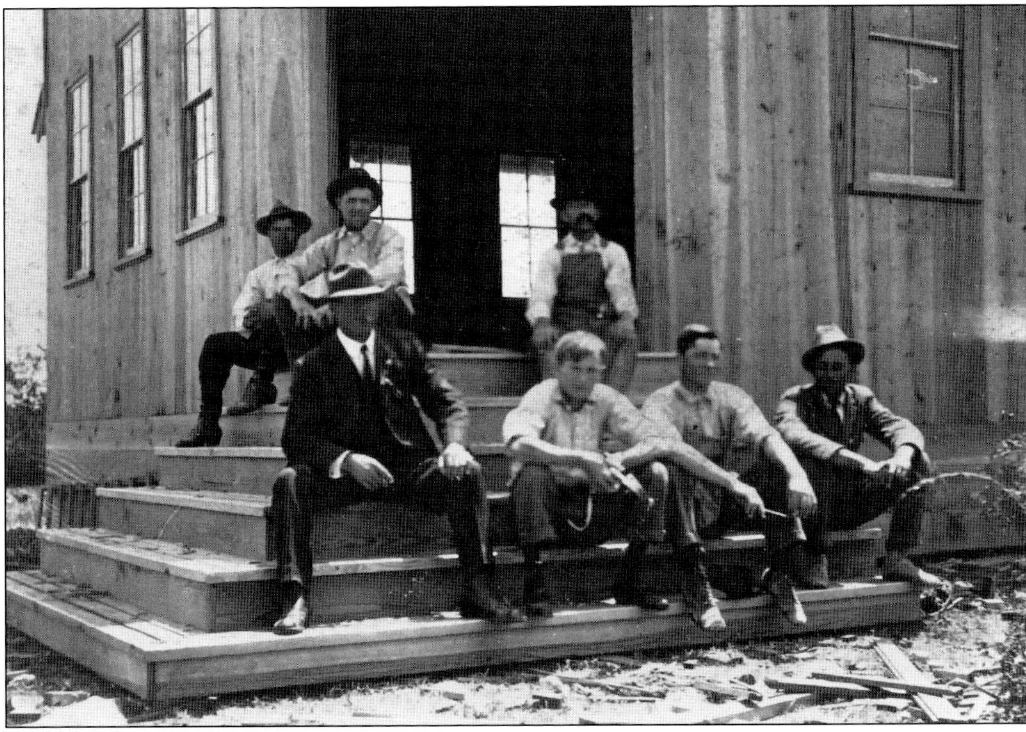

Bert Hileman (dark suit) sits with employees and friends in front of his dance hall, which has housed various businesses over the years, including a meat market, restaurant, and retail shops. (Courtesy of Kyle Cunningham.)

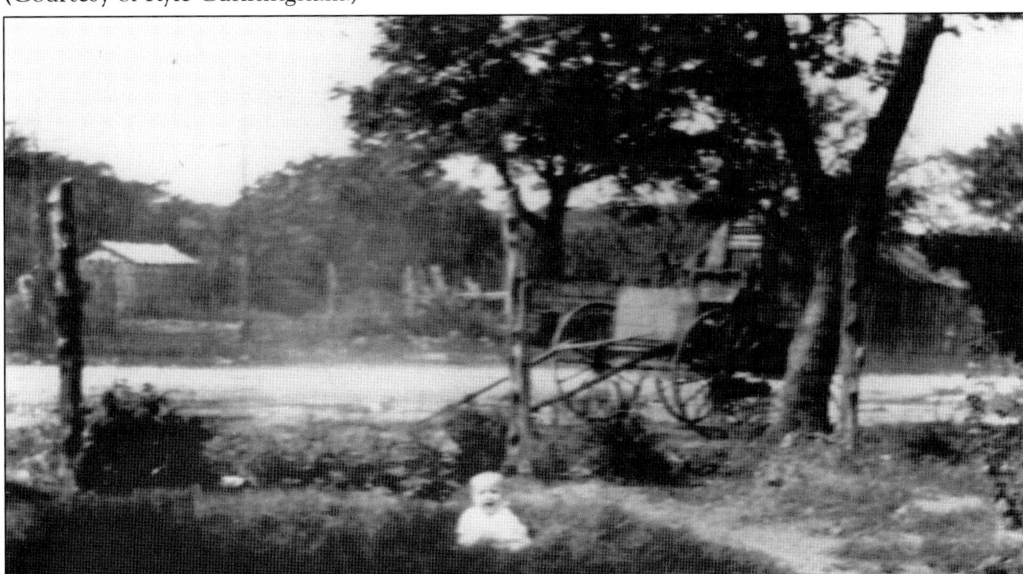

In the early 20th century, downtown Helotes was little more than a cow town surrounded by large farms and ranches—a few buildings on either side of a dusty, packed-earth road wide enough to accommodate cattle drives. This 1916 photograph of Stella Hileman in the grass in front of the Gugger homestead shows Bandera Road in the background. Note the simple wood structures across the street. (Courtesy of Kyle Cunningham.)

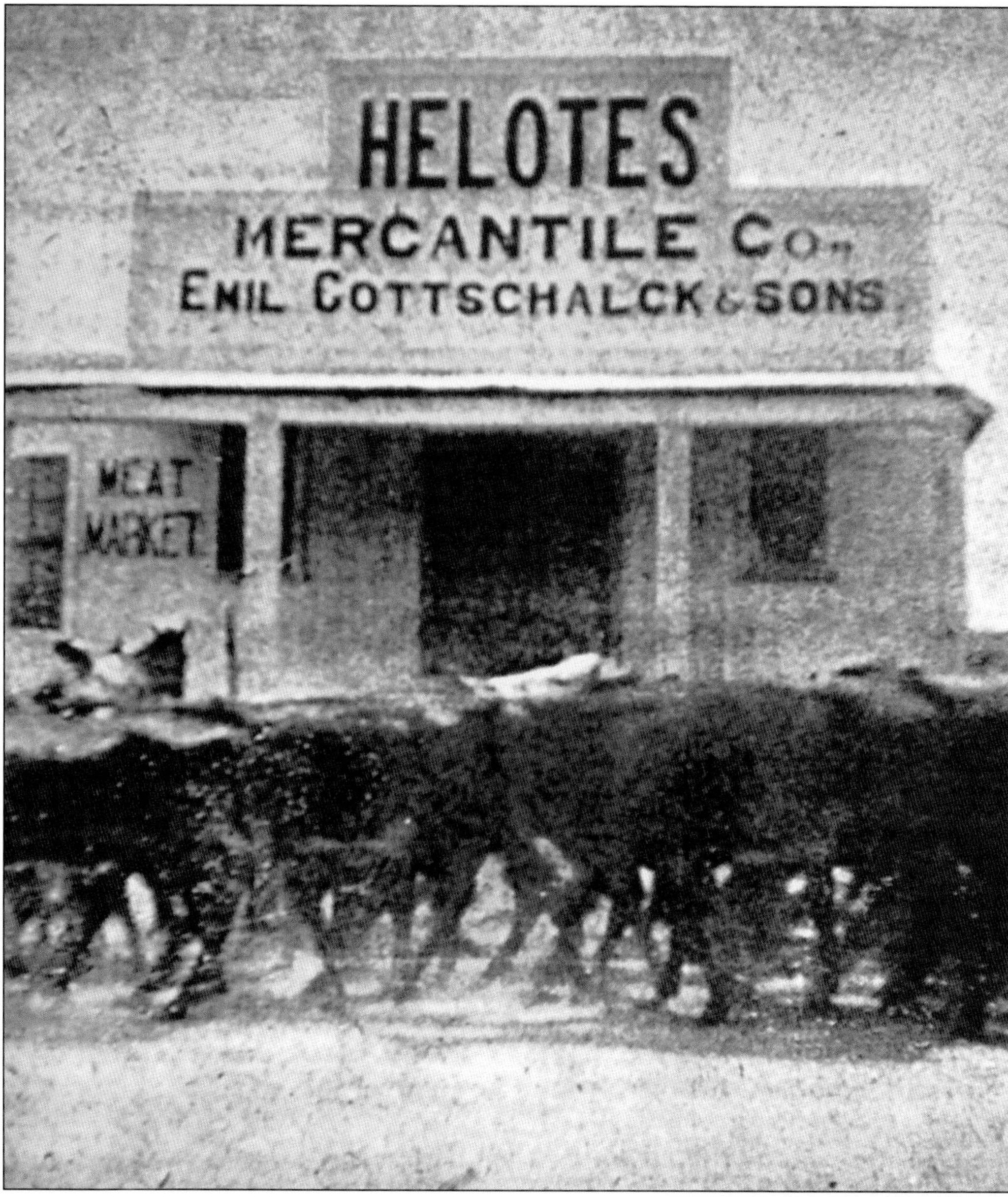

Emil Gottschalck and sons Emil H. and Rudolph purchased the Hileman property in the summer of 1916. They closed the dance hall—much to the chagrin of local dance enthusiasts—and reopened the wood-frame building as a mercantile. The Gottschalck family, which also included Emil Sr.'s wife, Julia, their daughter Litta, and Rudolph's wife, Stella, regularly witnessed cattle drives through town, as this 1916 photograph shows. (Courtesy of HSH.)

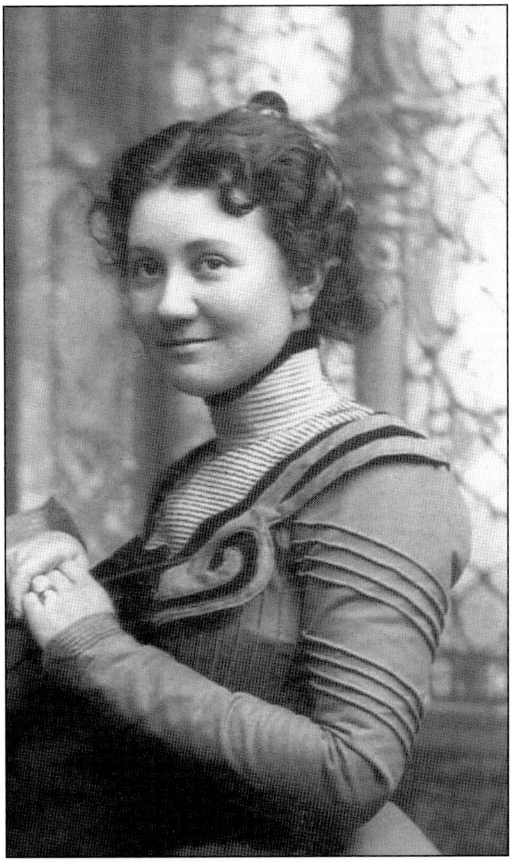

The summer of 1919 saw a new owner of downtown Helotes: Kate (Niernberg) Logan (1879–1946), shown in this 1900 photograph. Logan, who was divorced, purchased the Gottschalck property as a "feme sole." However, soon after, she married James Riggs (1879–1964), and the couple moved into the boardinghouse Bert Hileman had built for his mother-in-law. In 1923, they sold the northeast portion of the property that included the Gottschalck store, the old Gugger General Store, and the Gugger house to Albert and Maude Fuller. The Riggs built a grocery store next to their downtown home, which Kate managed. James Riggs, shown in the 1930s-era photograph below, opened a garage and service station across the street. (At right, courtesy of Cheryl Ryder; below, courtesy of Valda Terry.)

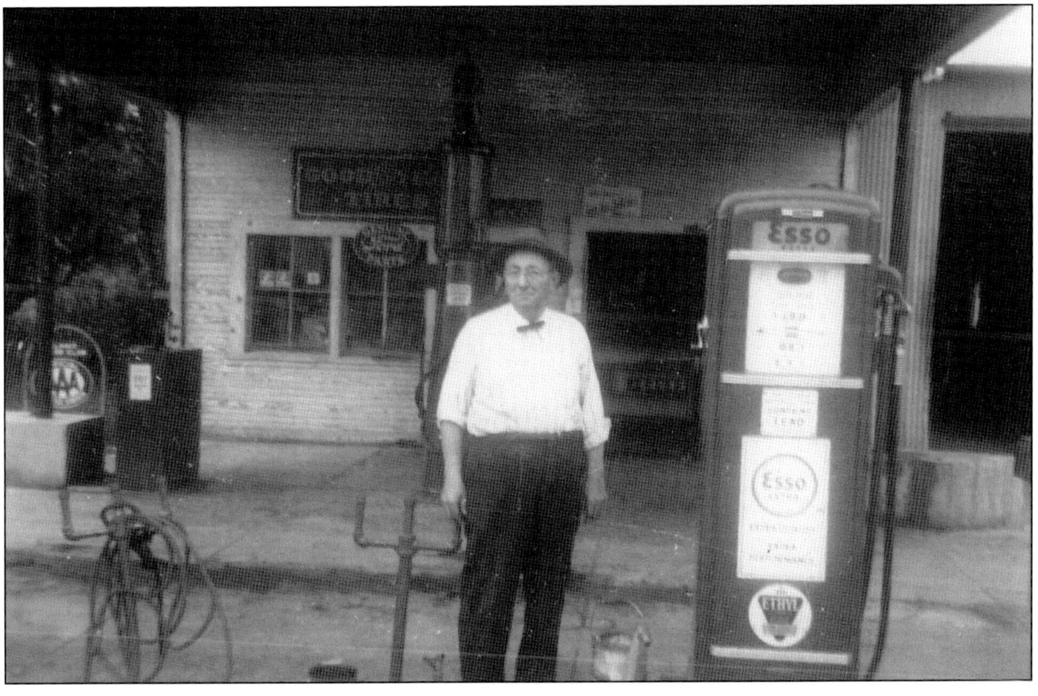

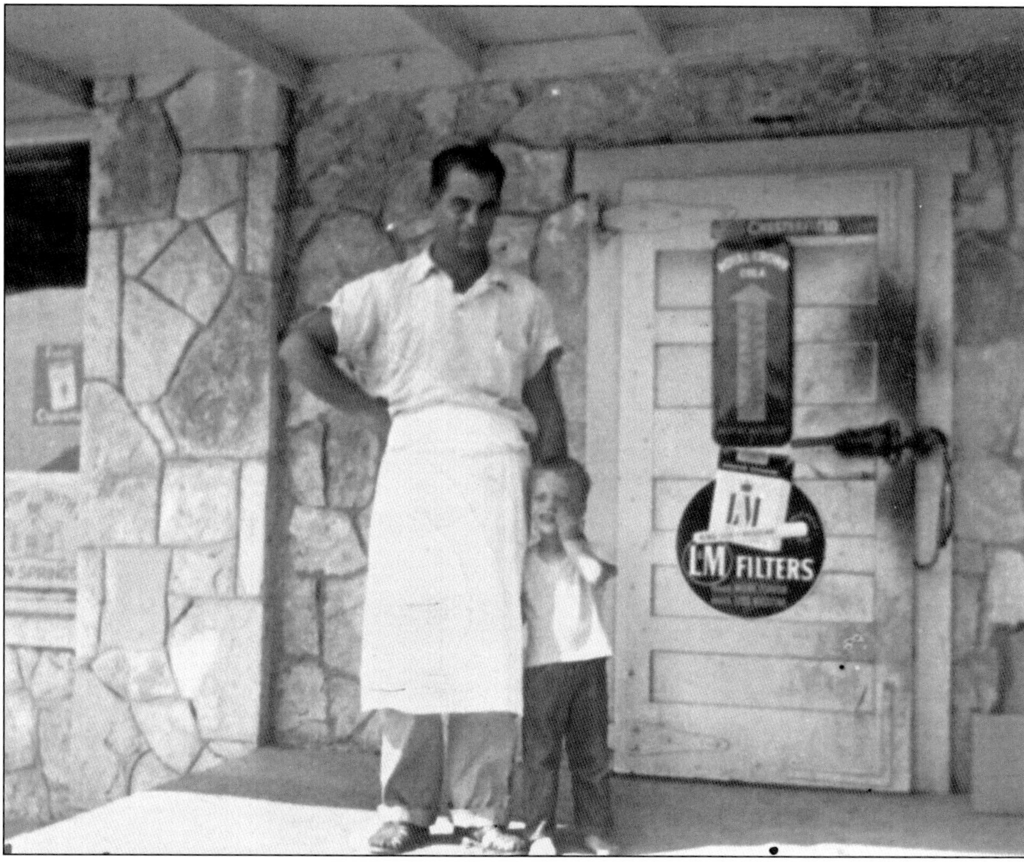

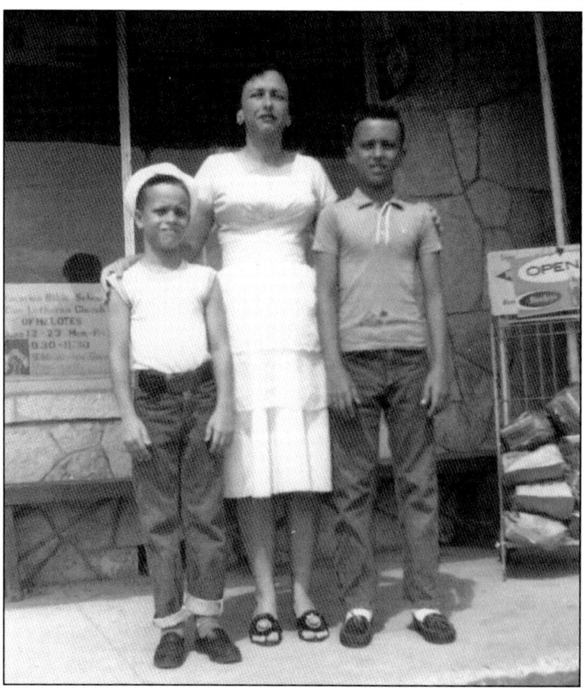

James Riggs's nephew Martin Terry is shown in this photograph with son Timothy in front of the Red and White grocery store he managed for his uncle in downtown Helotes from 1953 until 1962. Below is Martin's wife, Valda, flanked on her left by Timothy and on her right by Martin "Marty," in front of the store. Terry inherited his uncle's property and continued various enterprises until his death in 2000. The Terry family still owns the old Riggs garage, now an antique store. (Above and at left, courtesy of Valda Terry.)

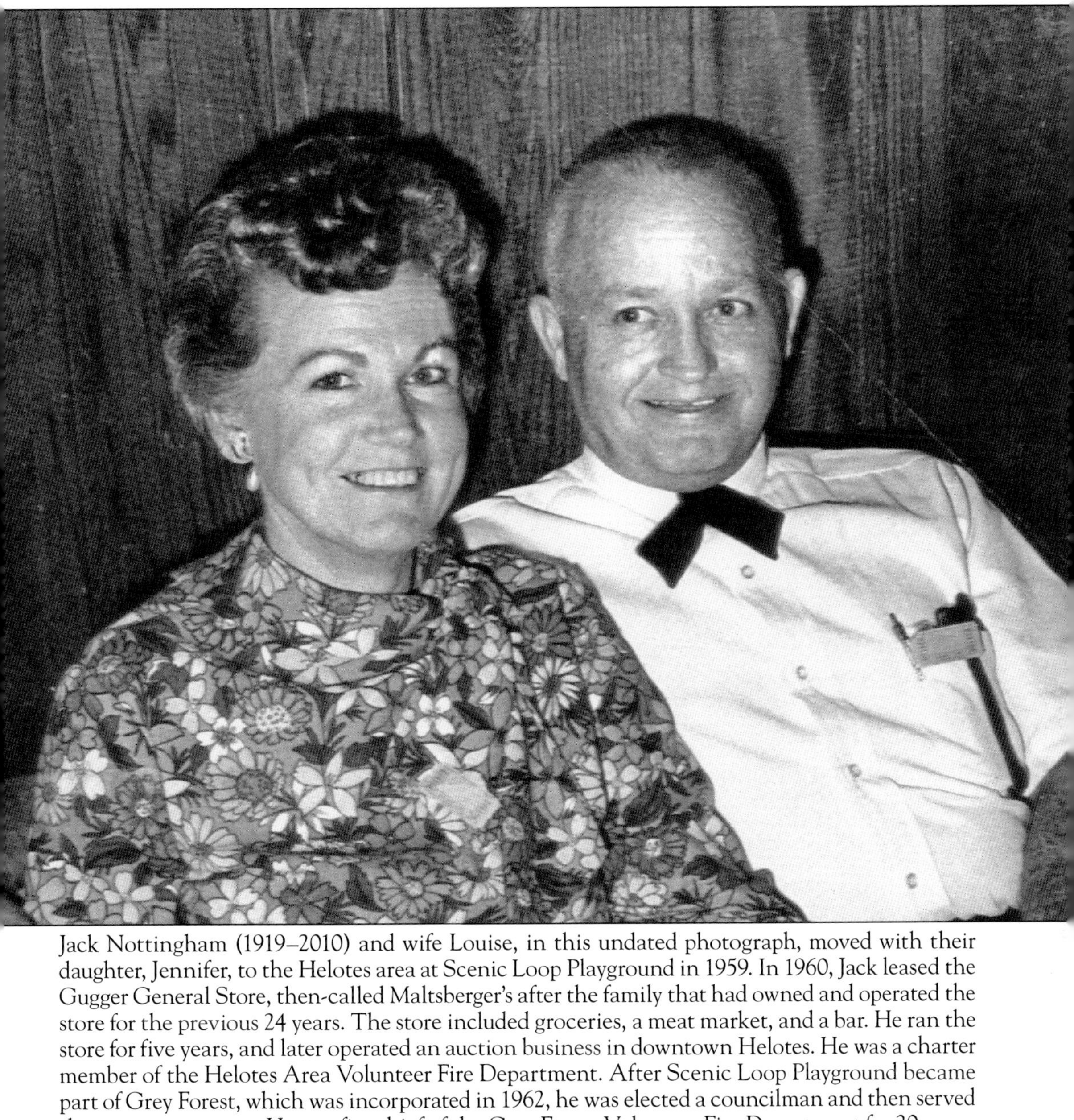

Jack Nottingham (1919–2010) and wife Louise, in this undated photograph, moved with their daughter, Jennifer, to the Helotes area at Scenic Loop Playground in 1959. In 1960, Jack leased the Gugger General Store, then-called Maltsberger's after the family that had owned and operated the store for the previous 24 years. The store included groceries, a meat market, and a bar. He ran the store for five years, and later operated an auction business in downtown Helotes. He was a charter member of the Helotes Area Volunteer Fire Department. After Scenic Loop Playground became part of Grey Forest, which was incorporated in 1962, he was elected a councilman and then served three terms as mayor. He was fire chief of the Grey Forest Volunteer Fire Department for 20 years. One of Nottingham's most important contributions was his work to bring a natural gas system to the area in 1967. He served as project manager for the contracting, installation, and initial management of the Grey Forest Utilities, which is located in Helotes. (Courtesy of HSH.)

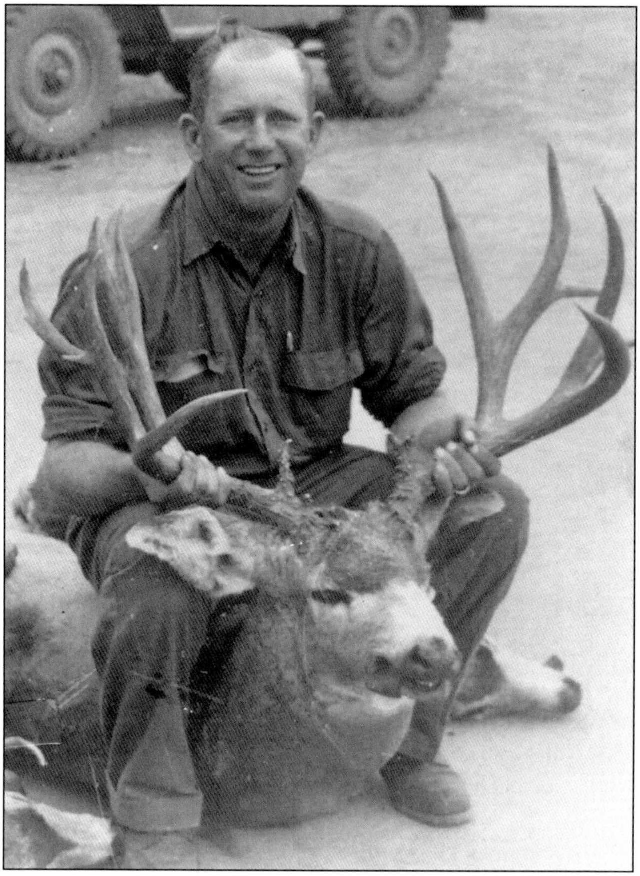

Commerce was localized in downtown Helotes until the 1950s when farmers began to sell their properties along Bandera Road. Max Toepperwein Jr. purchased a five-acre tract on the southwest corner of Bandera and Leslie Roads and opened Toepperwein's—a sporting goods, gas station, and icehouse—in 1951. The store, shown in the 1970s-era photograph below, was the first business visitors saw as they approached Helotes after driving several miles through open countryside. Joanne, Max "Butch" III, Charles, William, Hugh, and Harry helped their father and mother Lottie run the store. Toepperwein's was one of the longest-running stores in Helotes, operating from 1951 until 1977. After Max Jr., passed away in 1975, Lottie and their children operated the store, then leased the property, finally selling it in 2001, after Lottie's death. (At left and below, courtesy of HSH.)

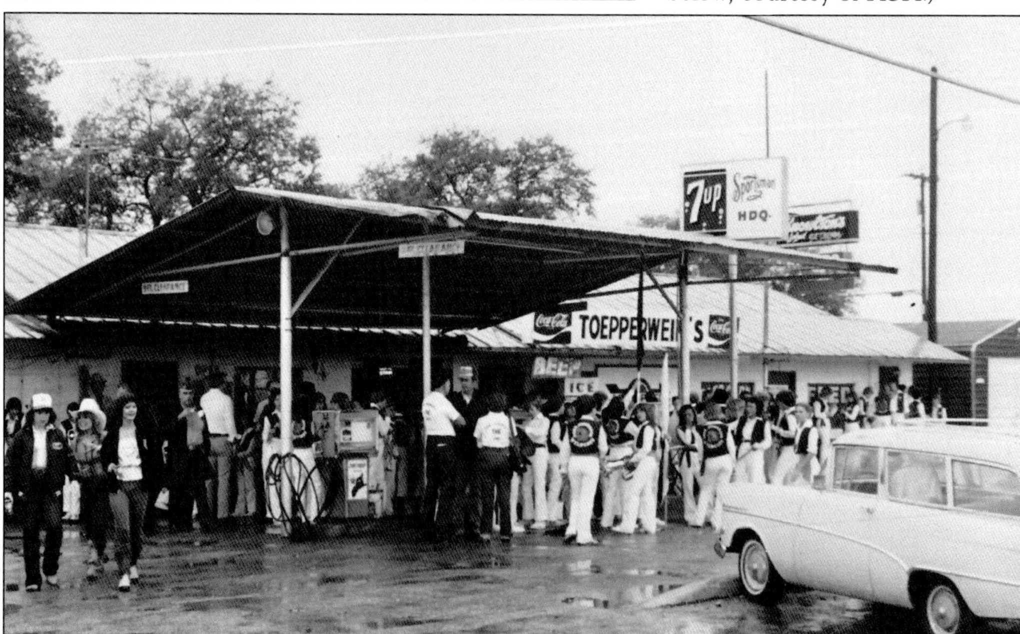

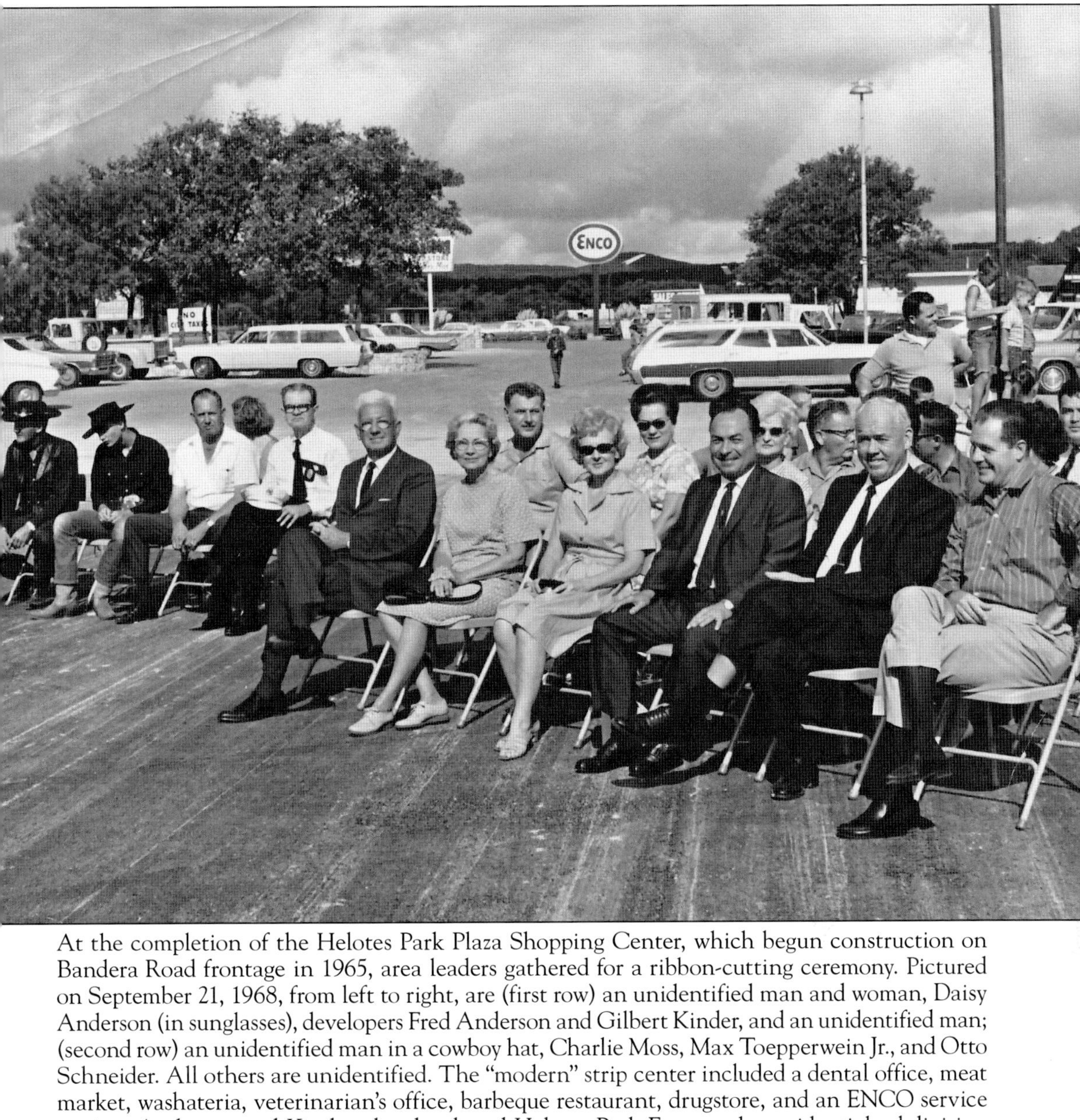

At the completion of the Helotes Park Plaza Shopping Center, which begun construction on Bandera Road frontage in 1965, area leaders gathered for a ribbon-cutting ceremony. Pictured on September 21, 1968, from left to right, are (first row) an unidentified man and woman, Daisy Anderson (in sunglasses), developers Fred Anderson and Gilbert Kinder, and an unidentified man; (second row) an unidentified man in a cowboy hat, Charlie Moss, Max Toepperwein Jr., and Otto Schneider. All others are unidentified. The "modern" strip center included a dental office, meat market, washateria, veterinarian's office, barbeque restaurant, drugstore, and an ENCO service station. Anderson and Kinder also developed Helotes Park Estates, the residential subdivision adjacent to the shopping center. One of the buildings in the center burned down in 2006 and was rebuilt in 2010. (Courtesy of HSH.)

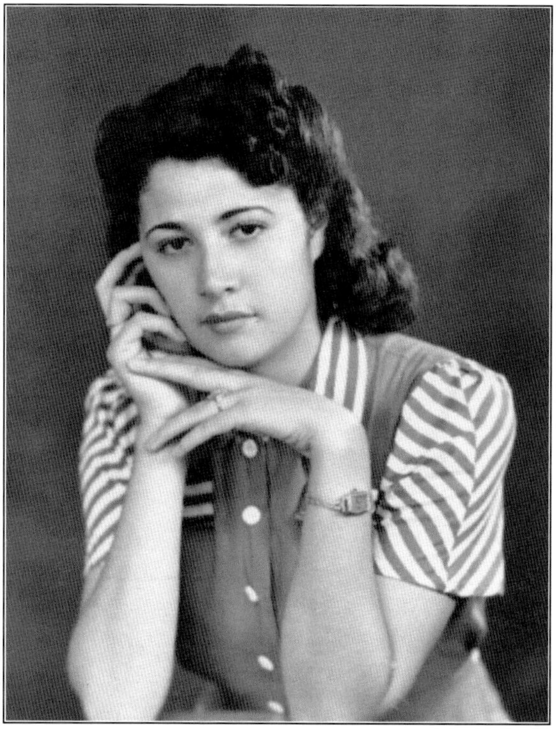

The longest-running business in Helotes is Ella's Barber Shop and Beauty Salon at Helotes Park Plaza, which opened in May 1966. Ella (Sanchez) Dunford, shown at age 19 in this 1943 photograph, started the salon with daughters Elaine and Doris. After they went to college, daughter Carol joined the business in 1974. Carol's daughter, Kimberly, began as a stylist in 1995. Dunford is a descendant of the Cadena clan on her father's side and the Hernandez and Morales pioneers on her mother's side. Her family traces its lineage to Canary Islanders who formed the first municipal government of San Antonio de Béjar. Shown from left to right in the November 1969 photograph below are Elaine, Doris, and Ella, with customers Jim Sofge, Larry Ayres, and Perry Thomas Smith. (Above, courtesy of Ella Dunford; below, courtesy of HSH.)

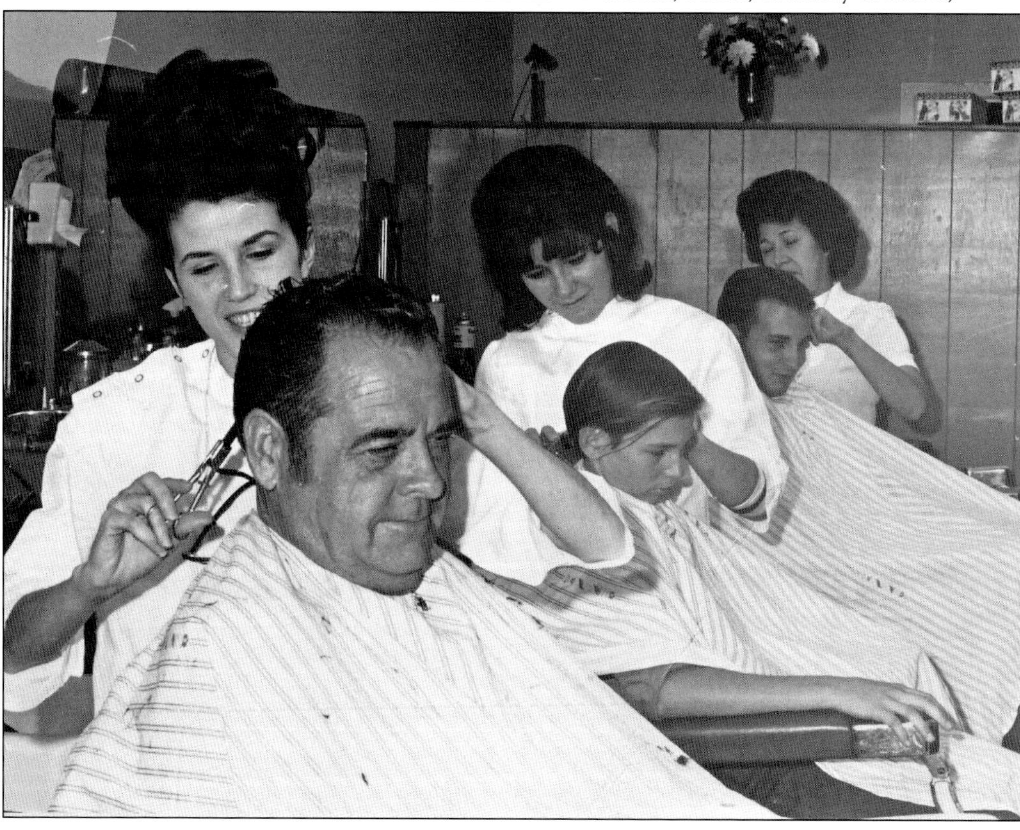

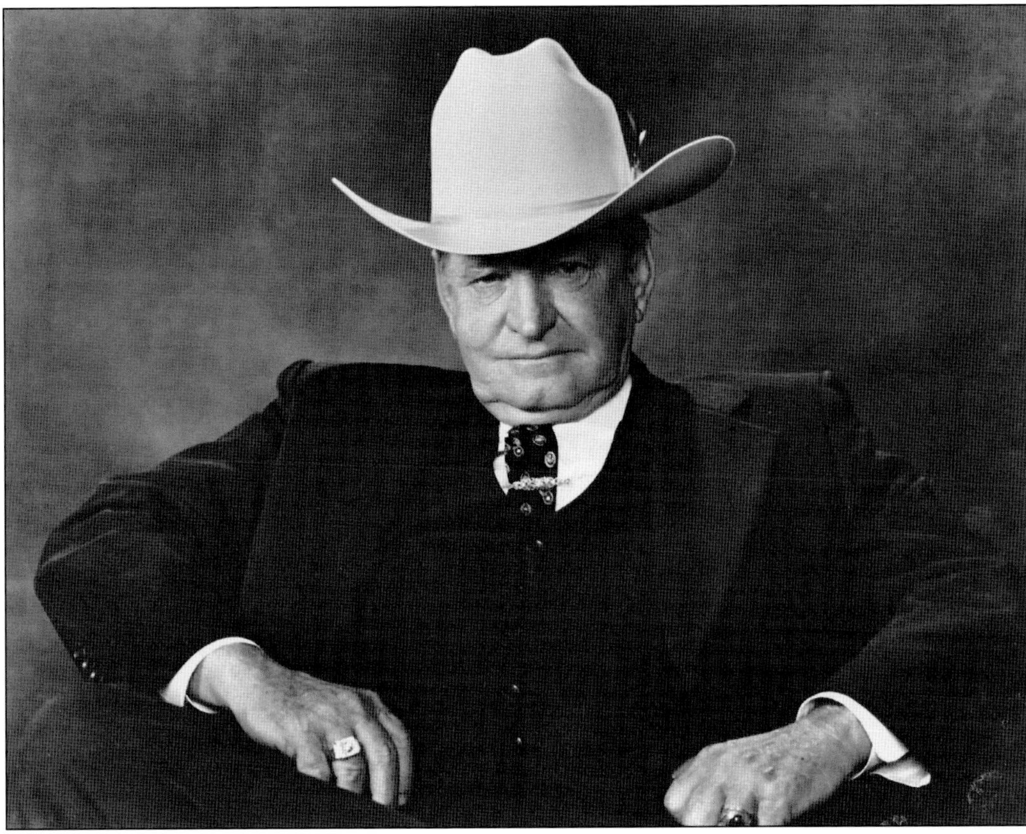

Arch C. Holden Sr. (1919–2002), "the last of the old-time traders," purchased the Erich Menger Ranch in northwest Helotes in 1972. He kept 80 acres around the original house and developed the remaining 477 acres into a residential subdivision called Chimney Creek. In the cattle, land, and oil business, Holden became a civic leader and was the driving force behind the establishment of Helotes's first bank. (Courtesy of HSH.)

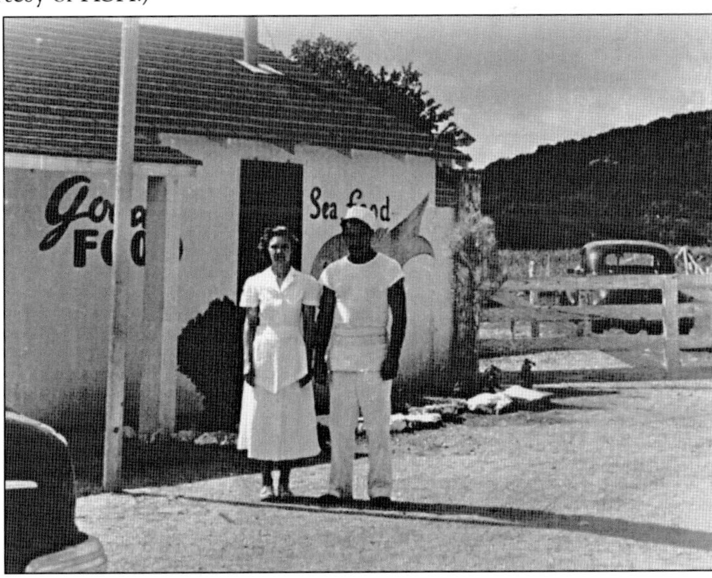

Rudy and Irene Zepeda moved to Helotes in 1946. They opened a restaurant called "Rudy and Irene's" on the northern outskirts of town along Bandera Road. Their eatery, which specialized in Mexican food, was the most popular restaurant in the 1950s and 1960s. In this 1950s photograph, co-owner and cook Irene Zepeda stands next to a kitchen helper in front of the restaurant. (Courtesy of the Lions Club of Helotes.)

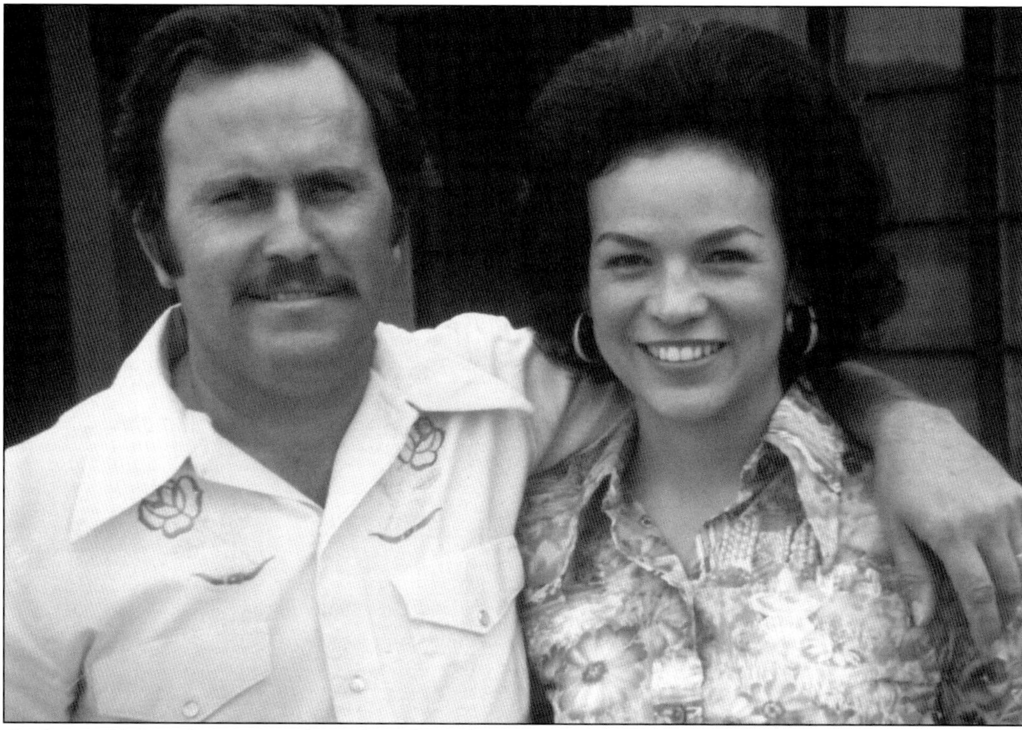

Carlos and Mary Garcia purchased Rudy and Irene's in 1972 and changed the restaurant's name to El Chaparral. The Garcias sold their San Antonio home to purchase the business and lived with their three children—Jessica and twins Gabriel and Carlos—in a small living area connected to the restaurant. Carlos worked in the kitchen, and Mary ran the dining room and cash register. Their sacrifice paid off, and they often had to turn away business because their little Tex-Mex restaurant, shown in the 1972 photograph below, didn't have enough room. (Above and below, courtesy of Carlos and Mary Garcia.)

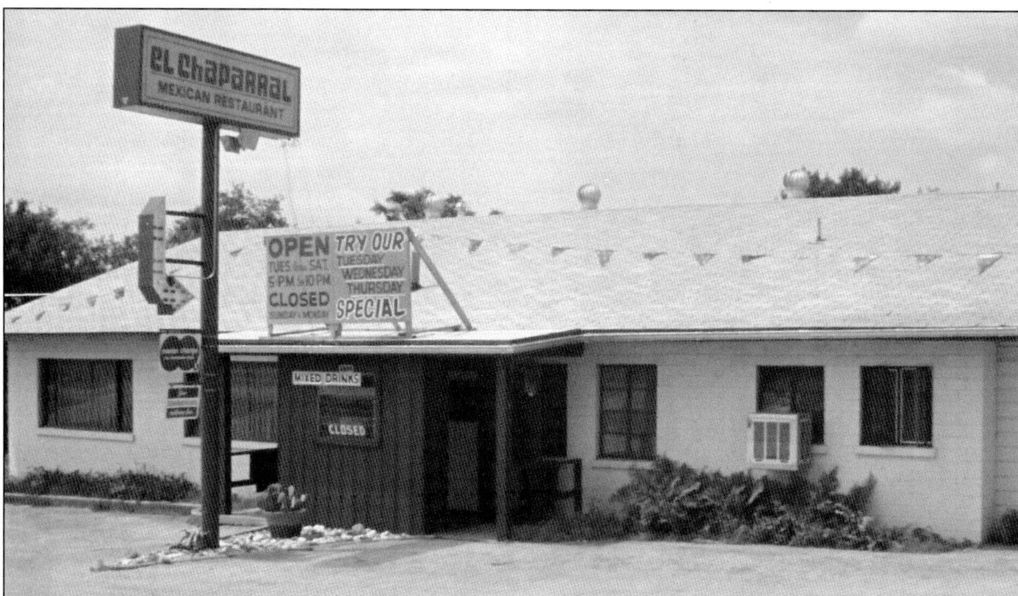

Jessica Garcia, four when her parents opened El Chaparral, often donned an apron to help in the kitchen. A graduate of St. Mary's University, she was in a car accident on Bandera Highway and passed away in 1996. The family keeps her memory alive throughout the restaurant with murals and with a lovely outside patio called "Jessica's Jardin." (Courtesy of Carlos and Mary Garcia.)

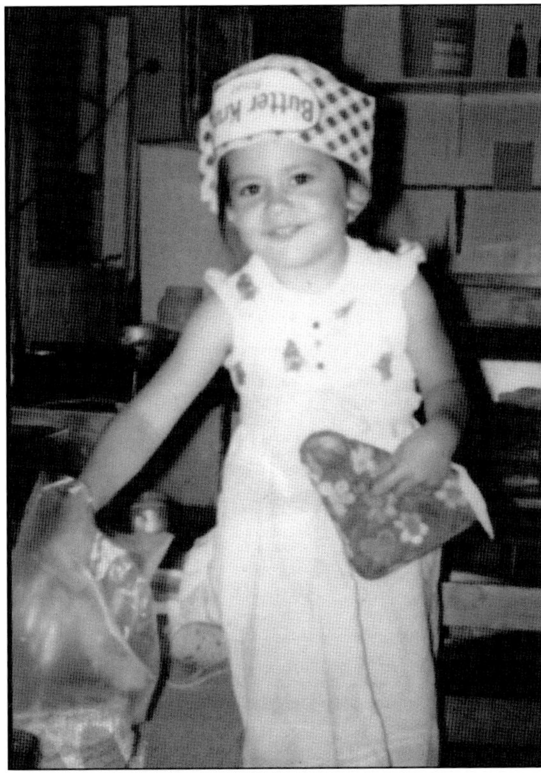

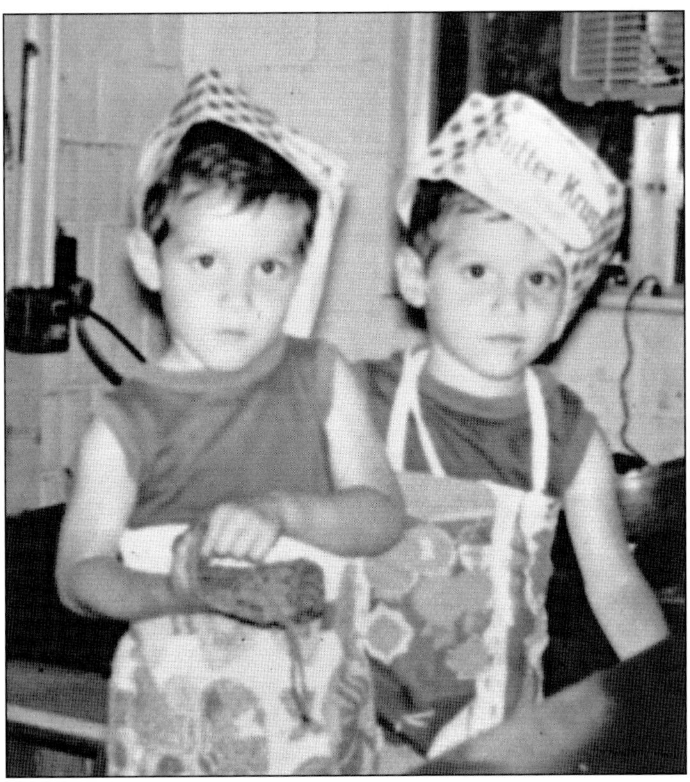

Gabriel and Carlos Garcia were two when their parents moved to Helotes. After their sister's death, the brothers, graduates of the University of North Carolina and professional soccer players, retired from the sport and joined the family business. Now co-owners, they spearheaded an expansion of the restaurant in Helotes in 2002 and the opening of two more locations in Boerne, Texas, and in northeast San Antonio. (Courtesy of Carlos and Mary Garcia.)

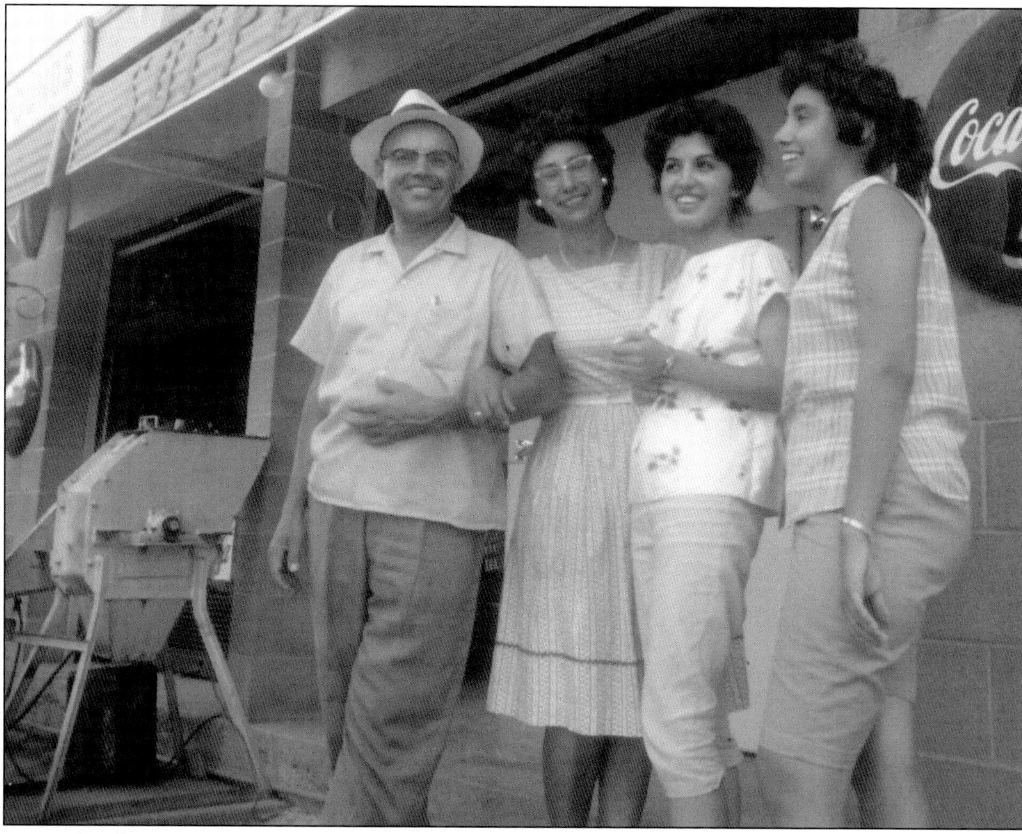

Manuel Villarreal, wife Nora (Treviño) Villarreal, daughter Christine, and Nora's niece Fredericka stand in front of Villarreal's Ice House in 1962. Located on Bandera Road a few miles north of Helotes, the store was established in 1956. The original building, in the 1962 photograph below, was on the west side of Bandera Road. After the county purchased several acres in the 1970s to run the four-lane highway through his property, Manuel moved the store to the east side on a more prominent elevation. He built a large dance hall and a smaller combination dance hall/icehouse that still stand today. Villarreal was one of the few remaining original proprietors at one of only 19 icehouses in Bexar County. When he passed away in 2006 at age 92, he had run the business just shy of 50 years. (Above and below, courtesy of Nora Villarreal.)

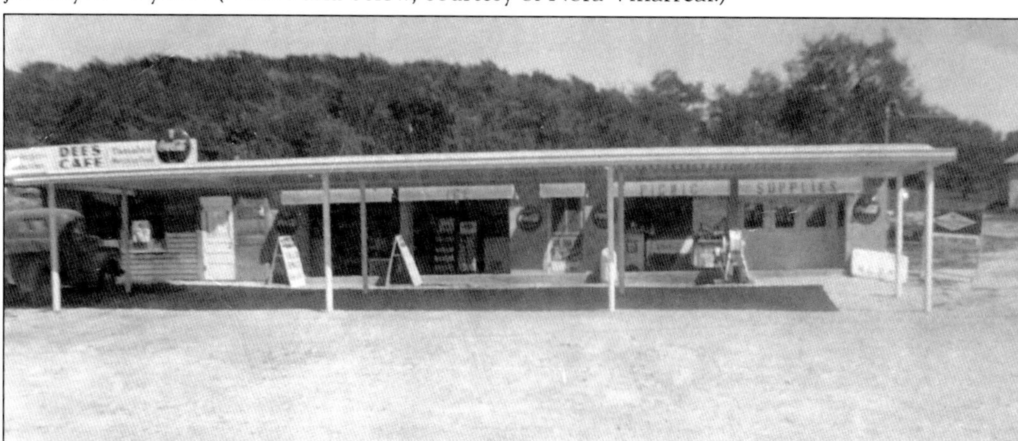

Three

Schools and Churches

After the pioneers built their homesteads and began producing sustenance from their farms and ranches, they turned to the next important endeavors in a community—education and communal worship. Before the first public schools were built, settlers taught their children at home, or they hired someone to teach them. When enough families had settled in the area, the first order of business was to build a school on land donated by civic-minded individuals, and to hire teachers to come live in the community. In the 19th and early 20th centuries, Helotes students walked, rode horses, or drove wagons to a one-room schoolhouse tucked away in the hills, as was Los Reyes School, or situated on farmland, in the case of the Helotes School. Both schools were in operation in the early 1870s. The churches didn't form until the beginning of the 20th century; before that, missionary priests and pastors came to the community for special occasions, but more often, Helotes settlers traveled to San Antonio churches for their religious needs. Finally, in 1906 and 1908, respectively, Lutheran and Catholic congregations built church buildings in Helotes. These two churches filled the needs of the area for more than 50 years, until three more Protestant denominations joined the fold. Today two elementary schools and a high school are within the city limits, and several new churches have joined the first five, promoting a strong ecumenical community.

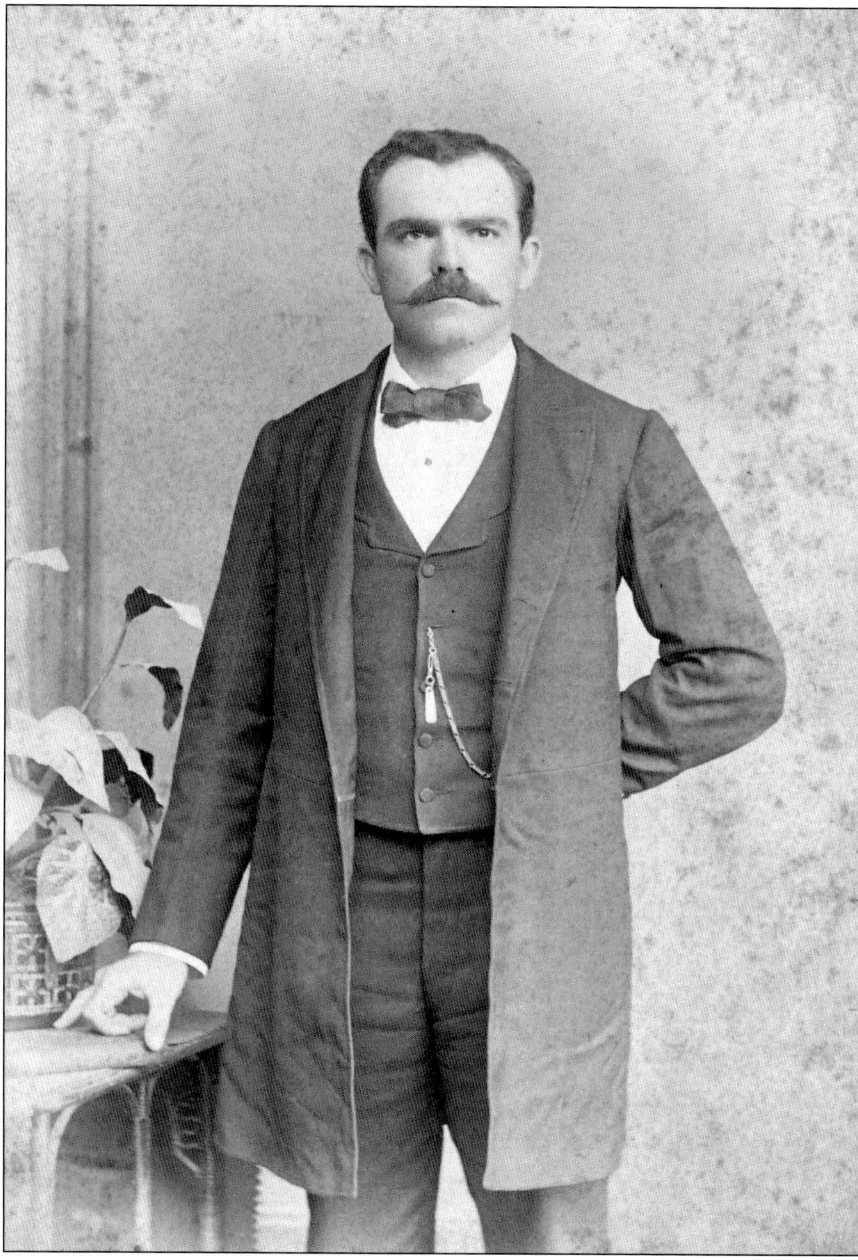

Henry T. Brauchle (1870–1958) arrived in Helotes in 1895 and became one of the settlement's most renowned schoolteachers and civic leaders. Born in Guadalupe County to German settlers, he taught at the Helotes School where his students spoke mostly German. After his July 29, 1897, marriage to Eleanora Jane Robinson (daughter of Augusta Ballscheit and her second husband, Robert E. Robinson), the couple lived in a room adjoining the rock facade schoolhouse. After an eight-year stint there, he taught at the Los Reyes School, 7 miles northwest of Helotes. A school trustee, election judge, owner and operator of the Helotes telephone system, and father of 10, Brauchle owned a 175-acre farm where the Helotes municipal buildings now stand. In 1990, an elementary school in northwest San Antonio was named in honor of this exemplary educator. (Courtesy of Ruth Lampman.)

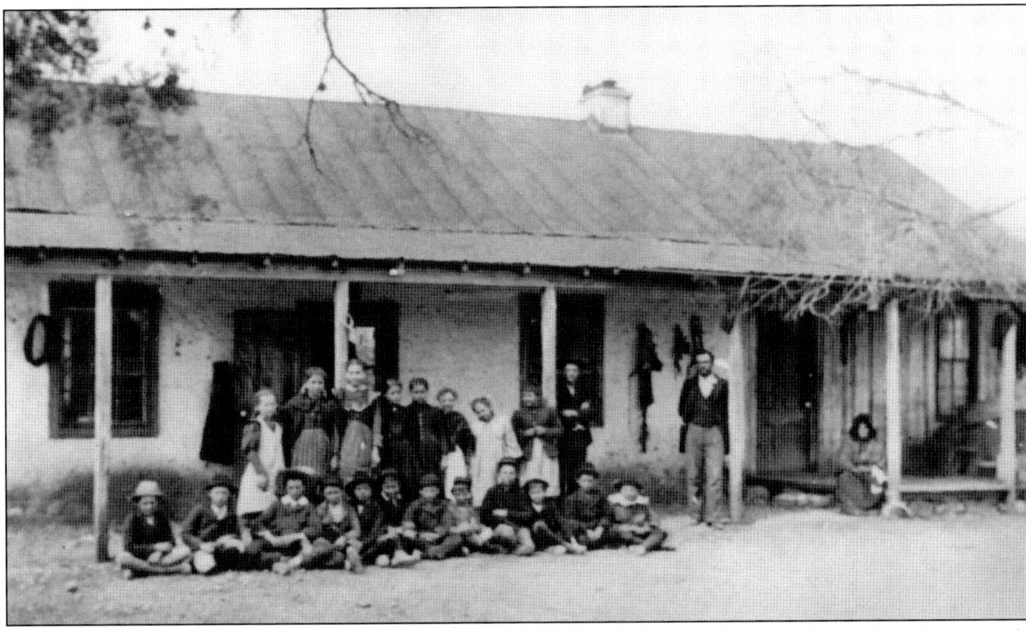

Henry T. Brauchle and his students pose in front of the Helotes School in this 1896 photograph. Also called the Boerner School for the family that donated the land in 1874, the rock schoolhouse was near today's Sandra Day O'Connor High School. Brauchle had 20 to 40 students, depending on the season. During planting or harvesting, the number decreased when the children helped their families in the fields. (Courtesy of Northside Independent School District, NISD.)

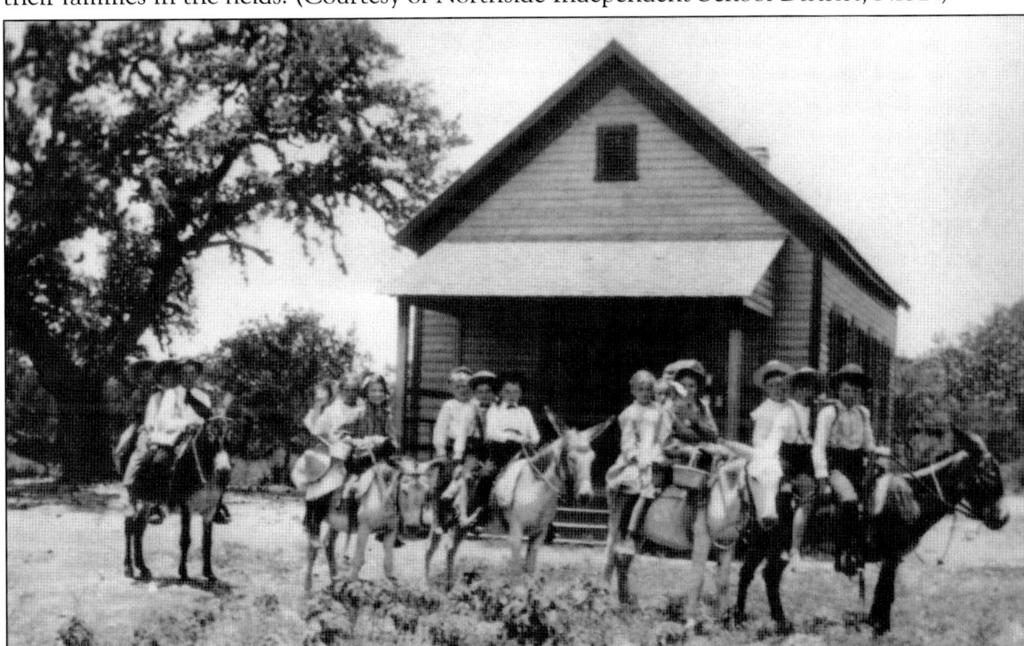

Students traveled to school in various ways. In this photograph, taken about 1908, students pose on their burros in front of the wood-frame 1902 Helotes School, built on the west side of Leslie Road, about 1 mile south of Bandera Road. This school replaced the old Boerner School. (Courtesy of NISD.)

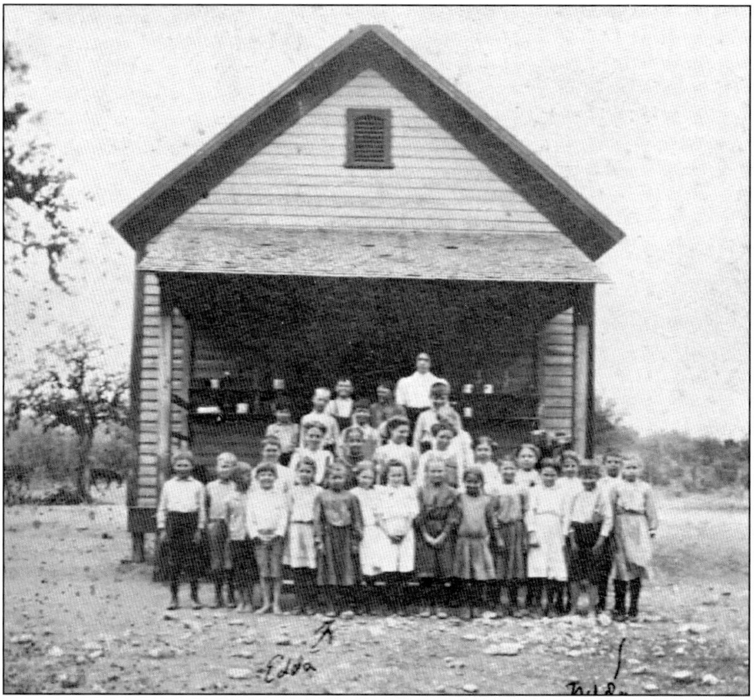

Leah Sales taught grades one through eight in this one-room Helotes schoolhouse from 1908 to 1910. Students who lived in rural communities often stopped going to school after eighth grade unless their parents had relatives with whom their children could board in town near a high school. The only individuals identified in this 1908 photograph are the teacher, and Edda and Thusnelda Braun, who are tagged on the image itself. (Courtesy of Fred W. Wendt.)

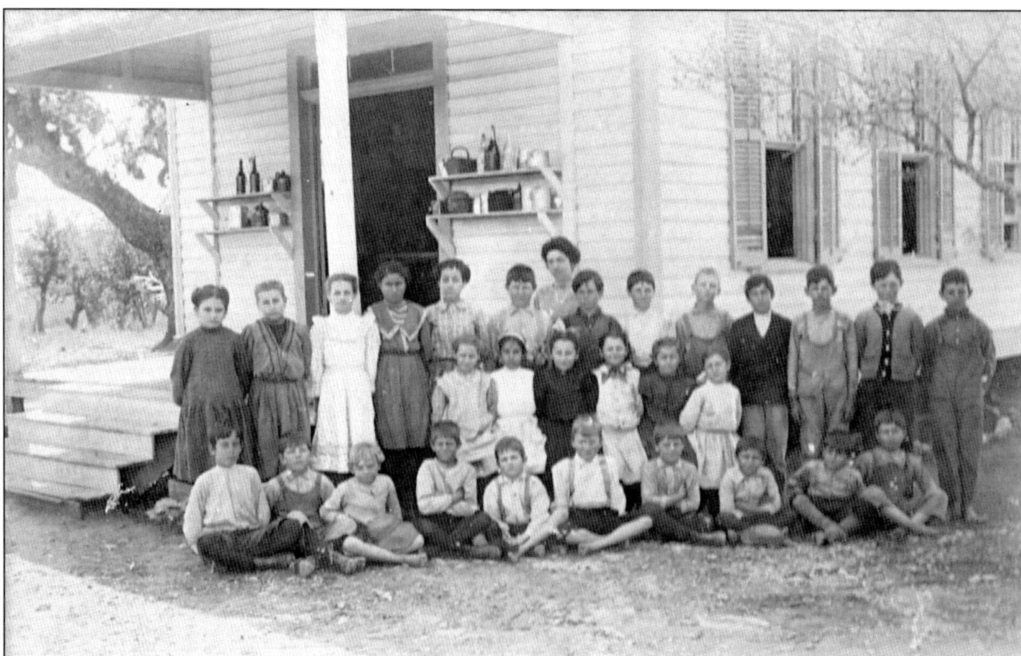

Among the students in this photograph taken about 1909 are Thusnelda and Sabrina Braun. Thusnelda thought school was "lots of fun," according to a comment written on the back of the picture. (Courtesy of Fred W. Wendt.)

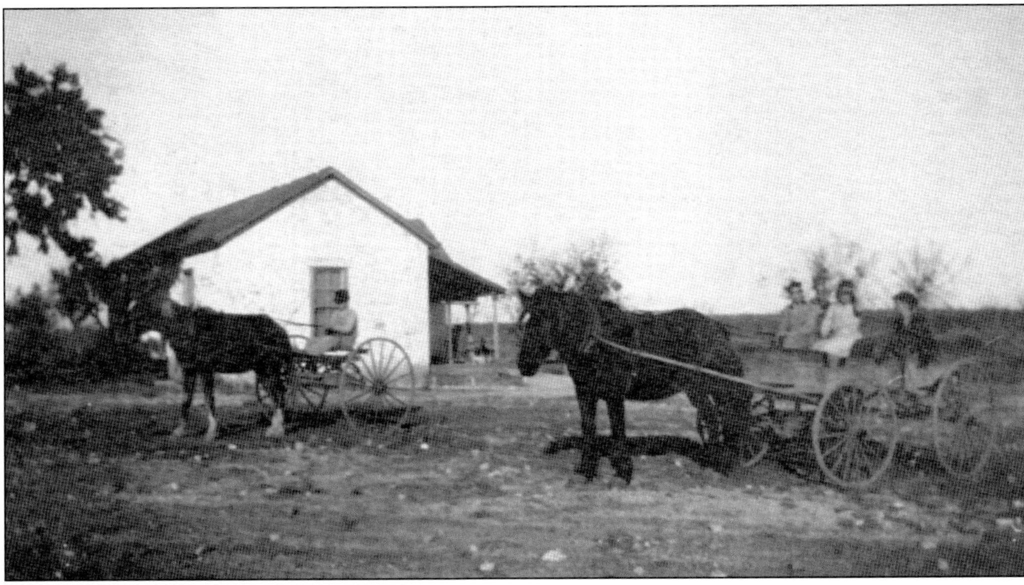

In this 1908 photograph, Thusnelda, Edda, and Felix Braun, riding in a buggy, are either arriving home or going to school accompanied by Tom Campbell in a gig. Campbell, the adopted son of Henry and Emma (Braun) Wehmeyer and a cousin of the Braun children, died of the Spanish Influenza during the 1918 epidemic. (Courtesy of Fred W. Wendt.)

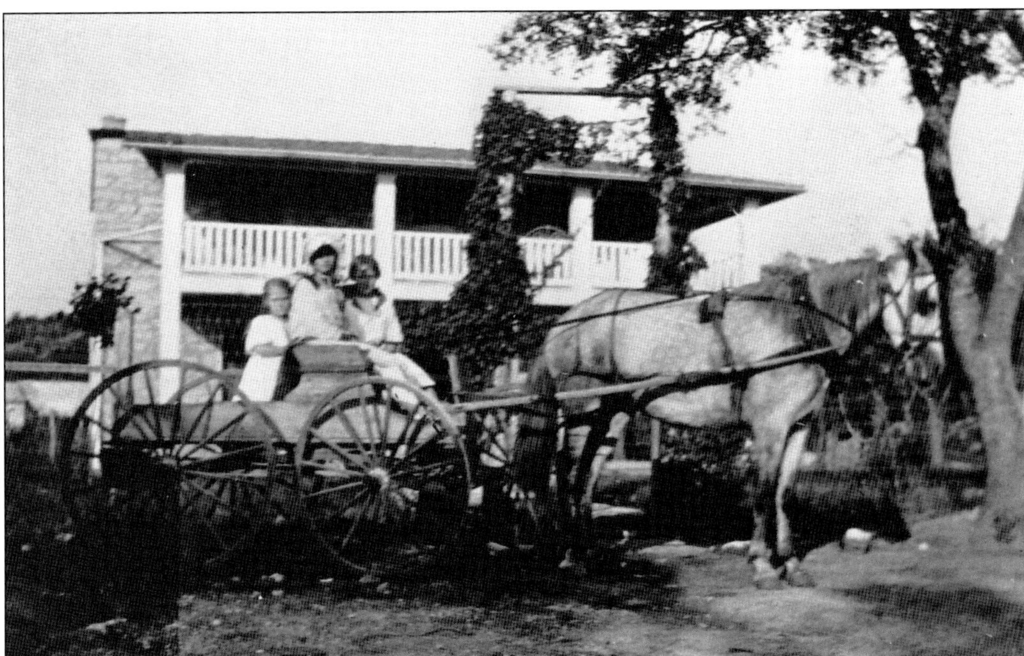

Alta Hileman drove herself and her two sisters, Ruth and Vera, to the Helotes School from their home in downtown Helotes. The girls are shown here in 1914. According to Alta, her horse hurried home after school to be with her colt. (Courtesy of Kyle Cunningham.)

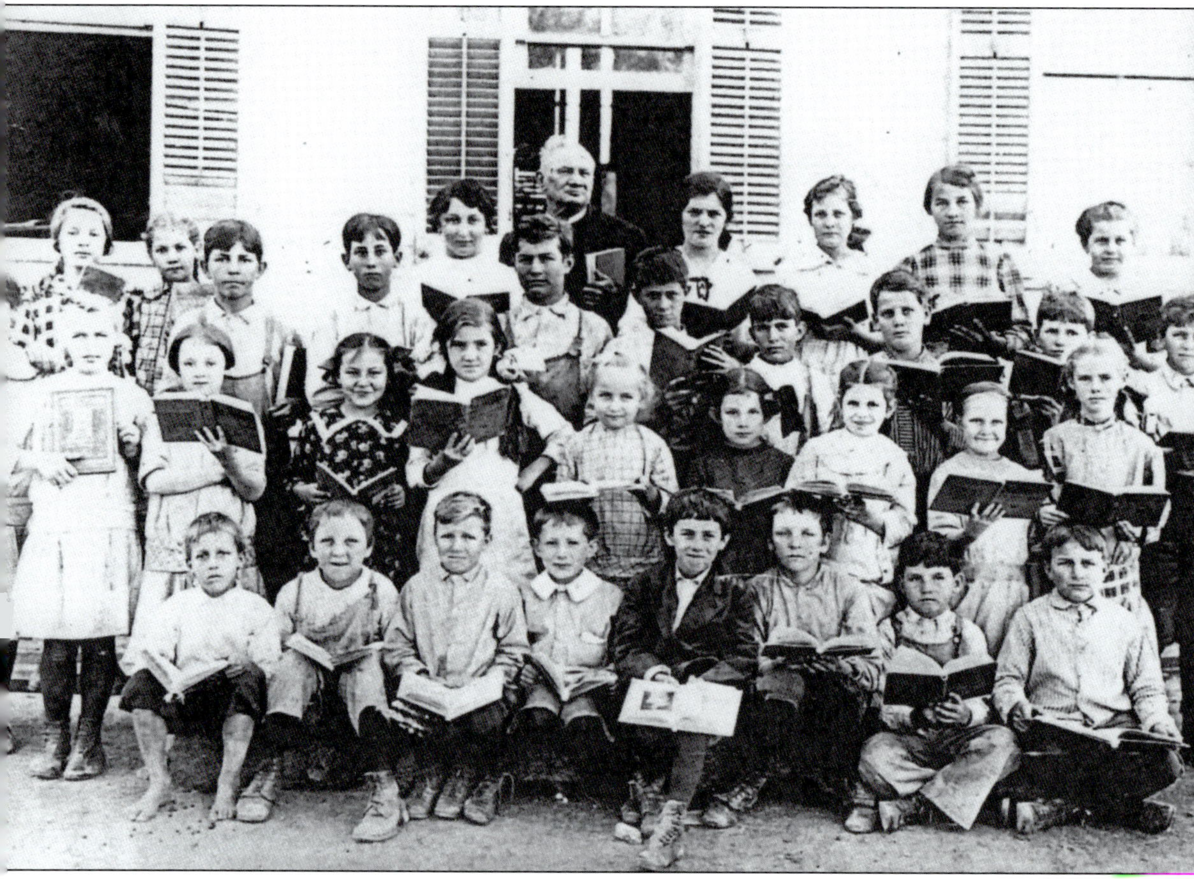

The Helotes School class of 1914 is shown here. From left to right, they are (first row) Freddie Biering, Clarence Galm, Arnold Mosmann, Carl Zettner, Bennie Lee, Freddie Galm, Roy Brauchle, and Fritz Mosmann; (second row) Alta Hileman, Nettie Braun, Ruth Hileman, Thelma Tezel, Gladys MacDonald, Amanda Braun, Elizabeth Zettner, Ellen Brauchle, Vera Hileman, and May Spizers; (third row) Gertrude Woller, Ada Woller, Henry Brauchle, George Lee, Felix Braun, Max Benke, Gussie Mosmann, Robert Biering, Hugh Brauchle, and Eugene Weimer; (fourth row) Alma Scheffler, teacher Simon Zettner, Emmy Brauchle, Elsie Biering, Rosie Biering, and Etta Braun. (Courtesy of Ruth Lampman.)

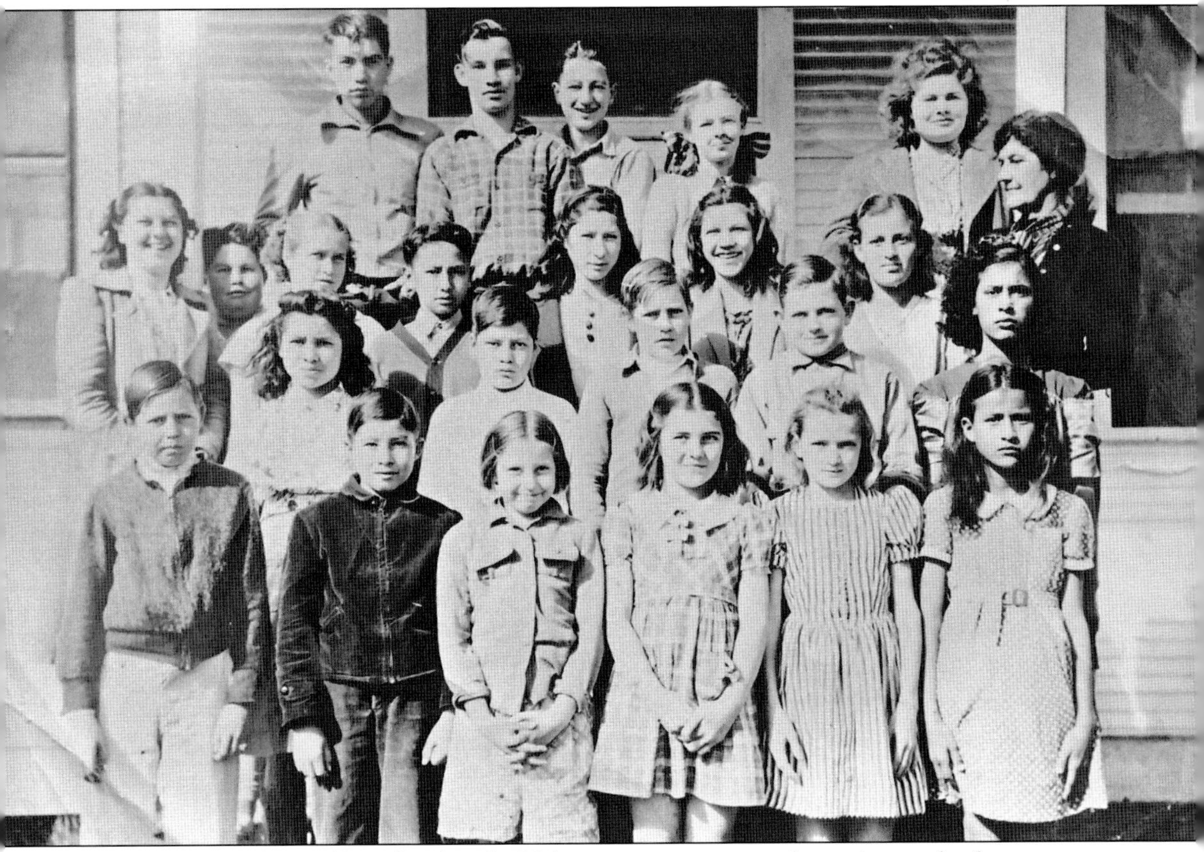

Los Reyes was the first public school in the Helotes area, operating a few miles north of town near Los Reyes Creek starting about 1870. Built on Morales family land, it was later reestablished on the Frank Madla Ranch. In 1939, Los Reyes and the Helotes School united to form the Helotes Common School District. Two one-room wooden structures were moved to Riggs Road, just south of downtown Helotes on land donated by James and Kate Riggs. The Los Reyes class of 1940–1941 is shown in this photograph. From left to right, they are (first row) Floyd Ott, Matthew Madla, Etta Mae Ott, Lottie Hendrick, Frances Josephine "Frankie Jo" Whetstone, and Aurelia Valdez; (second row) Maria Padilla, Frank ?, Cecil Ott, Donald Sims, and Maria Valdez; (third row) Joyce ?, William Owens, Flossie Miller, Robert Rosas, Matilde Morales, Margaret Menchaca, and Pauline Valdez; (fourth row) Jesse Menchaca, Frank Maltsberger, Chris Demans, Imogene Stolle, Dorothy Owens, and teacher Mrs. Mosely. (Courtesy of Matilde Morales Diaz.)

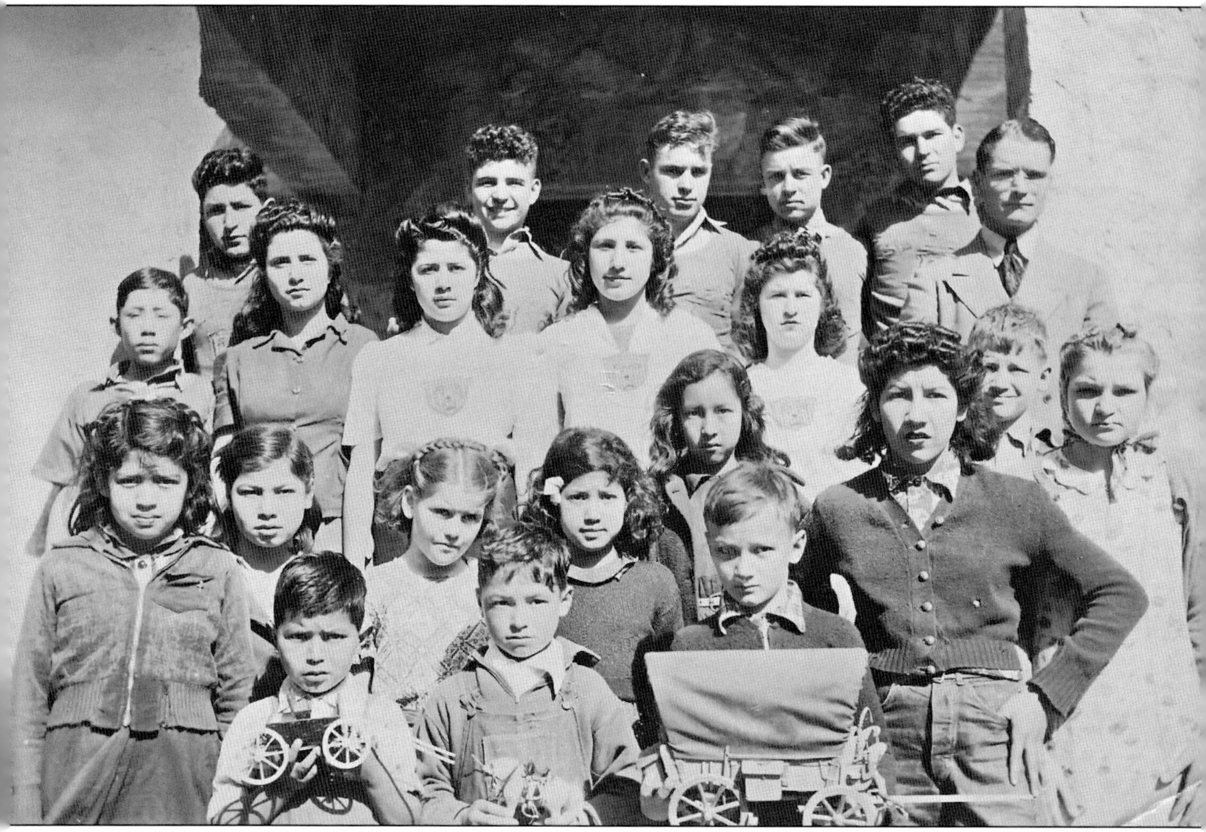

Clifton (also called Clifden), a planned community that never developed, was located on Bandera Road 9 miles northwest of Helotes. The Clifton School operated from 1882 to 1950, when it was discontinued and its students were transferred to the Helotes School in the newly formed Northside Common School District. Seen from left to right in this 1940 class photograph are (first row) Emilio Martinez, Felix Hernandez, Thomas Schott, and Victoria ?; (second row) two unidentified girls, Faye Brauchle, two unidentified girls, an unidentified boy, and another unidentified girl; (third row) Joe Casillas, Gloria Martinez, Ella Sanchez, Beatrice Sanchez, Bertha Hernandez, and teacher Dub Carter; (fourth row) Arthur Martinez, Armando Hernandez, Alexander "Sandy" Logan, James Logan, and Johnny Hernandez. The boys in front are displaying wagons and a horse made by the Logan brothers. (Photograph courtesy of Felix Hernandez.)

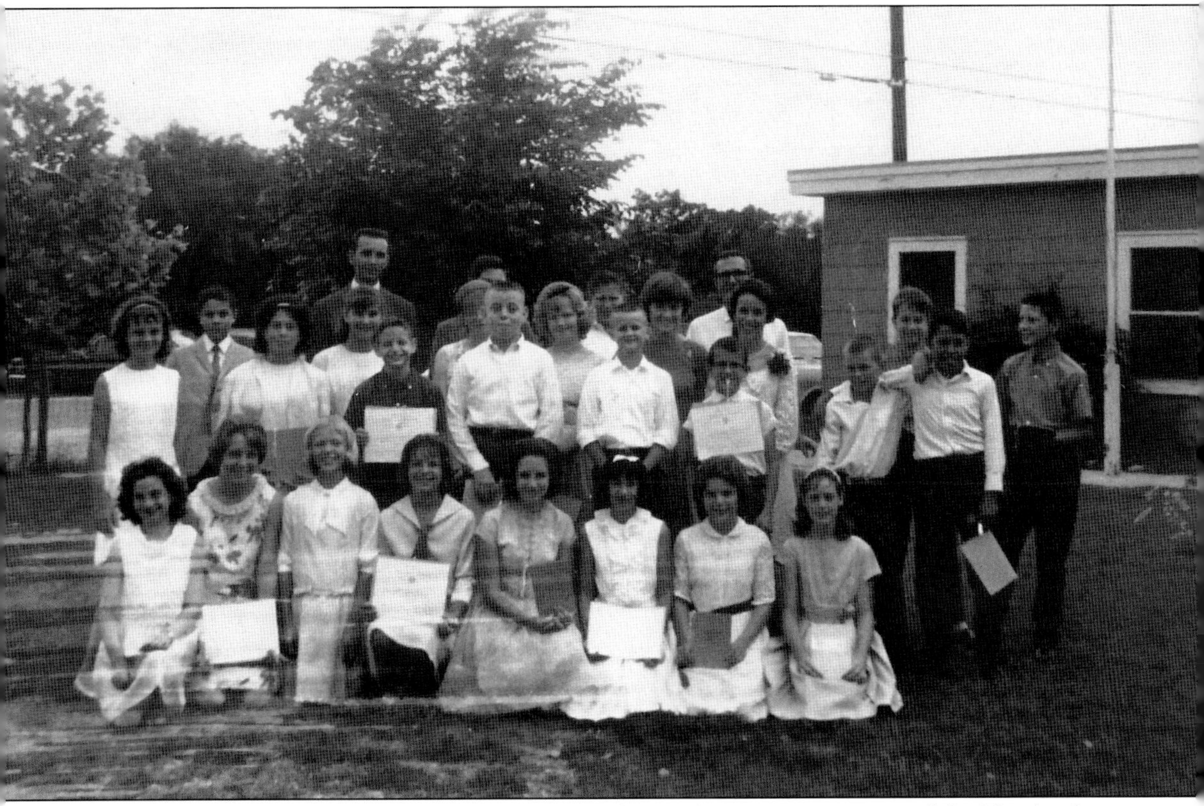

When this picture was taken on May 28, 1965, Helotes Elementary was part of the Northside Independent School District. Seen here is the 1965 sixth-grade graduating class of Helotes Elementary. From left to right, they are (kneeling) Ann Hernandez, Jeffrea Hughey, Jackie McCarter, Robin Wynn, Tommie Lou Cunningham, Mary Jane Logan, D'Laine Parrot, and Sally Mayfield; (standing) Becky Collier, Alexander "Sandy" Logan, Margaret Perez, teacher Tom Zuberbueler, Julie Darnell, Curtis Nichols, Deby Smith, James Logan (behind Smith), Jay Miller, Debbie Duecker, Benny Menchaca (behind Duecker), Glenn Snapp, Melody Mikel, Danny Poor, Lee Ann Laremore and principal Leslie Fulenwider (both behind Poor), Larry Ayers, Nelson Surles, Sammy Rodriguez, and Ray Menchaca. (Courtesy of Mary Jane Blanco.)

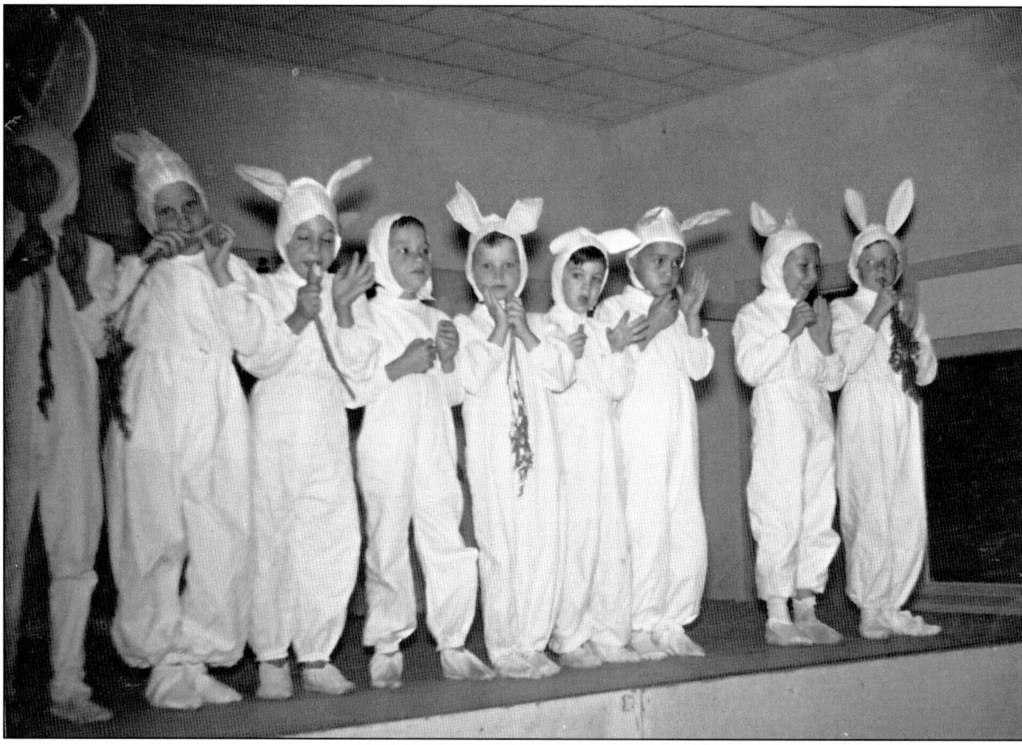

This Easter program at Helotes Elementary School in 1951 featured several bunnies. The first three on the left could not be identified. The others, left to right, are Ralph Madla, Freddie Schmitt, Jimmy MacAllister, David Rodriguez, Manuel Balero, and Mickey Birch. (Courtesy of Ralph Madla.)

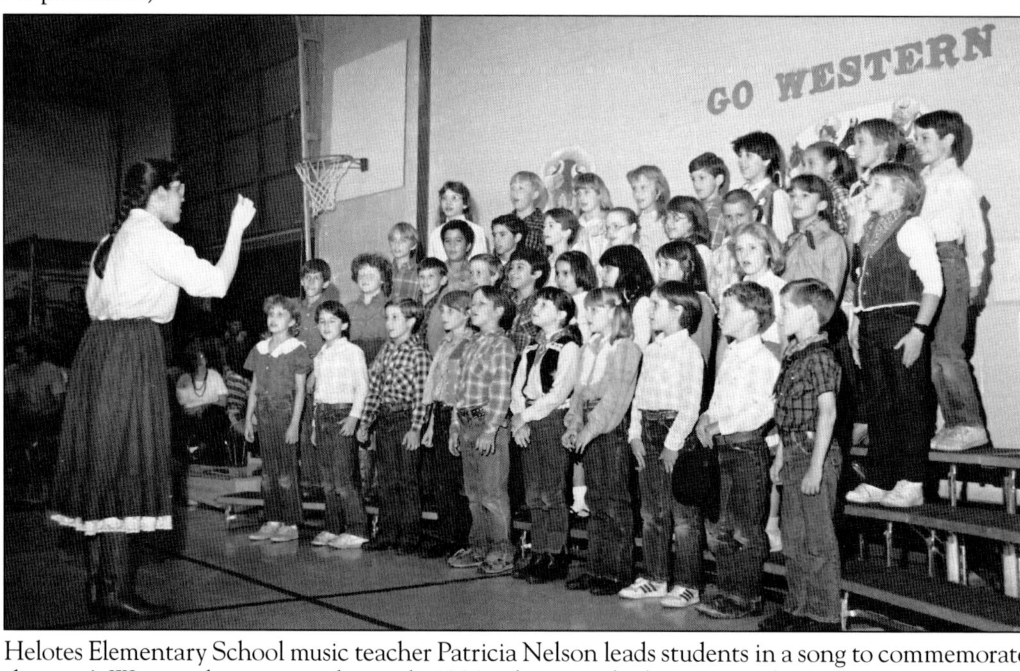

Helotes Elementary School music teacher Patricia Nelson leads students in a song to commemorate the area's Western heritage in this early 1980s photograph. (Courtesy of HSH.)

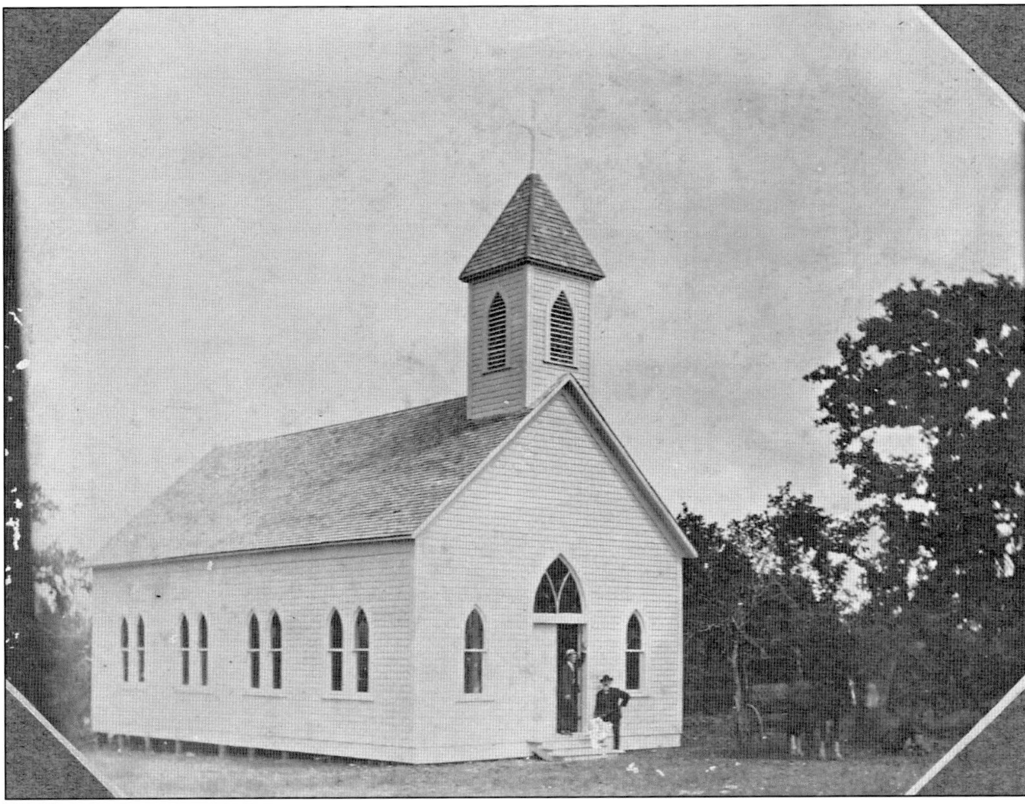

The Gugger family donated land for the building of Zion Lutheran Church of Helotes, which was dedicated June 10, 1906, and included the gravesite of Anton Gugger. Zion Lutheran, shown in this 1915 photograph, was the first church in northwest Bexar County, and its cemetery was the final resting place for many Helotes pioneers. The grave in the photograph below is that of Friedrick Braun who died December 25, 1915. The cemetery and church on Leslie Road near the intersection of Braun Road and Loop 1604 received Texas Historic Landmark designation in 1986 and 1997, respectively. Two more churches were built in later years; the original church building is now used for special occasions. (Above and at right, courtesy of Fred W. Wendt.)

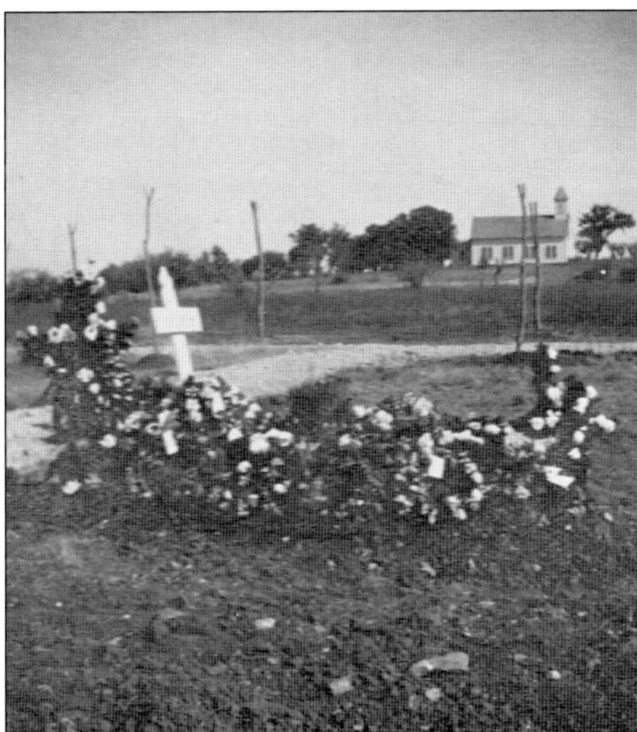

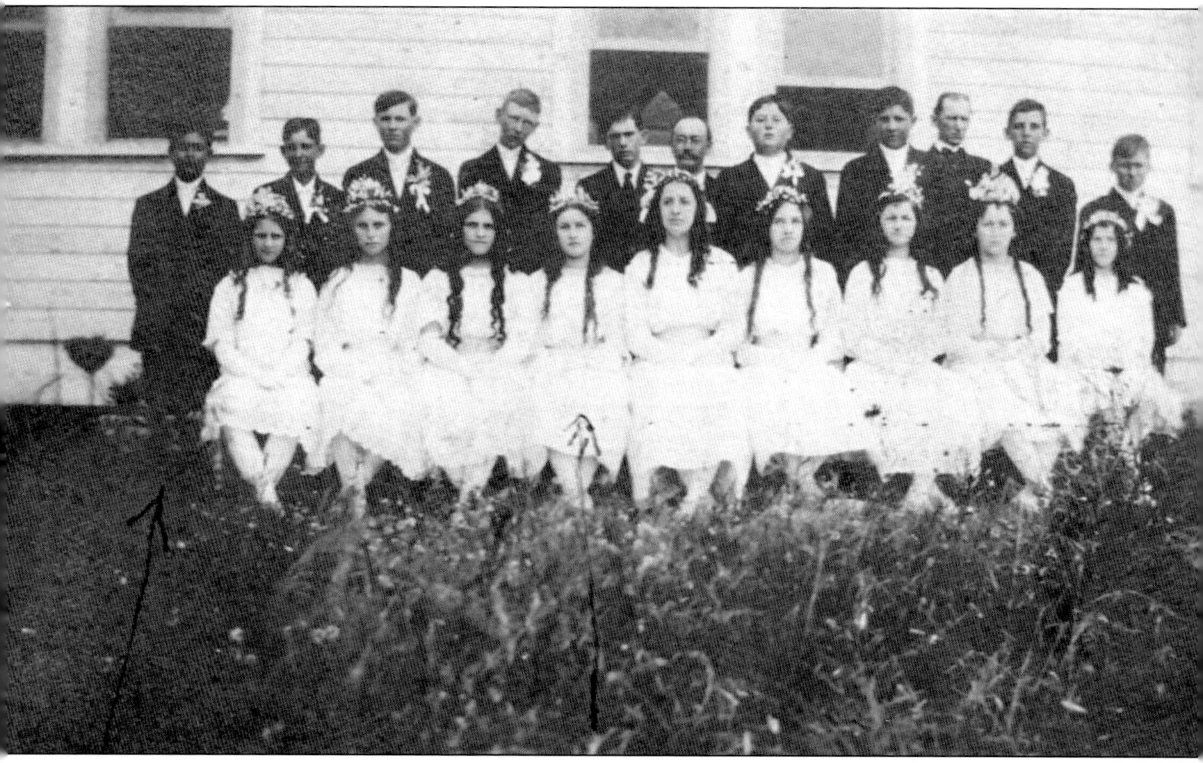

This photograph taken March 17, 1914, shows Zion Lutheran Church's Confirmation class, left to right, (first row) Elsie Biering, Hilda Steubing, Emmie Brauchle, Thusnelda Braun, Lena Biering, Rosie Biering, Dorothea Benke, Alma Scheffler, and Mabel Steubing; (second row), Felix Braun, Dallas Steubing, Richard Steubing, Max Benke, George Brauchle, pastor Nicolas Frueh, Erwin Steubing, Arthur Steubing, an unidentified person, John Galm, and Julius Mosmann. (Courtesy of Fred W. Wendt.)

Our Lady of Guadalupe Catholic Church, also called Los Reyes Church, was located on Bandera Road on land donated by Pedro and Manuela Treviño. Built in 1908, it burned down in 1924, and the church used the land for a Catholic cemetery. This photograph, taken in 1914, shows parishioners assembled in front of the church after celebration of a First Holy Communion Mass. The photograph below was taken inside the church and shows communicants at the altar. From left to right, they are Ada Woller, Anna Woller, an unidentified person, and George Marnoch. (At right, courtesy of Our Lady of Guadalupe Catholic Church, OLG; below, courtesy of John Igo.)

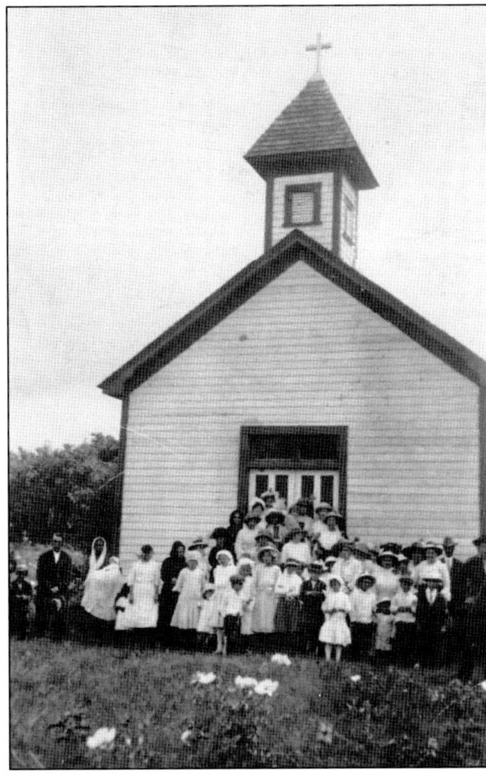

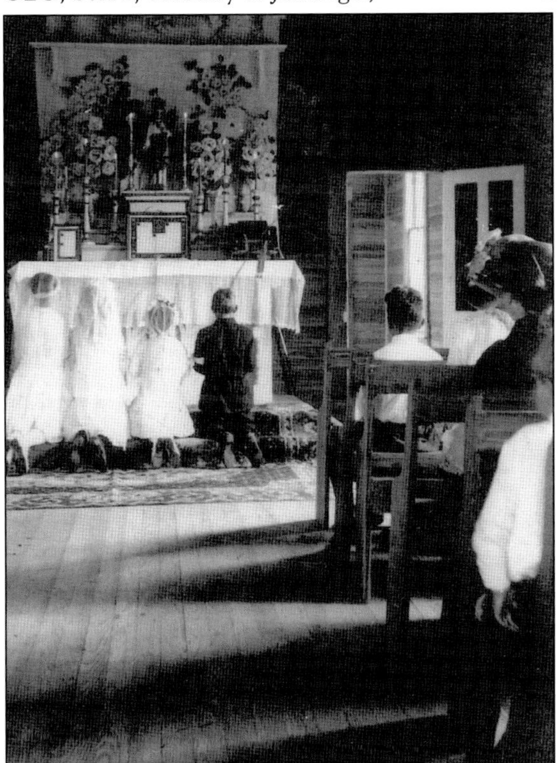

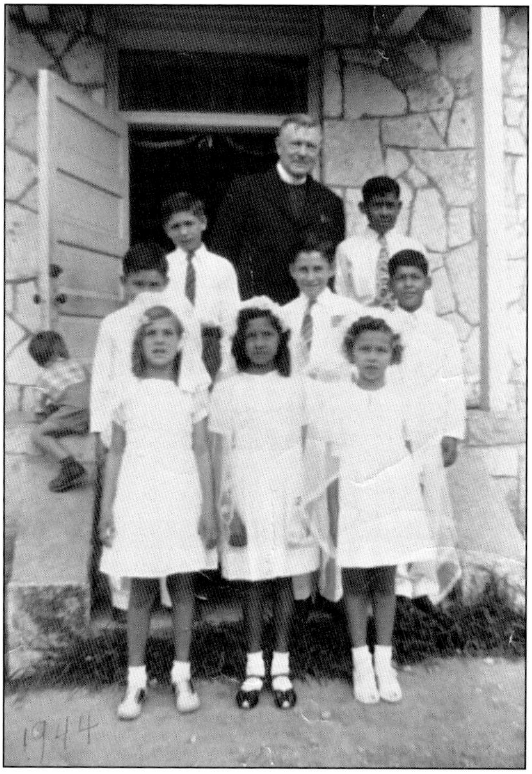

Before a new Catholic church was built, summer Bible schools and other types of services were held at Helotes Elementary School. This photograph shows the 1944 Communion class standing on the steps of the school. From left to right, they are (first row) Ophelia Barrera, Margaret Rosas, and an unidentified student; (second row) Felix Madla, Jesse Madla, and Narcisco Padilla; (third row) Ernest Barrera, Fr. Alfred Rabe, and Tom Padilla. (Courtesy of Juanita "Janie" Madla.)

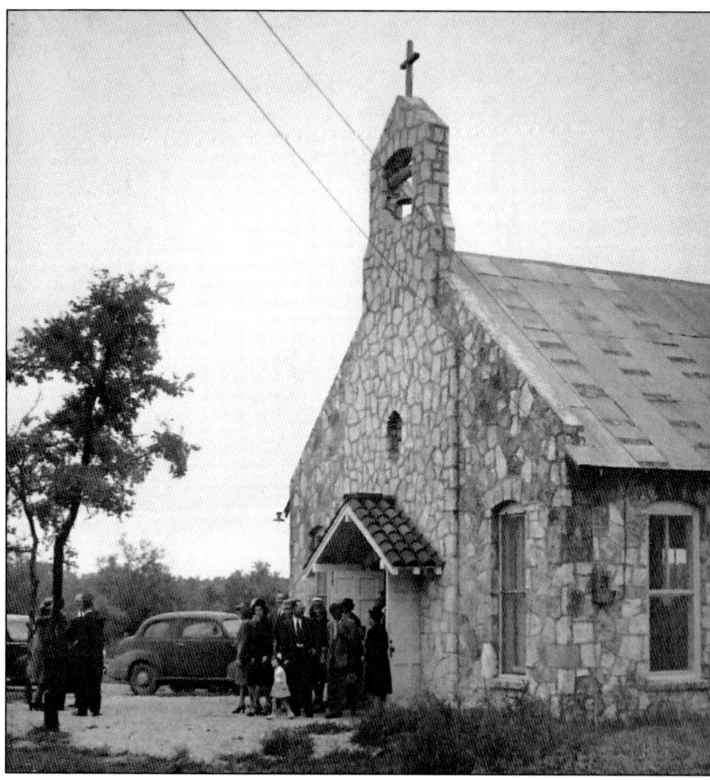

On August 5, 1943, a group of parishioners, under the direction of Fr. William Lamm, broke ground for a new Our Lady of Guadalupe Catholic Church on land donated by Fernando and Kathryn Antonio. The church, located on Riggs Road across the street from Helotes Elementary School, seated 250 people and was completed in June 1944. This photograph, taken October 5, 1945, shows the church before the bell tower was added. (Courtesy of OLG.)

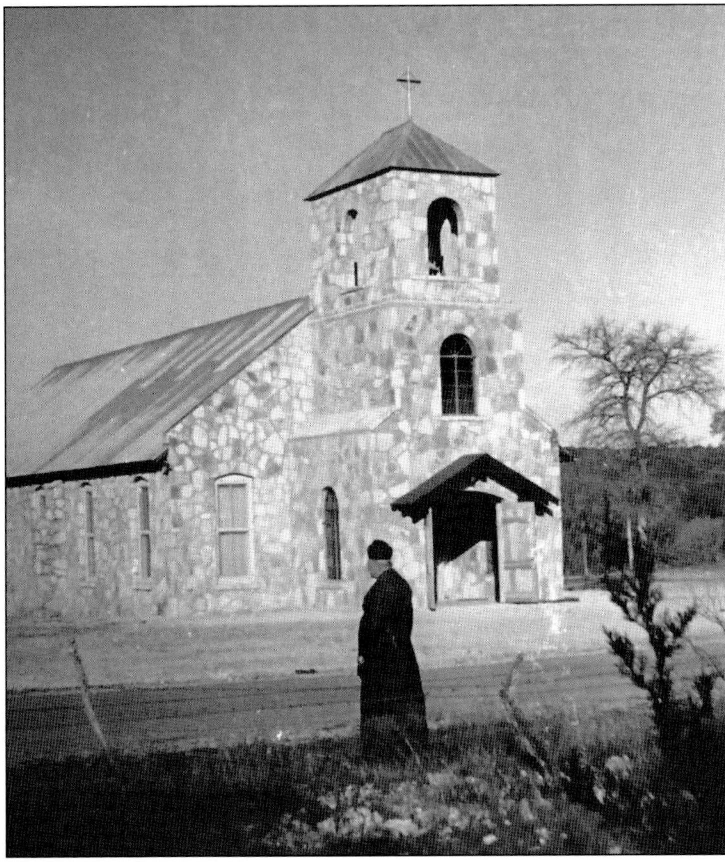

Fr. Alfred Rabe, the parish's first priest, stands in front of Our Lady of Guadalupe Catholic Church in January 1952, after the bell tower, which included a vestibule, was added. The photograph below, taken in 1985, shows the rural church before a new sanctuary seating 1,000 parishioners was built five years later. The new church, built of native limestone, incorporated a portion of the original building, which is now used as a day chapel. (At right, courtesy of OLG; below, courtesy of Nora Villarreal.)

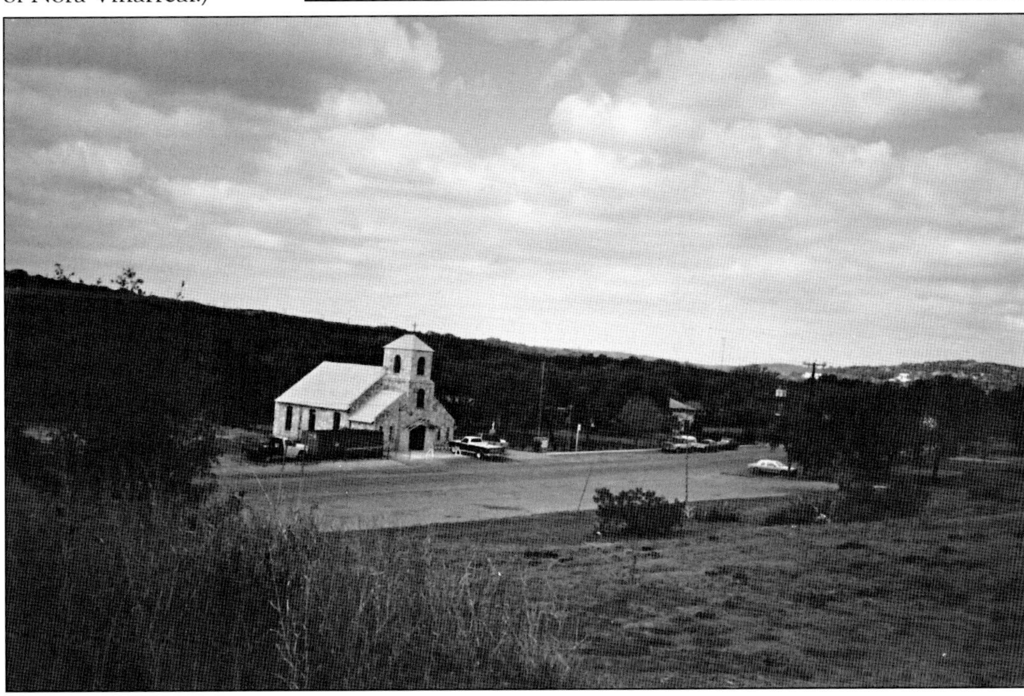

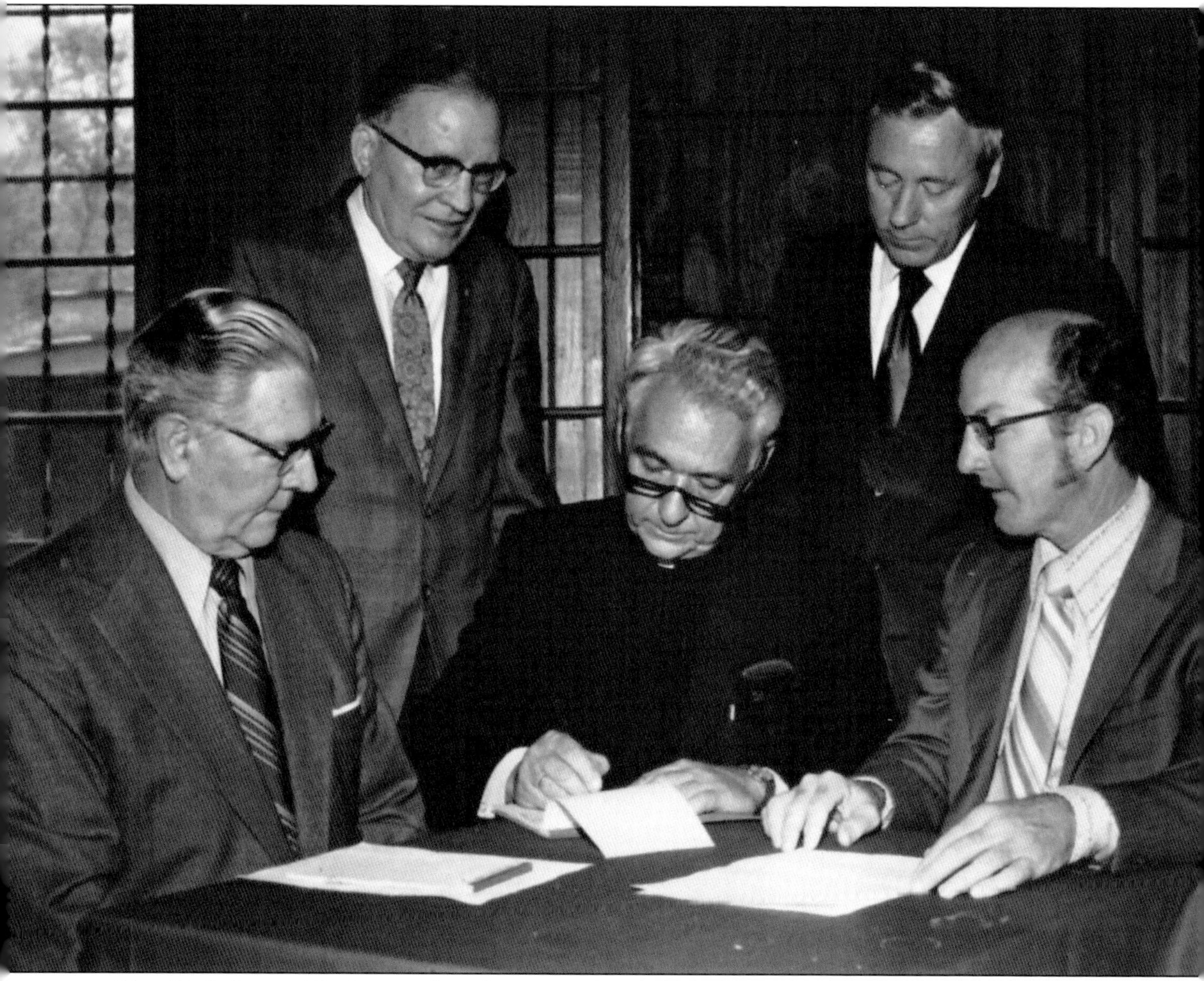

The Catholic and Lutheran churches were the only denominations in Helotes for many years; however, within the first six years of the 1960s, three new denominations—Baptist, Presbyterian, and Methodist—joined their ranks. In 1972, local pastors drew up plans for the Father's Day observances in their respective churches. Seen here from left to right, are (seated) Rev. Samuel Terry of Forest Hills Presbyterian, Fr. Louis Trawalter of Our Lady of Guadalupe Catholic, and Rev. W. C. Maddox of Helotes Baptist; (standing) Rev. C. L. Bohls of Zion Lutheran, and Rev. Collin Furr of Helotes Hills Methodist. (Courtesy of HSH.)

Four

Recreation and Civic Activities

Creeks for fishing and swimming, hills for hiking, valleys for horseback riding, and plenty of game for hunting—Helotes provided a choice of places and activities for recreation. The beauty of the landscape called out to both residents and city folk. After a laborious workweek in the fields, on the range, or at an office in the city, Sunday afternoons saw people mingling with their neighbors at the local shooting club, where they could not only practice their gun skills, but also partake in cold mugs of beer. They cooled themselves off at the nearest swimming hole or went for a hike in the hills. Some harnessed their favorite horse for a trot along a creek while others went for hayrides—by wagon in the early years, in later years by truck. Those with musical interests joined the brass band, and people with an artistic bent formed an art guild. As the community grew, so did efforts to sponsor activities to keep local youth busy. Baseball and softball teams were formed, and a Boy Scout troop was chartered. Civic organizations sprang from the need for safety, charity, and preservation, and fortunately for the posterity of the town, someone saw the need to record what was happening in that most civic of organizations—the town newspaper.

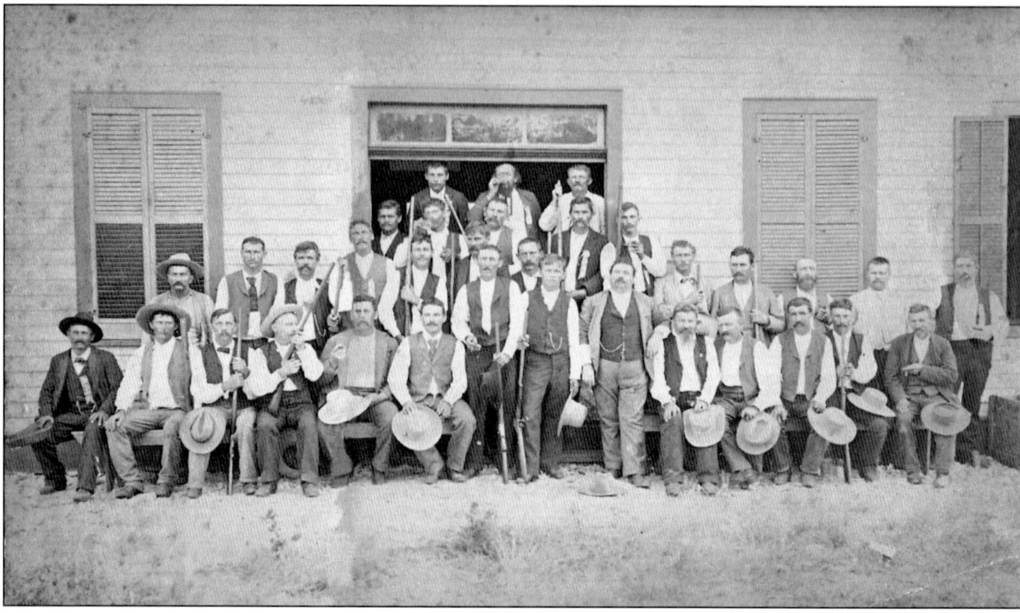

The Braun family deeded six acres to the newly formed Helotes Shooting Club on December 9, 1889. Called *Schuetzen Verin* in German, the shooting club was a popular Sunday afternoon entertainment and often held target or turkey shoots at its rifle range using muzzle-loaded guns. This photograph shows club members at a prize shoot on September 10, 1893. (Courtesy of Ruth Lampman.)

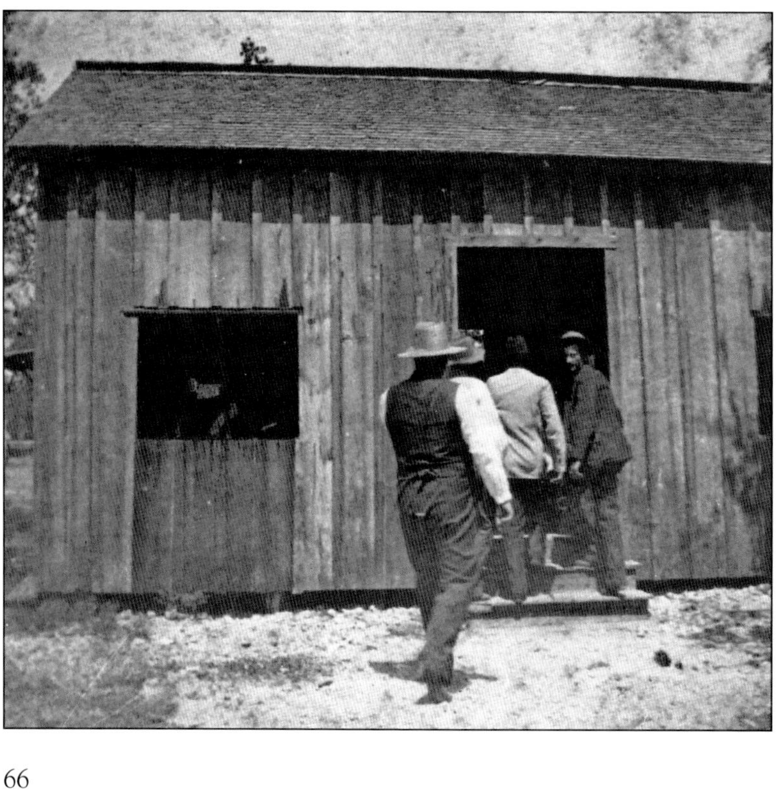

This photograph taken at a prize shoot on September 10, 1893, at the Helotes Shooting Club grounds shows patrons going into a saloon there. Members and guests could purchase keg beer for 5¢ a mug. For 10¢, a patron could purchase a tin bucket filled with beer to take home. (Courtesy of Institute of Texan Cultures, Laura Long Collection.)

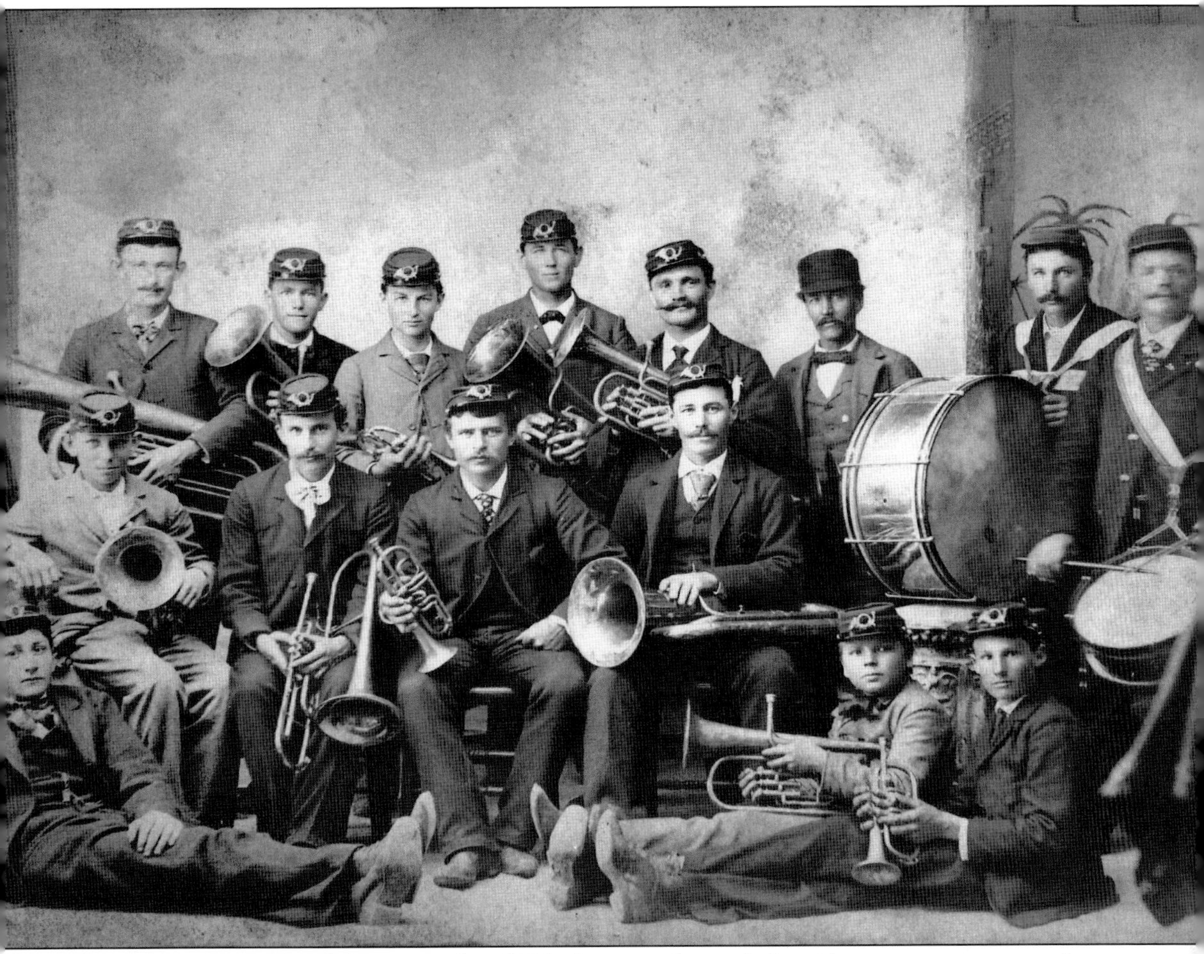

The Helotes Brass Band shown in this 1896 photograph regaled residents at town events for several years. The German fraternal organization, Hermann Sons, which chartered Lodge 76 in Helotes on June 3, 1893, sponsored the band, which often practiced and held concerts at the Helotes Shooting Club Hall. In the top row are Theodore Biering (first from left), Henry Steubing Jr. (fourth from left), Herman Mosmann (fifth from left), and Alex Benke (second from right). (Courtesy of Institute of Texan Cultures, Pat Zettner Collection.)

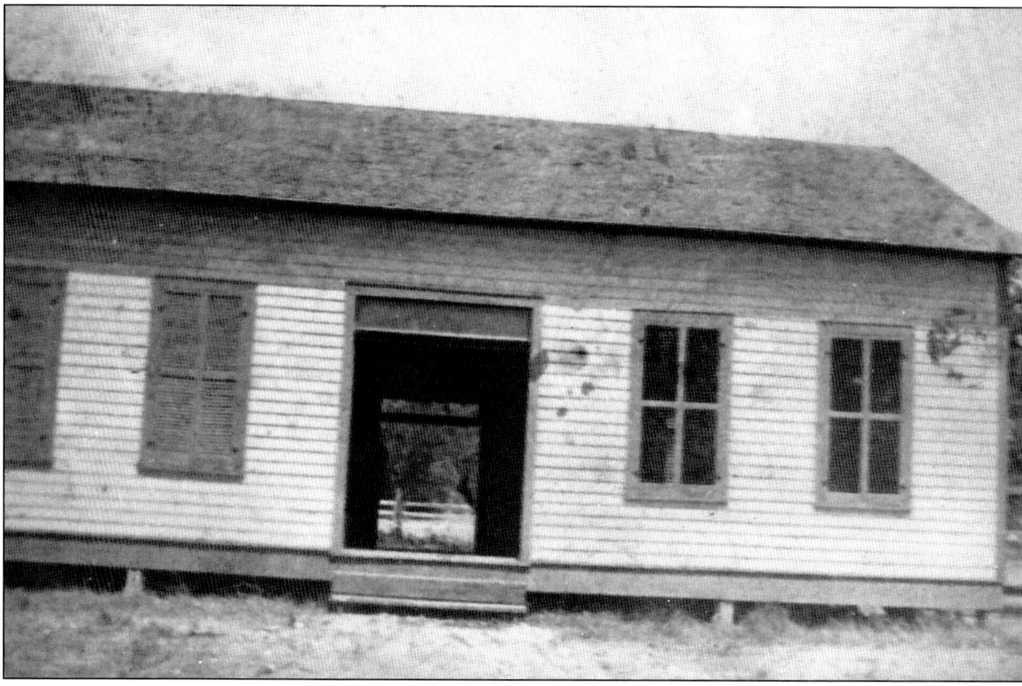

The Helotes Shooting Club Hall, or *Schuetzen Halle,* was built in the style of a dogtrot cabin. The hall was used as a gathering place for dances and other events. Although the exact date of its construction is not known, the building was in place by September 10, 1893, when this crooked photograph was taken. Today this building—as shown in the 1983 photograph below—is known as Braun Hall. On December 22, 1922, the Helotes Shooting Club sold the property to Hermann Sons of Texas Helotes Lodge 76, which still owns it. (Above, courtesy of Institute of Texan Cultures, Laura Long Collection; below, courtesy of HSH.)

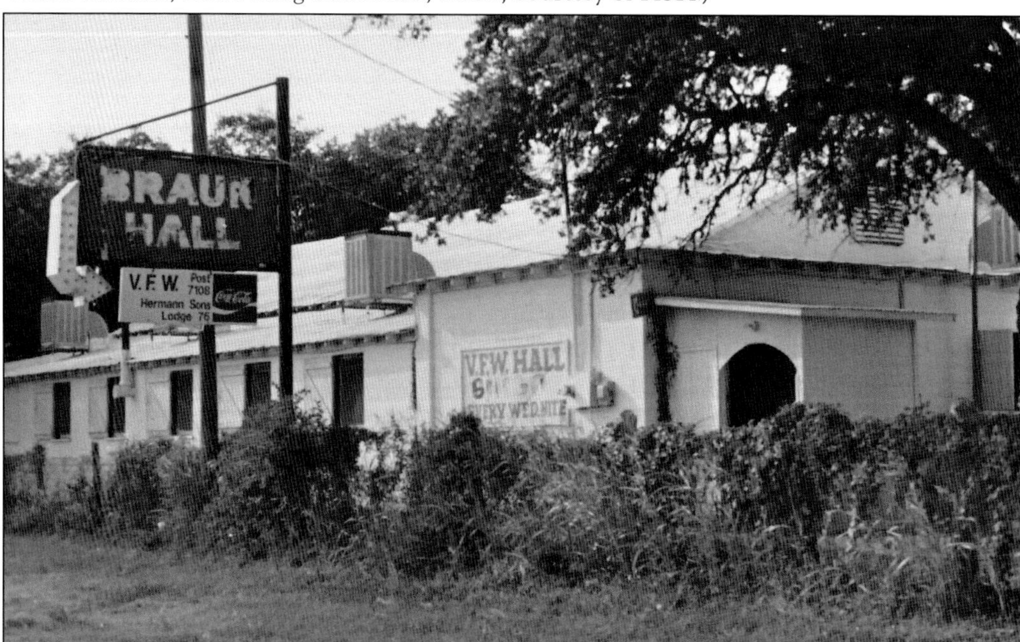

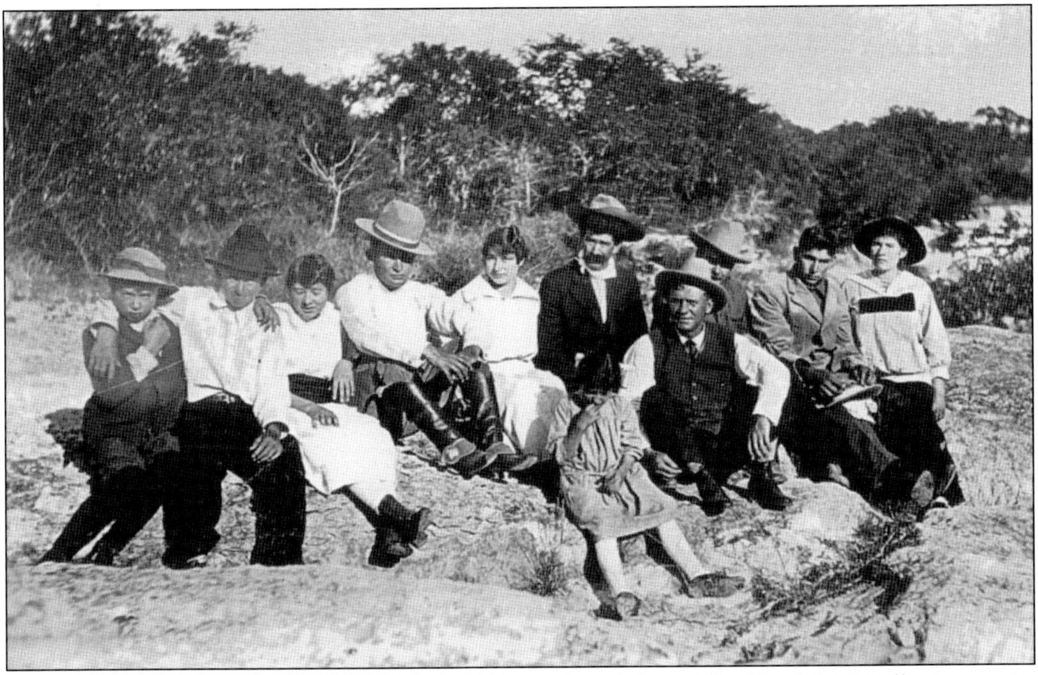

Hikers taking a rest at the Madla Ranch in 1916 are, from left to right, Frank M. Madla, Inocencio Torres, Concepción Madla, David Gallagher, Mary Madla, Manuel Hernandez, David Logan, Frank L. Madla, Cristobal Madla, Pasquelina (Madla) Hernandez, and Eloisa Madla sitting in the front. In the photograph below, Gallagher poses with Josephine Martinez before embarking on a horseback ride in the hills. (Above courtesy of Juanita "Janie" Madla; below courtesy of Emma Leal.)

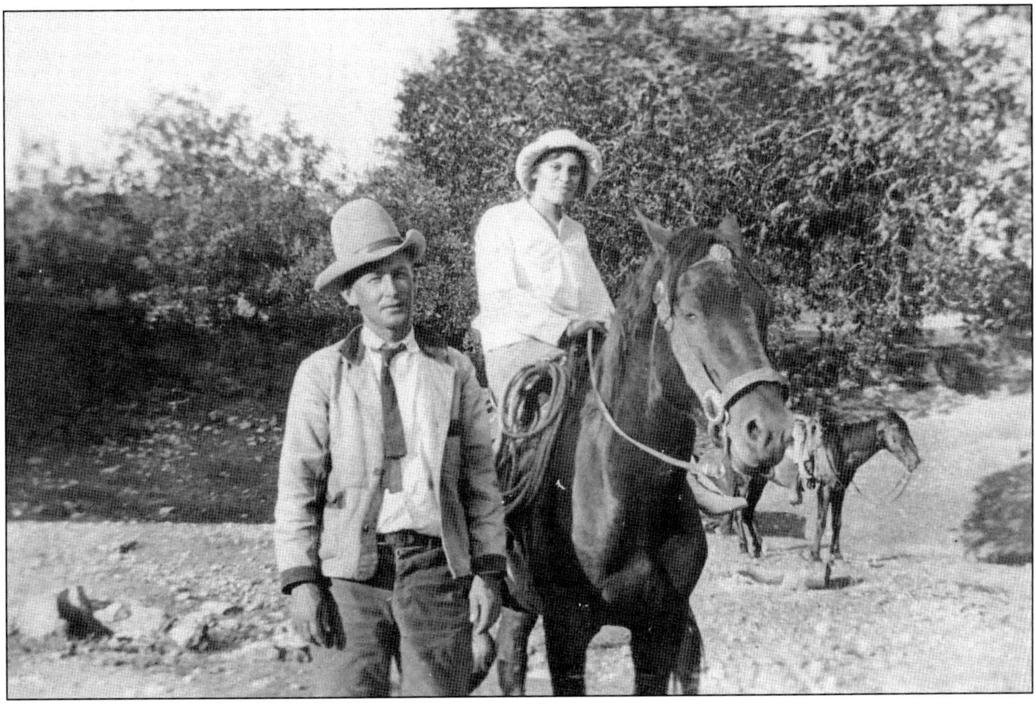

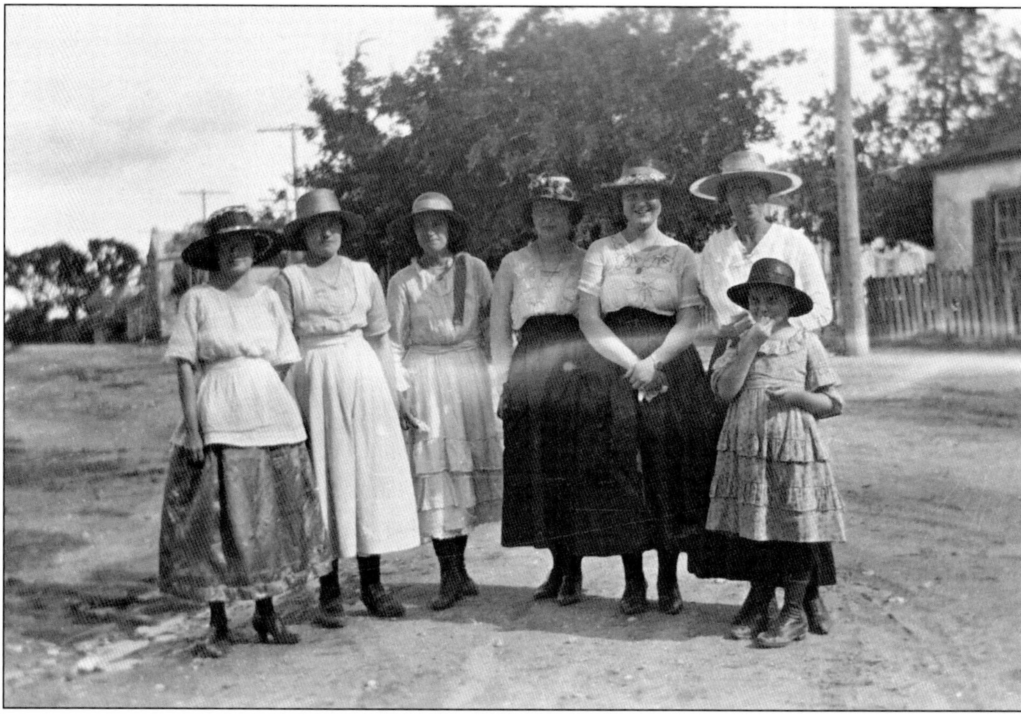

Enjoying a trip to Castroville via a hayride in the early 1920s are, left to right, Bertha Braun, Thusnelda Braun, Edda Braun, Alma Scheffler, Mary Merfels, Emma (Braun) Wehmeyer, and Alice Weymeyer. In the photograph below, hayriders pile into the bed of a truck. The only person identified in this photograph is Oscar Wood on the far right. (Above and below, courtesy of Fred W. Wendt.)

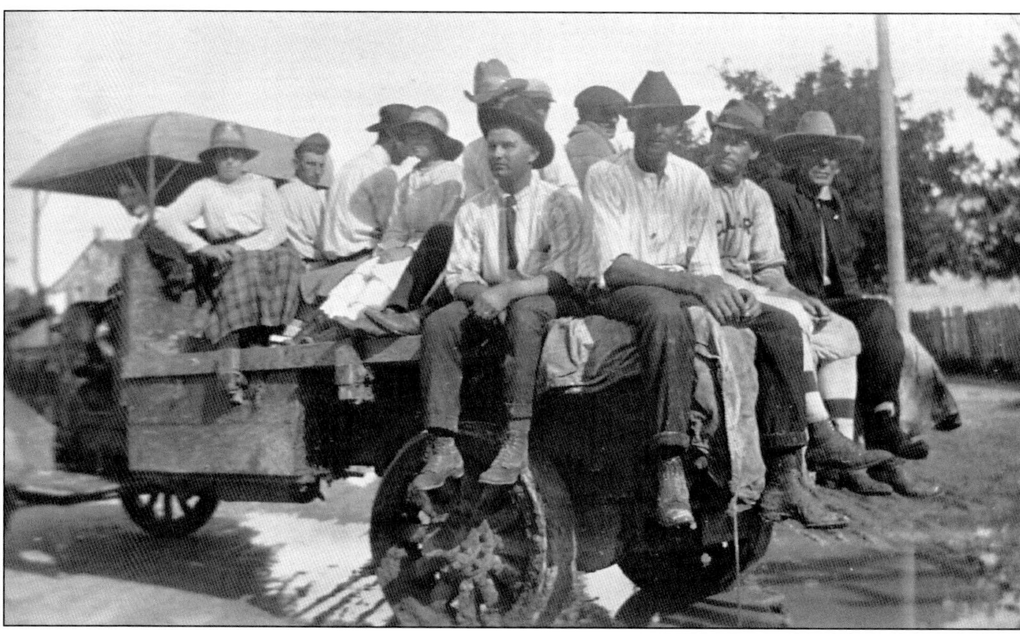

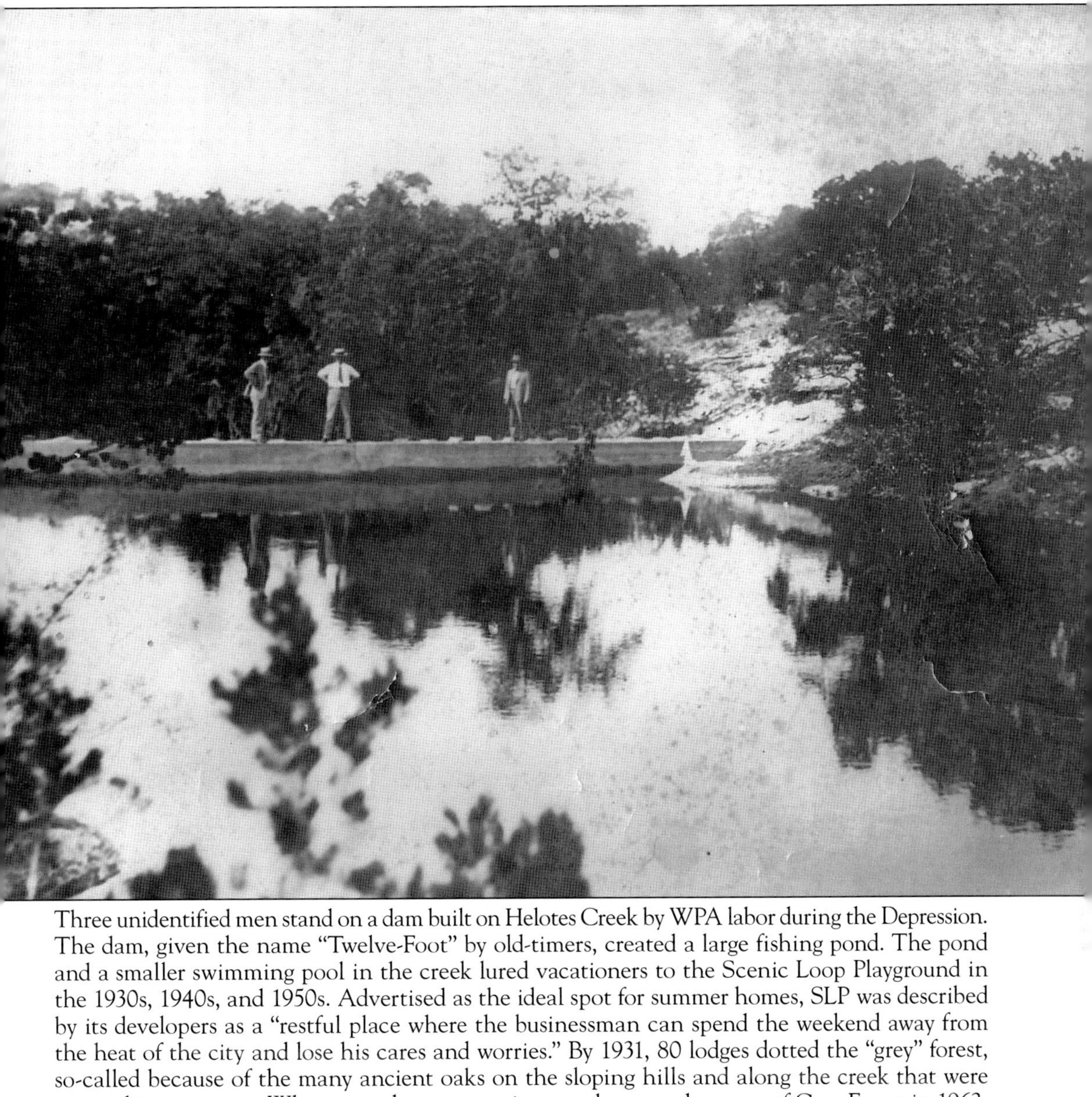

Three unidentified men stand on a dam built on Helotes Creek by WPA labor during the Depression. The dam, given the name "Twelve-Foot" by old-timers, created a large fishing pond. The pond and a smaller swimming pool in the creek lured vacationers to the Scenic Loop Playground in the 1930s, 1940s, and 1950s. Advertised as the ideal spot for summer homes, SLP was described by its developers as a "restful place where the businessman can spend the weekend away from the heat of the city and lose his cares and worries." By 1931, 80 lodges dotted the "grey" forest, so-called because of the many ancient oaks on the sloping hills and along the creek that were covered in grey moss. What started as a recreation area became the town of Grey Forest in 1962, 3.5 miles from Helotes. Scenic Loop Playground received Texas Historic Landmark designation in 2007. (Courtesy of HSH.)

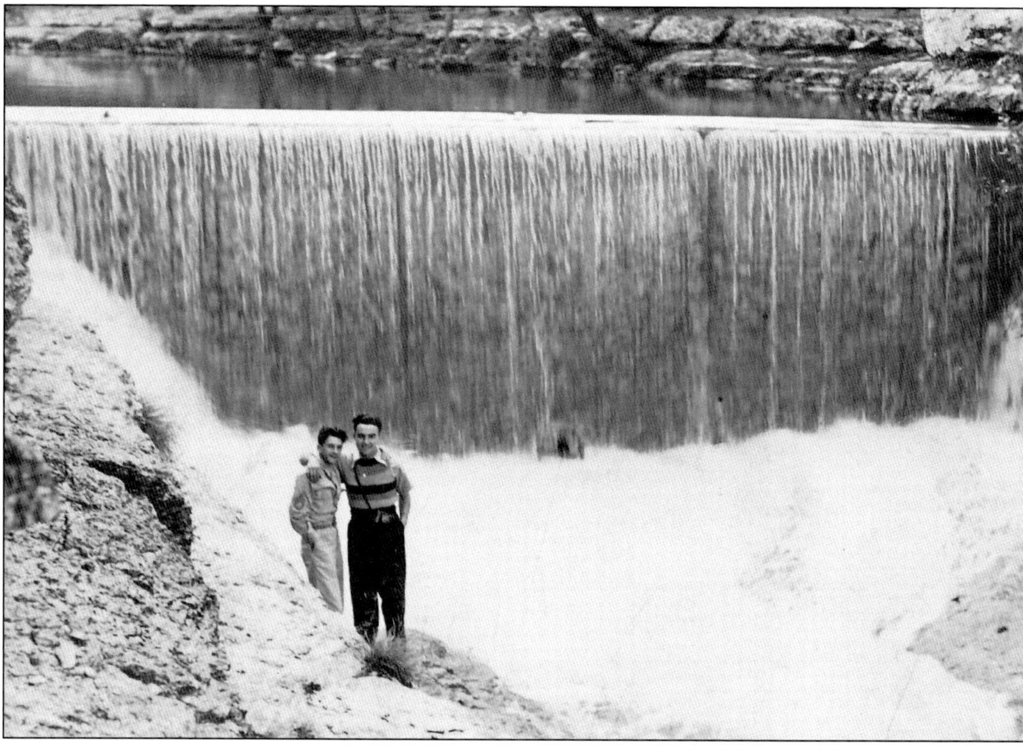

Jesse Madla, with the help of his brothers, built this dam on Chimenea Creek in the mid-1920s to create a swimming hole on his property. He opened a park called Madla Ranch Campground that attracted several thousand visitors until it closed in 1971. Madla's brother-in-law, Ray Alcalá, on the left, is shown in this 1938 photograph with a friend standing in front of the dam. (Courtesy of Juanita "Janie" Madla.)

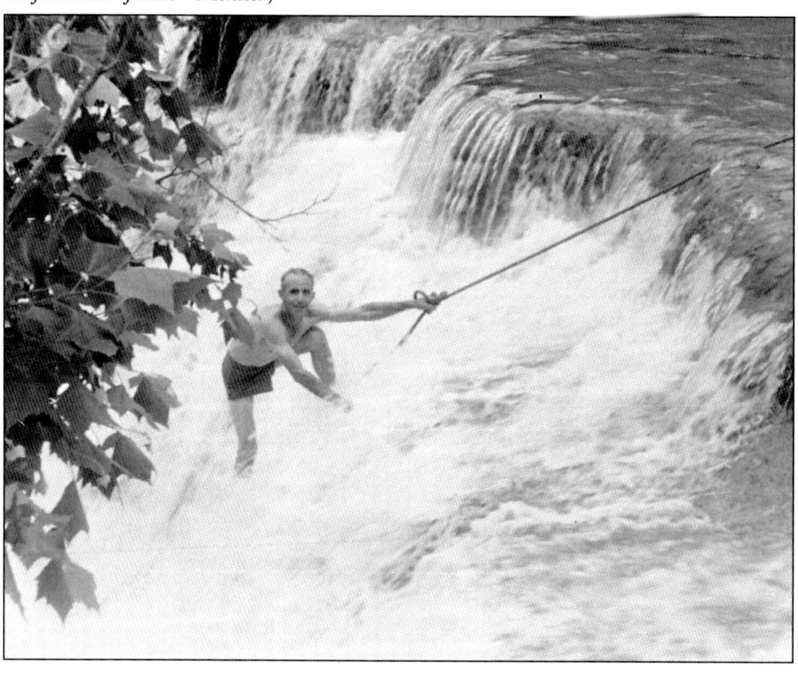

This waterfall on Chimenea Creek is upstream from the Madla dam. In this June 1957 photograph, Ignacio Alcalá appears to be having fun as he is pulled up the waterfall with a rope. (Courtesy of Mary Ellen Madla Ibarra.)

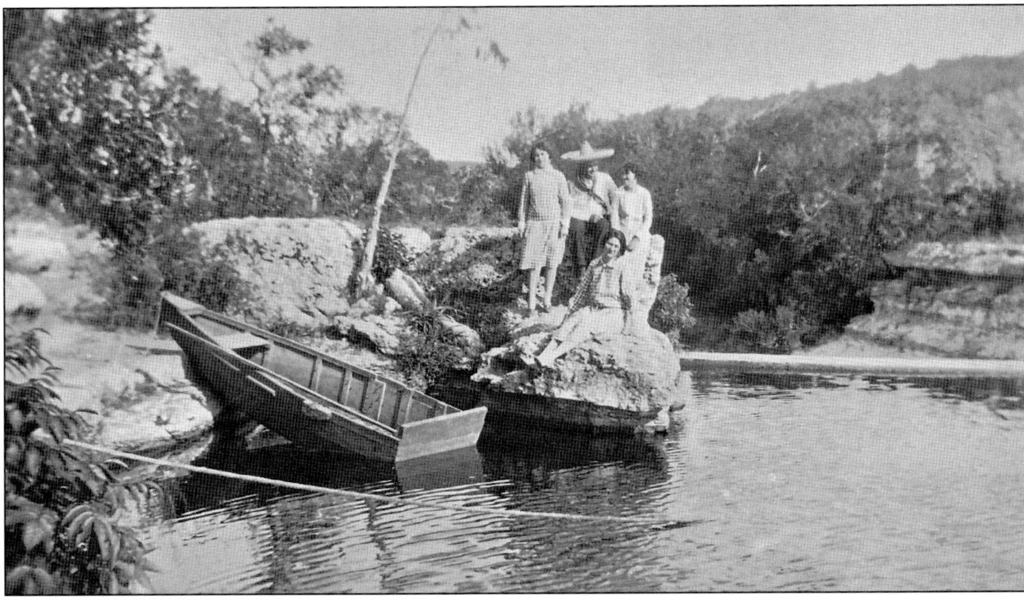

Shown from left to right in this 1932 photograph on a boulder near the Madla dam on Chimenea Creek are Aurora (Alcalá) Madla, husband Jesse Madla (wearing a sombrero), and two unidentified relatives. Also shown is a boat and rope that was used as a cable to pull the boat across the creek. (Courtesy of Juanita "Janie" Madla.)

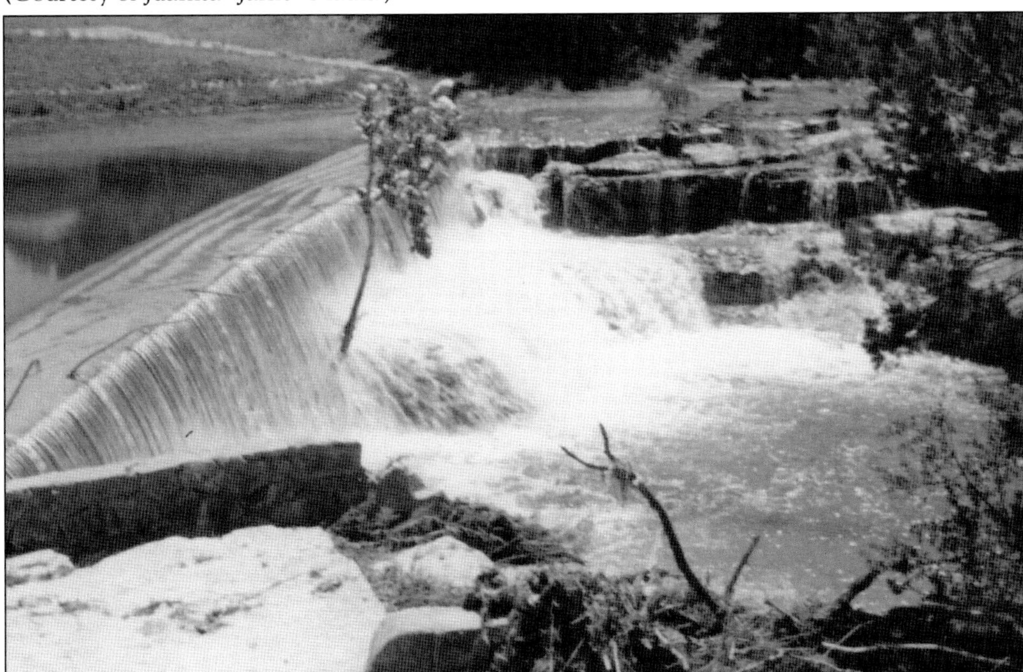

Seen here in 1973, Logan's Playground was a recreational area on San Geronimo Creek open to the public from 1948 until 1975. The playground offered fishing, camping, swimming, and a dance area, and was part of the Logan Ranch owned by Scottish immigrant David Logan and wife Mary Ann (Madla) Logan. Mary Ann opened the playground after her husband's 1947 death. (Courtesy of Mary Jane Blanco.)

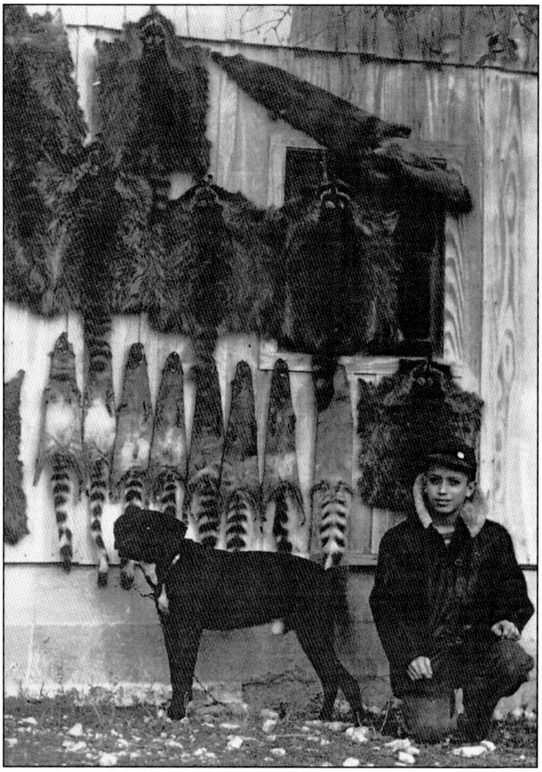

In this 1944 photograph, 11-year-old Bill Woller poses in front of the Frank Woller homestead with the results of a hunting expedition in the Helotes hills: pelts of raccoons, ringtails, foxes, and other animals. Woller's father sold the pelts to the Kallison store in downtown San Antonio and to Pete's Place in San Geronimo. The pelts were used for military aviator hats and collars needed for the war effort. (Courtesy of Bill Woller.)

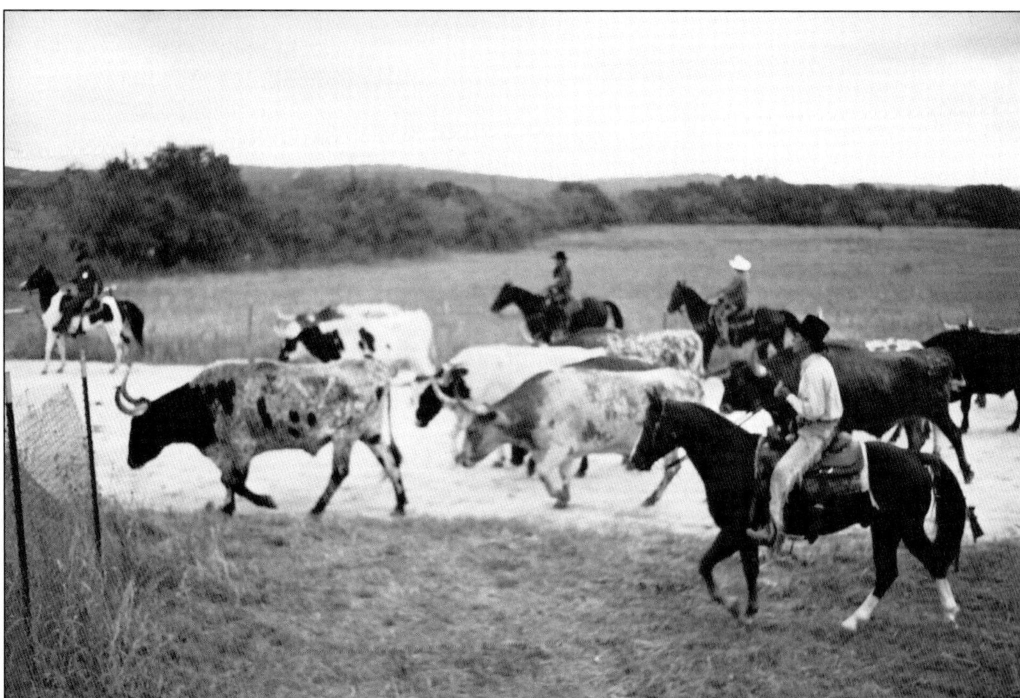

Helotes was a stopover for cattle drives until the early 20th century. This photograph shows a commemorative drive through Helotes in 1988. (Courtesy of HSH.)

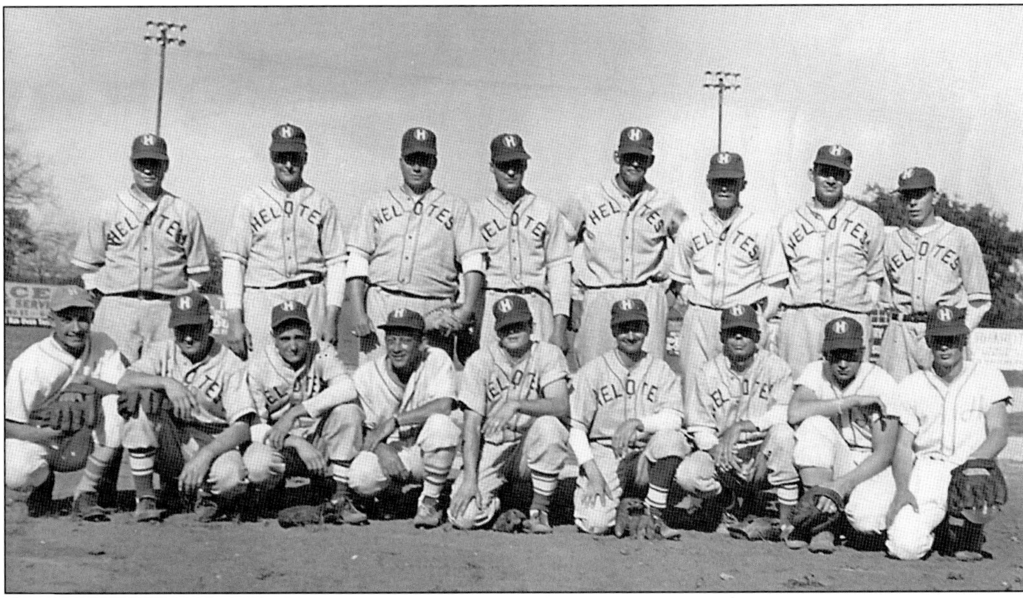

The 1951 Helotes baseball and softball teams played at Braun Hall field before they broke up when several of the players enlisted in the Korean War. The Helotes Boilermakers baseball team in the photograph above included (first row) Lloyd Bendele, Lee Nickel, Gerald Nickel, Alvin Brandt, Lee Tyson, Burton Braun, Lawrence Tezel, John Galm, and Kenneth Evers; (second row) Mgr. George Michalczak, Calvin Galm, Melvin Michalczak, Sammy Galm, Leroy Galm, Stanley Becker, James Gussen, and John Tezel. Listed in the same order, the softball team members below are (first row) Henry Braun, Edmond Krueger Jr., Oscar Gass, Burton Braun, G. Nickel, Lester Krueger, and Paul Ott; (second row) Mgr. Milton Krueger, Harold Galm, M. Michalczak, Sam Galm, Charles Gass, C. Galm, K. Evers, and Claude Steubing. The young boy is Curtis Krueger, the manager's son. (Courtesy of Sam Galm.)

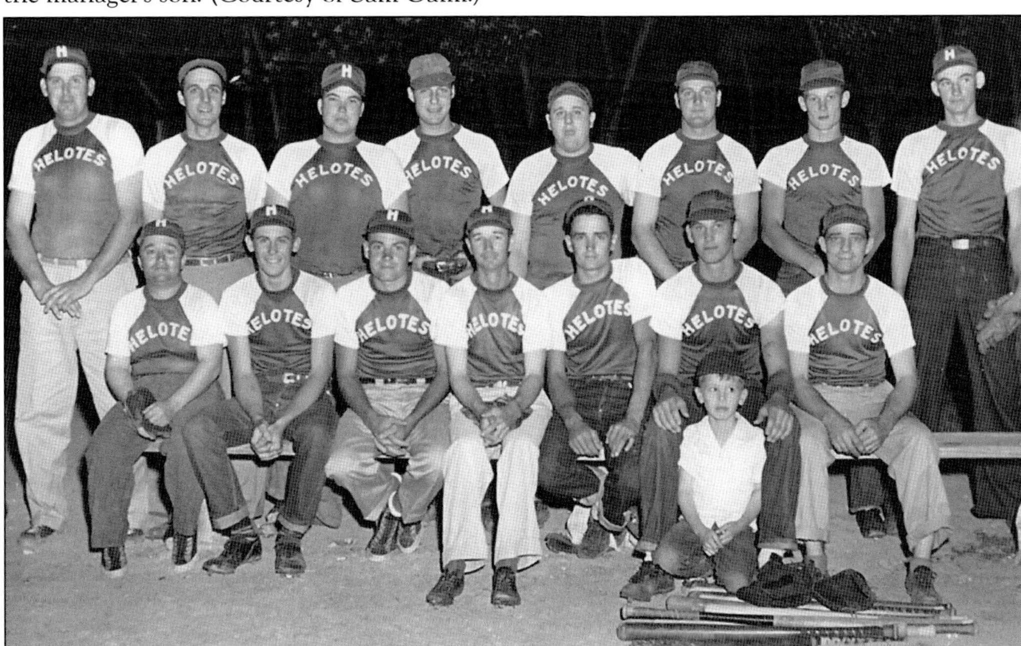

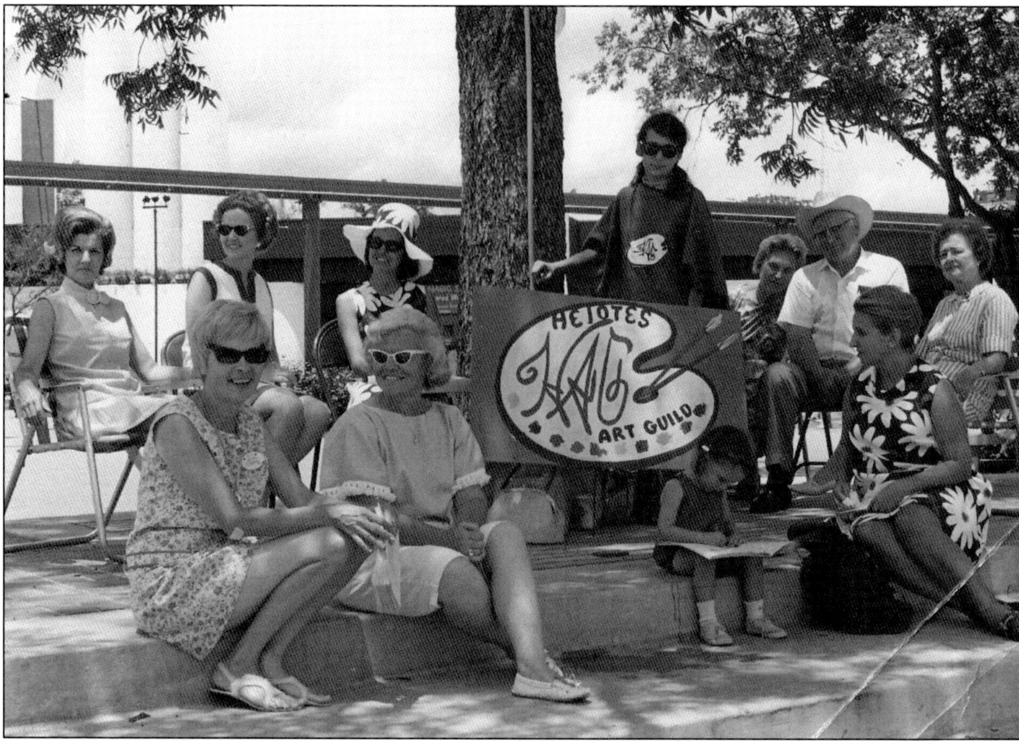

Helotes Day at Hemisfair, the World's Fair in San Antonio, June 24, 1968, featured a big outdoor show in which the Helotes Art Guild displayed more than 107 paintings at the Special Events Plaza. (Photograph by Dade Rayfield; courtesy of HSH.)

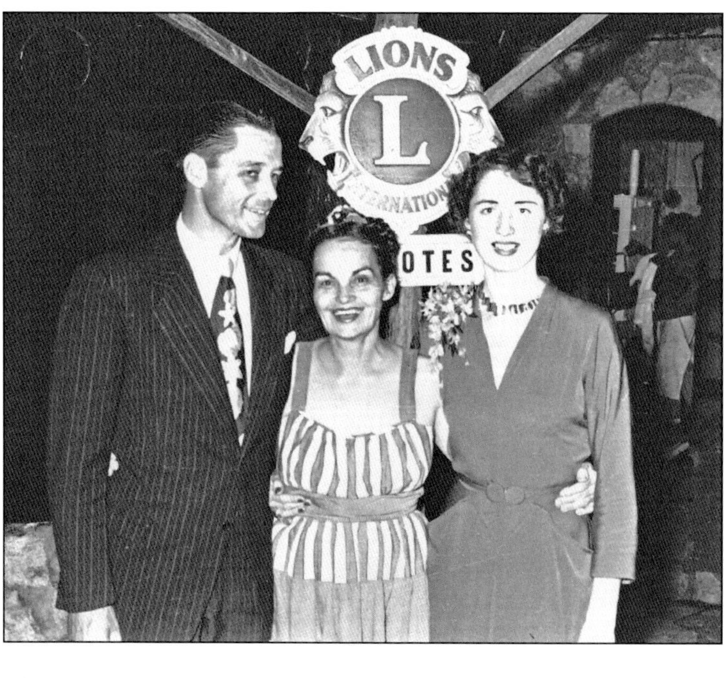

The Lions Club of Helotes, chartered September 8, 1950, with 34 members, has spearheaded many of the town's civic activities, from establishing the volunteer fire department to founding the town's Cornyval Festival. In this photograph at the first Lions Club banquet at the Grey Moss Inn are Arthur Howell, his mother Mary Howell, owner of the Grey Moss Inn, and Arthur's wife Dorothy. (Courtesy of the Lions Club of Helotes.)

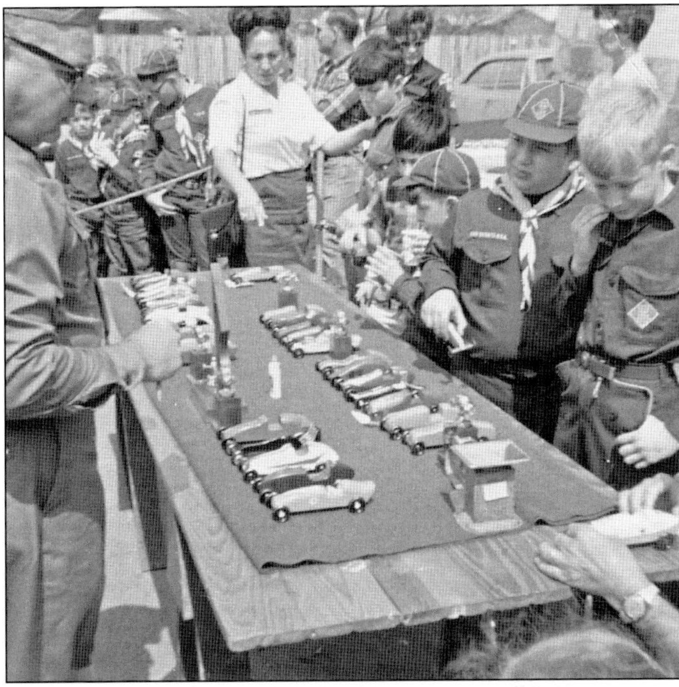

Helotes Hills United Methodist Church was the original charter organization for Helotes Boy Scout Troop and Cub Scout Pack 401. In this May 1968 photograph, Cub Scoutmaster James Logan, far left, directs the boys during the annual Pinewood Derby. Also identified in the photograph is Logan's wife, Rita, who has her hand on Ray Dunford's shoulder. On the far right are Billy Logan and Jimmy Stanley. (Courtesy of Bill Barker.)

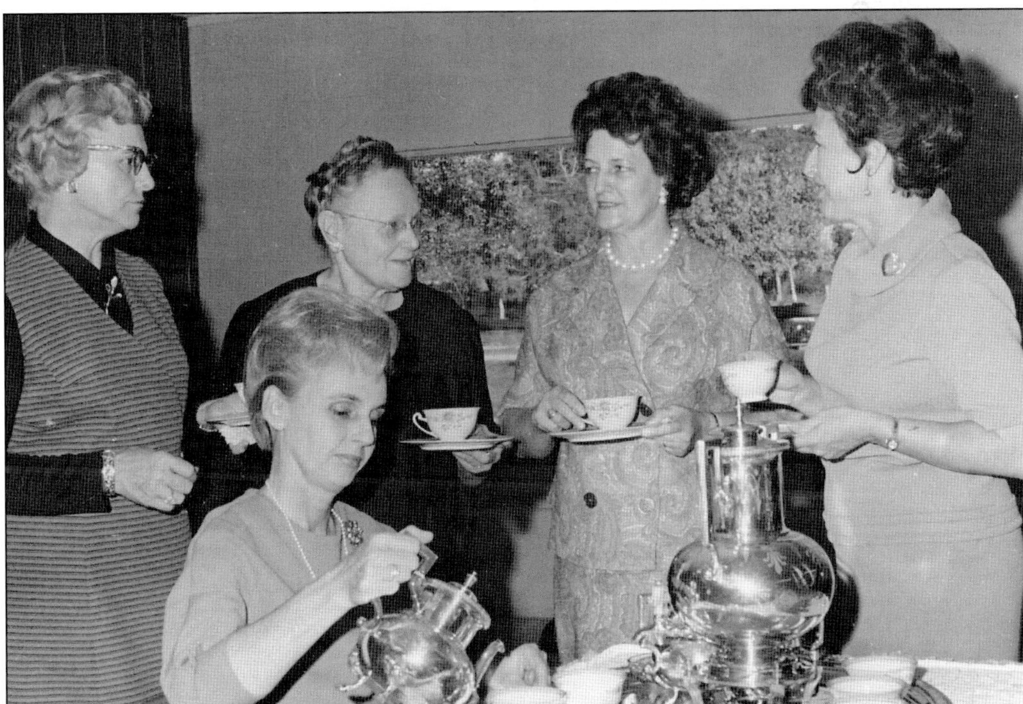

The Helotes Women's Club marked the 20th anniversary of the club's founding with a tea and open house at the Confraternity Building of Our Lady of Guadalupe Catholic Church, November 8, 1970. Sarah Melgaard, a past president, served the tea. The 1970 officers shown here are, from left to right, club president Loretta Ham, vice president Marie Parrigin, treasurer Virginia Surles, and secretary Valda Terry. (Courtesy of HSH.)

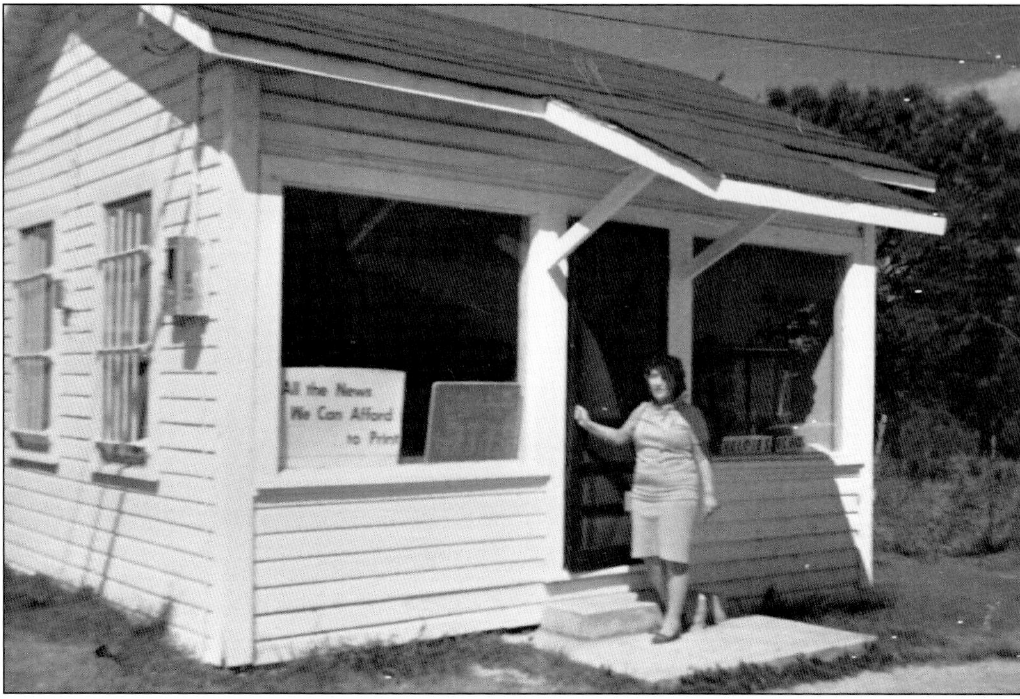

Lucy Perkins Brown (1916–1988), the town's first newspaper editor and cofounder of the historical society, stands in front of the first newspaper office in the early 1960s. Brown and husband Charles O. Brown (1916–2000), shown below, founded the *Helotes Echo*, with the first edition appearing September 1, 1961. Born with "ink in her blood," Lucy was from Sioux City, Iowa, where her father was editor of the *Sioux City Journal*, a paper founded by her grandfather. After her father's death, she moved with her mother and siblings to San Antonio, where she met her future husband. Both graduated from the University of Texas with degrees in journalism and became teachers. When the couple moved to Scenic Loop Playground in 1954, Lucy saw Helotes as the perfect place to fulfill her dream of starting a newspaper with her husband as publisher. She was editor of the *Helotes Echo* for 27 years. (Above and below, courtesy of HSH.)

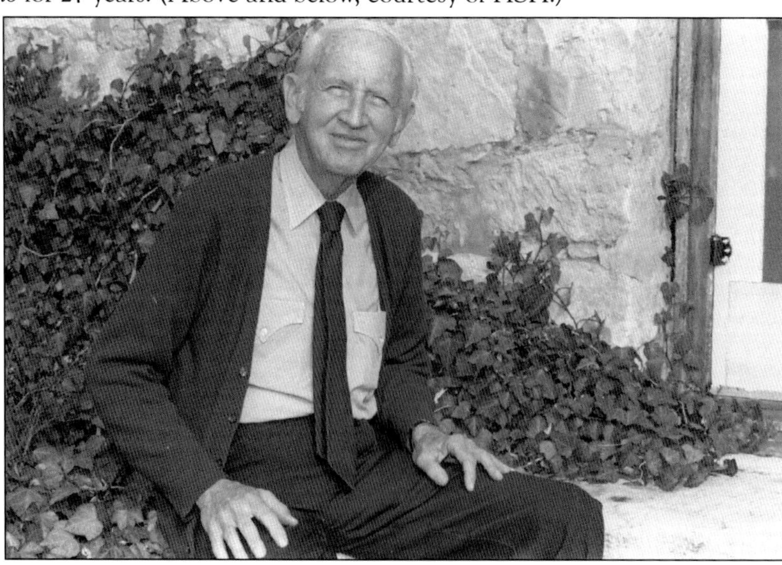

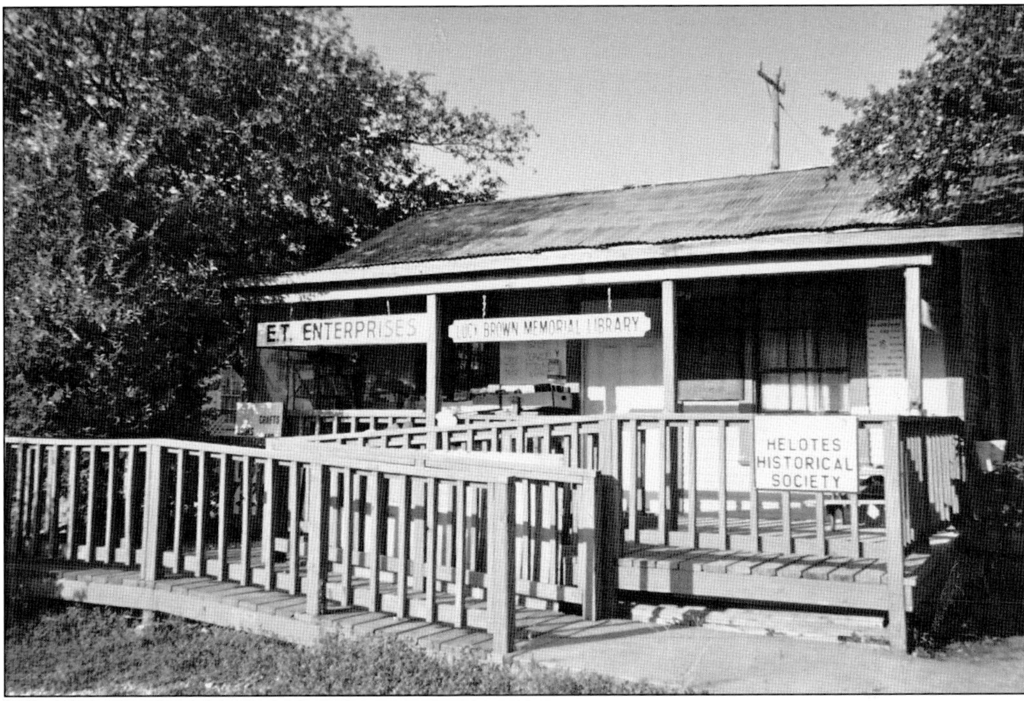

This cottage in downtown Helotes next to the Helotes General Store (then known as the Hickory Hut Restaurant) housed the Lucy Brown Memorial Library from 1988 until 2006. Run by historical society members, the library shown in this 1990 photograph held the town's archives. Books were also available for checkout. In the photograph below are historical society members at a 2001 event. From left to right, they are Anna Mae "Mas" Nichols, JoAnn Gillis, Mary McAfee, Irene Scharf, Wanda Terry, John Gillis, and Alma Kasparek. In 1966, Terry (1921–2005) cofounded the Helotes Historical Society with Lucy Perkins Brown. Co-owner of the Hickory Hut Restaurant with her husband, Corbin, Terry served several terms as society president. (Above and below, courtesy of HSH.)

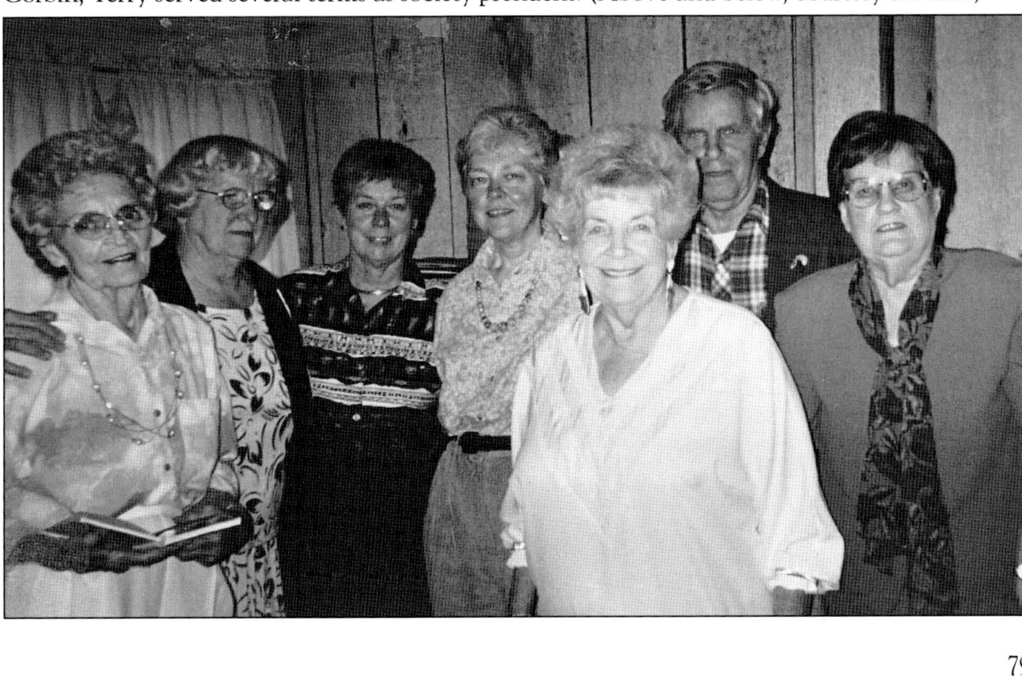

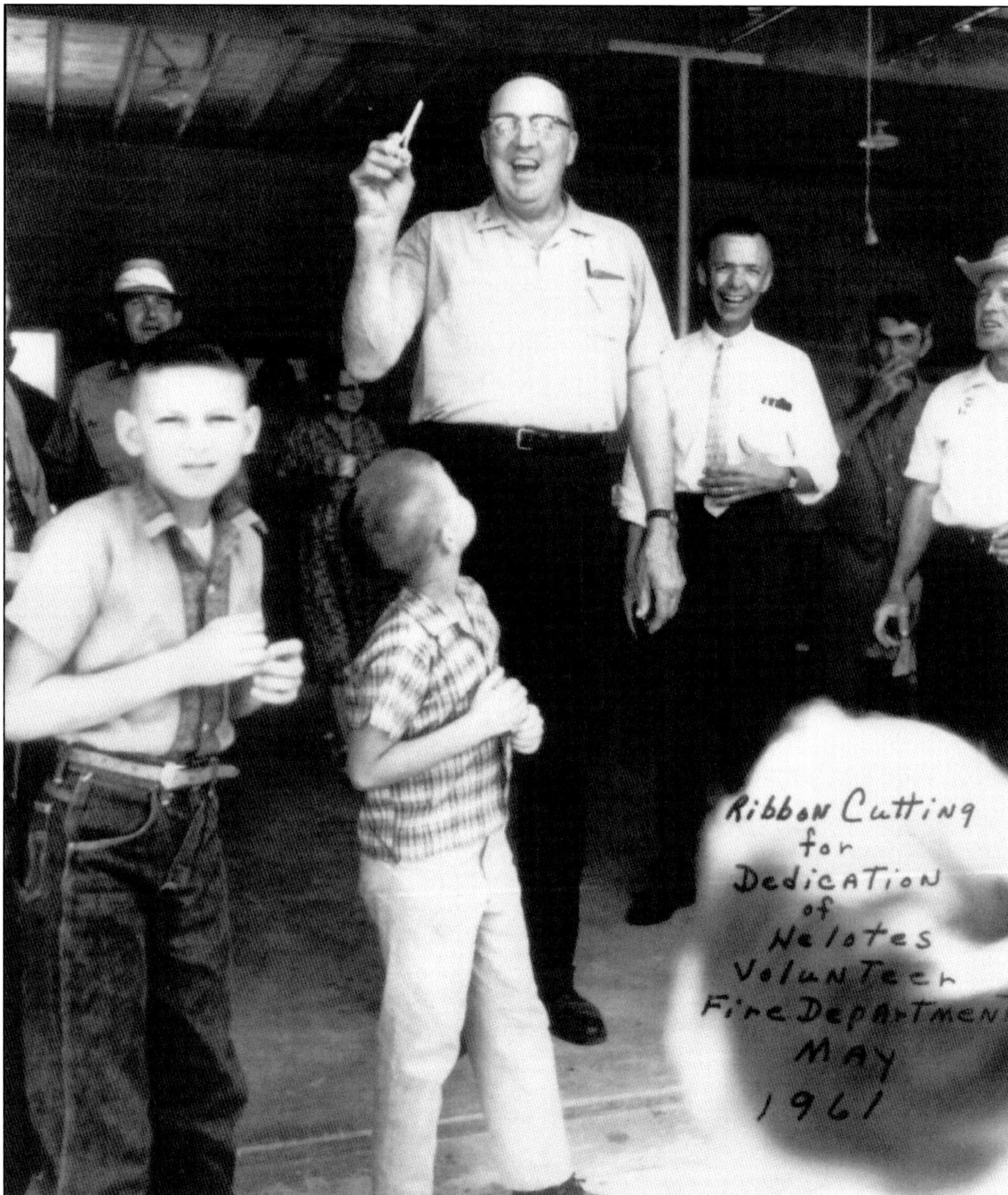

A prolonged drought in the 1950s hit farmers and ranchers hard and raised concerns about fire prevention. A Helotes Fire Corps was formed to assist the Bexar County Fire Department. With donations from business sponsors and fund-raisers, the Lions Club purchased land on Bandera Road to build a fire station. Civic leader Clarence Galm (1907–1987), the first president of the Helotes Area Volunteer Fire Department (HAVFD) board of directors, participated in the ribbon-cutting for the dedication of the new fire department building, May 19, 1961. Standing behind Galm, from left to right, are Charles Davis (wearing a hat), fire chief Ed Faust (1960–1961), Harvey Mayfield (fire chief, 1965), and Ralph Swift (fire chief, 1961–1965). In 1977, farmer and stockman Galm received the Joe Freeman Award for outstanding community service to agriculture. Galm, who spearheaded the effort to consolidate the schools into the Northside School District, established in 1950, was honored with a namesake school in 1987. (Courtesy of HSH.)

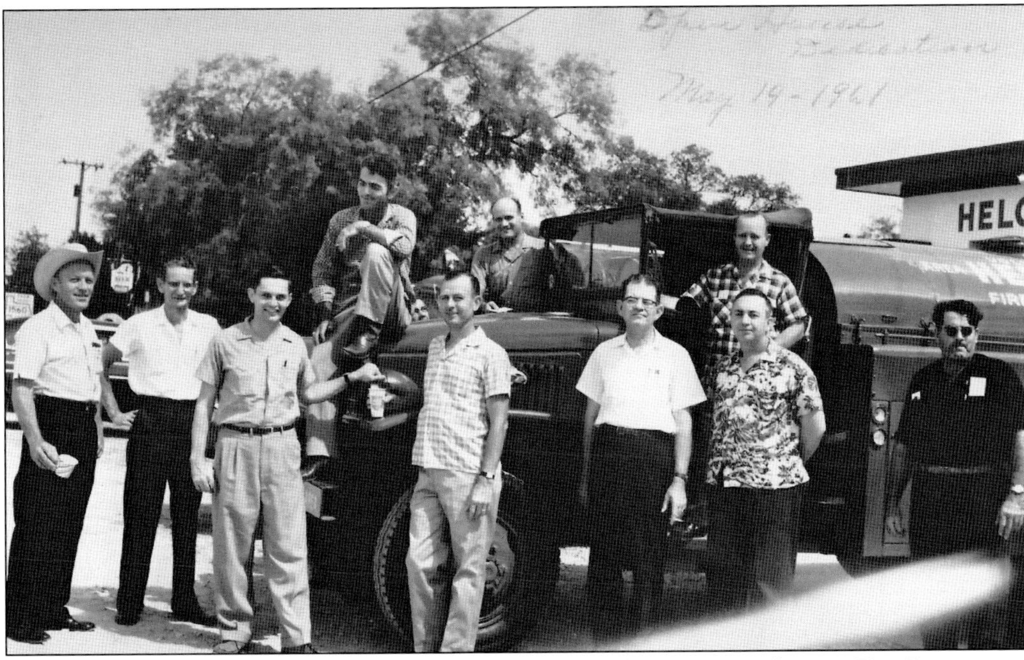

Seen here from left to right at the open house for the Helotes Area Volunteer Fire Department on May 19, 1961, are volunteers (standing) Ralph Swift, Ike Parrot, Baxter Melgaard, Gus Heisler, Otto Schneider, an unidentified volunteer, and Joe Wallace; (on truck) Harvey Mayfield, Sherwood Nelson, and Jack Nottingham. (Courtesy of City of Helotes.)

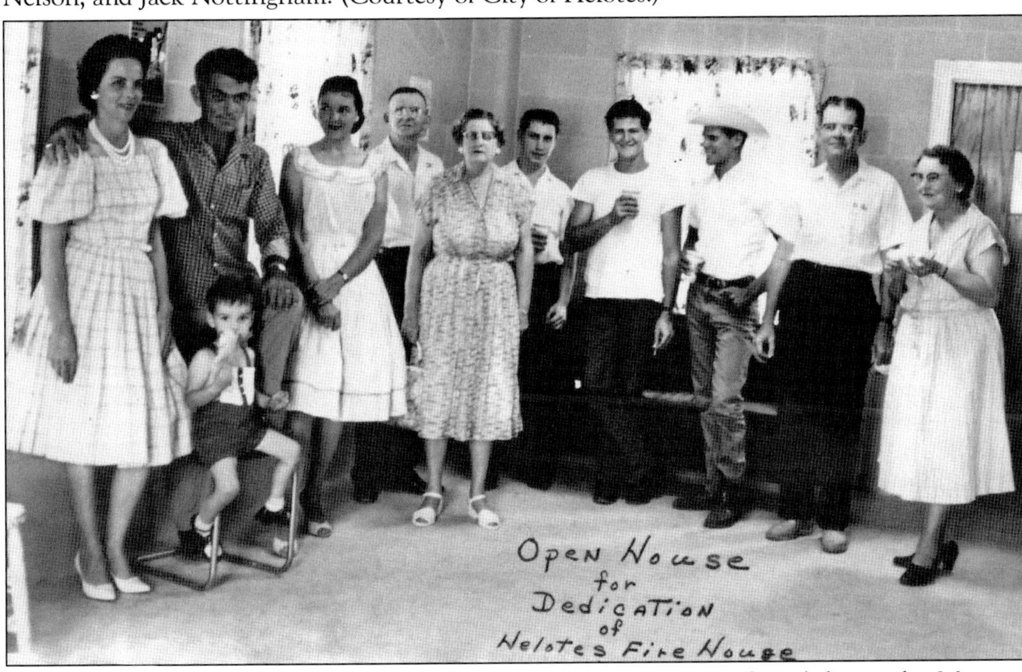

Guests seen here at the department's May 19, 1961, open house are, from left to right, Mammie Mayfield, her son Paul Mayfield, Harvey Mayfield, Ann Galm, Bill Saner, Elsie (Biering) Saner, Walter "Brownie" Schwarz, William Toepperwein, an unidentified guest, Otto Schneider, and Lillian Galm. (Courtesy of City of Helotes.)

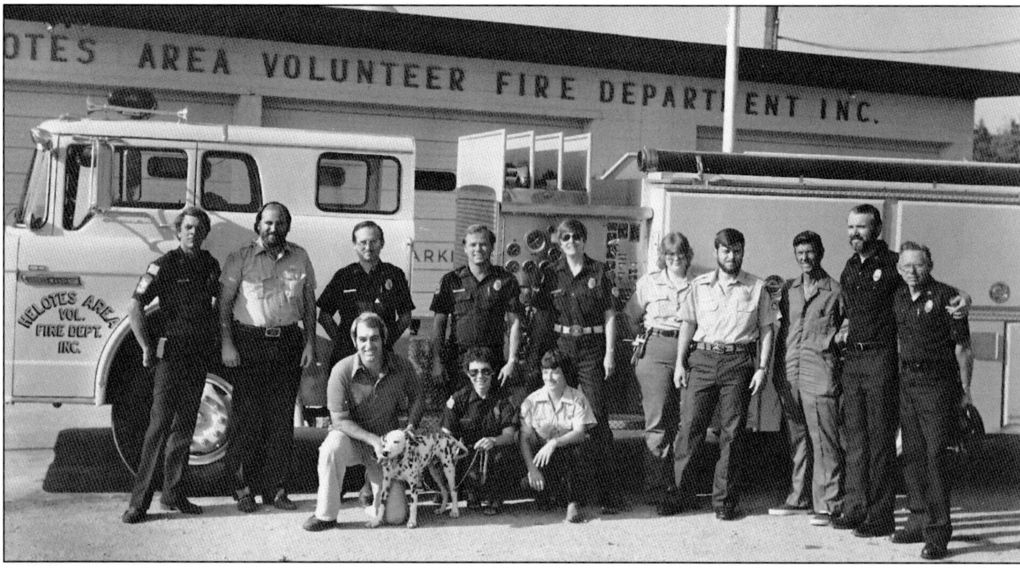

Every few years, a new crop of civic-minded individuals volunteered to work for the Helotes Area Volunteer Fire Department. From left to right, this 1981 photograph includes (first row) Leonard Hill with the mascot Dalmatian, Pat Armstrong, and Maggie Grabhorn; (second row) Ron Binks, Emory Rebresh, Wayne Chauffe, Richard DeHart, Judy Reichardt, Joi Harris, Doug Godfrey, John Widner, fire chief Tom Schoolcraft (1980–1986), and John Blalock. (Courtesy of City of Helotes.)

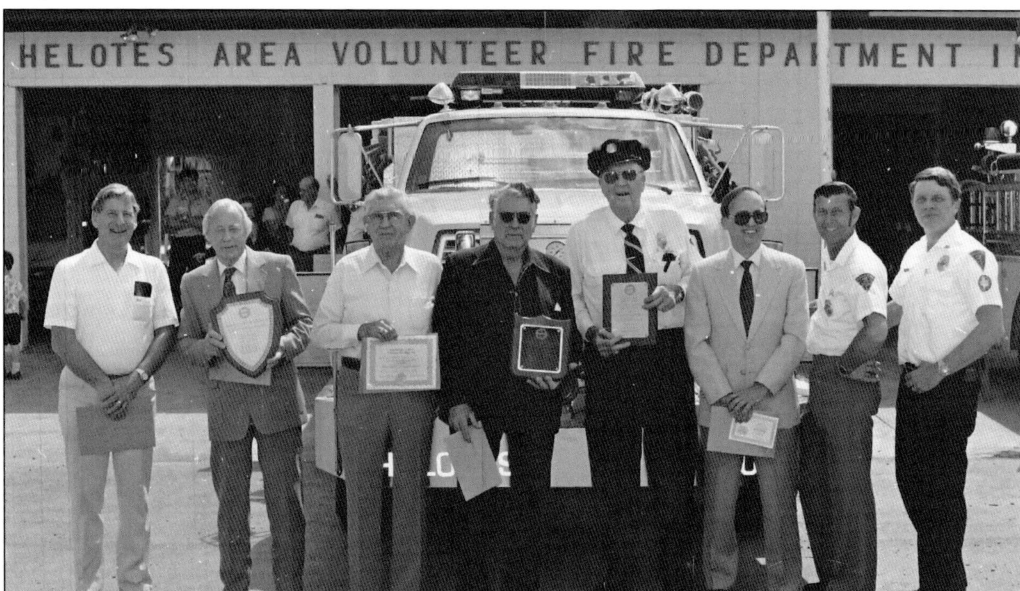

Former Helotes Area Volunteer Fire Department chiefs and board presidents were honored at a 1987 public reception at the station. Seen here from left to right, they are Norris Henley (president, 1986–1992), Collin Furr (president, 1972–1978), Charles Davis (president, 1966–1968), Joe Wallace (fire chief, 1966), Clarence Galm (president, 1961–1966, 1968–1972), Wayne Chauffe (fire chief, 1970–1975, 1978–1979), John Widner (fire chief, 1967), and Ron Binks (fire chief, 1986–1990). (Courtesy of City of Helotes.)

Five

Farm and Ranch Life

From its settlement in the 1850s until the mid-20th century, Helotes was a farm-and-ranching community. Farmers sold their produce at Market Square in San Antonio, while ranchers provided livestock for the meat market. Their livelihoods depended on hard work and long hours. In 1919, the Helotes post office handled mail for 64 area families; 60 of them were involved in farming. Dairy farms were predominant until the 1960s when prices fell and many owners began selling off their land. Although the majority of ranches and farms averaged 160 acres, some grew to thousands of acres. While many of the farms and ranches were subdivided among descendants of the early pioneers and/or sold to developers, several properties were acquired in the early 20th century by wealthy individuals who created large recreational ranches. Conservationists spearheaded an effort in the early 1990s to create a public park out of the Hoffmann Ranch. Government Canyon State Natural Area, which borders Helotes's western boundary, opened to the public in 2005.

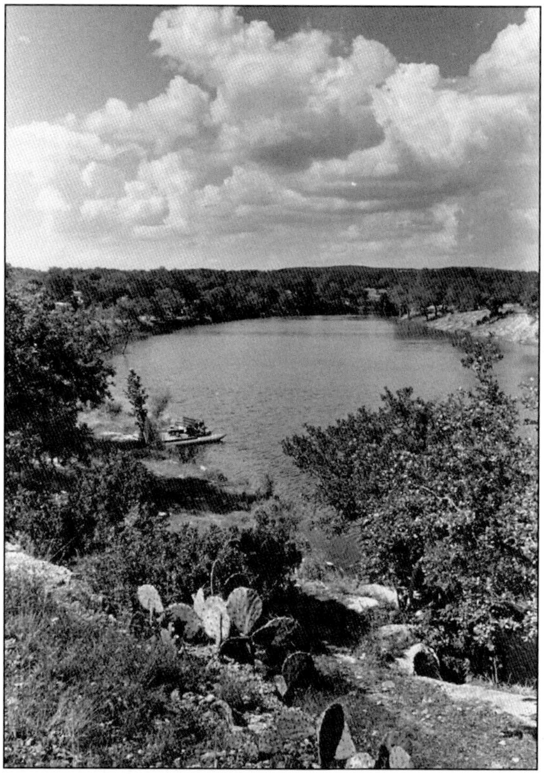

The Gallagher Ranch, 9 miles northwest of Helotes, was established after Irish immigrant Peter Gallagher was commissioned by Mexican president Antonio López de Santa Anna in 1833 to establish a military supply depot within 25 miles of San Antonio. Gallagher chose a site on San Geronimo Creek, gradually accumulating 10,000 acres. The property has served as a fort, post office, stagecoach stop, cattle and dude ranch, and as a Western movie set—most notably 2000's *All the Pretty Horses*. Gallagher created a dam on the creek to form the lake shown in this 1967 photograph. In 1927, Vachel and Amy McNutt purchased the property, which included several buildings designed in the Spanish-Colonial style seen in the photograph below. "Mrs. Mac" was a familiar figure in Helotes, where she picked up her mail and shopped. She made the Gallagher the foremost dude ranch in Texas. (Photographs by Dade Rayfield; courtesy of HSH.)

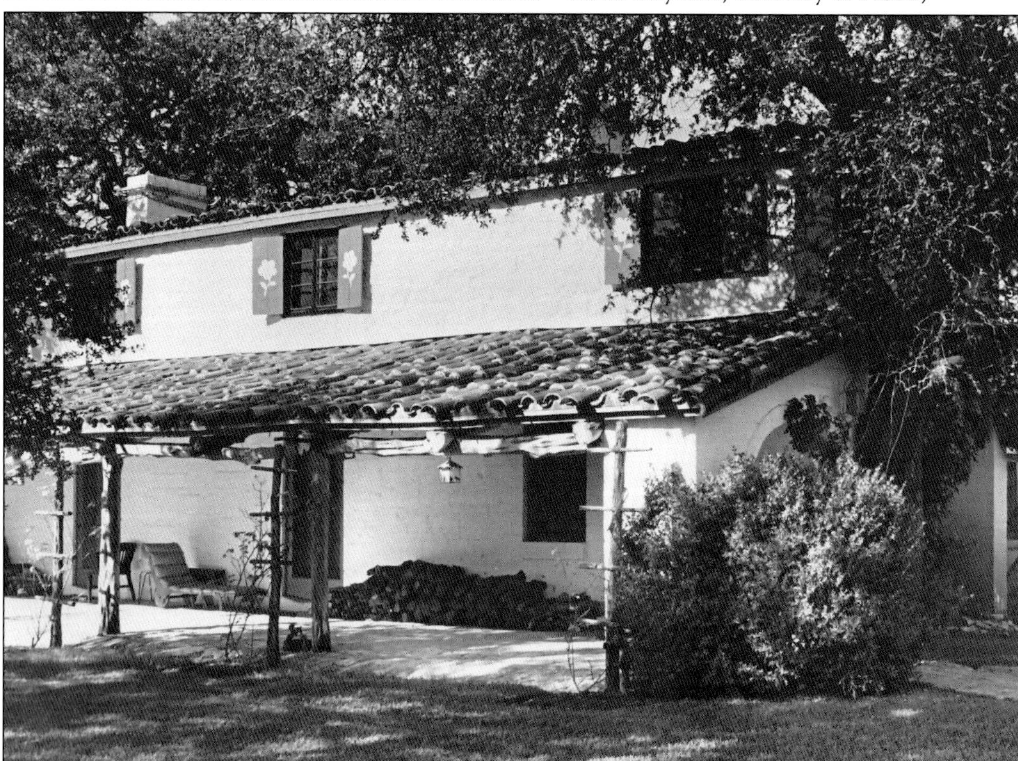

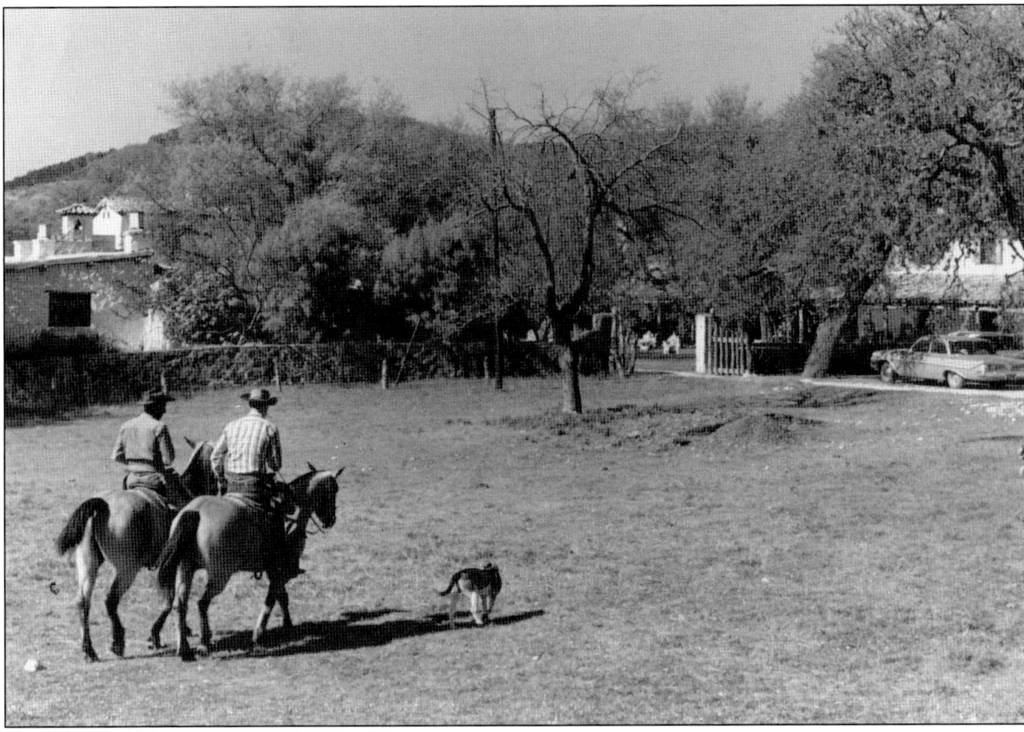

Working cowboys ride toward the headquarters of the Gallagher Ranch in this 1967 photograph. The image below shows ranch hands spraying cattle. Today the portion of the ranch that includes the original buildings is known as the Gallagher Ranch Headquarters and is owned by the Christopher Hill family. (Photographs by Dade Rayfield; courtesy of HSH.)

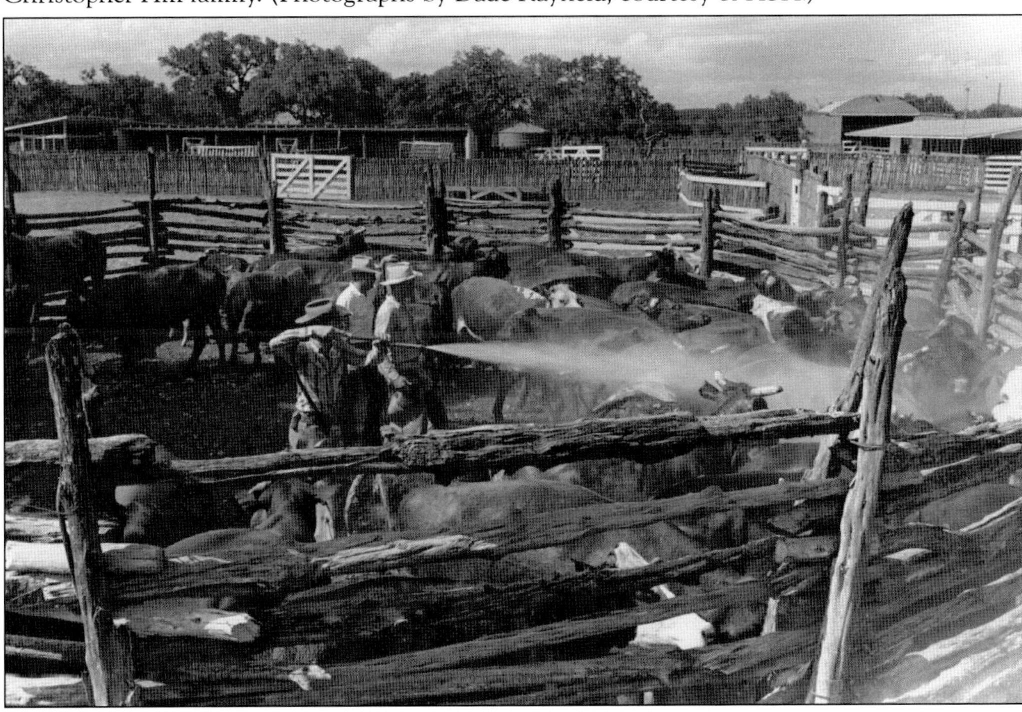

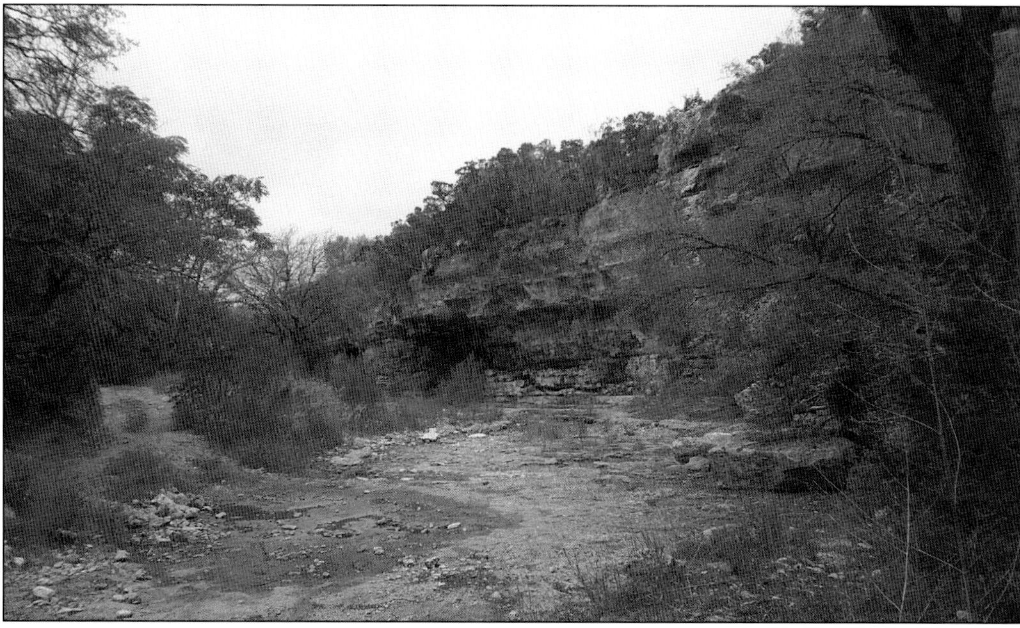

Seen on the left in this photograph, Joe Johnston Road was a military road made in the early 1850s from San Antonio to Bandera through land making up today's rugged, 11,500-acre Government Canyon State Natural Area (GCSNA). The GCSNA, adjacent to Helotes' western border, was once part of a large cattle ranch owned by Carolina (Ernst) Hoffmann (1842–1927) and Jacob Hoffmann (1838–1903). (Courtesy of Cynthia Leal Massey.)

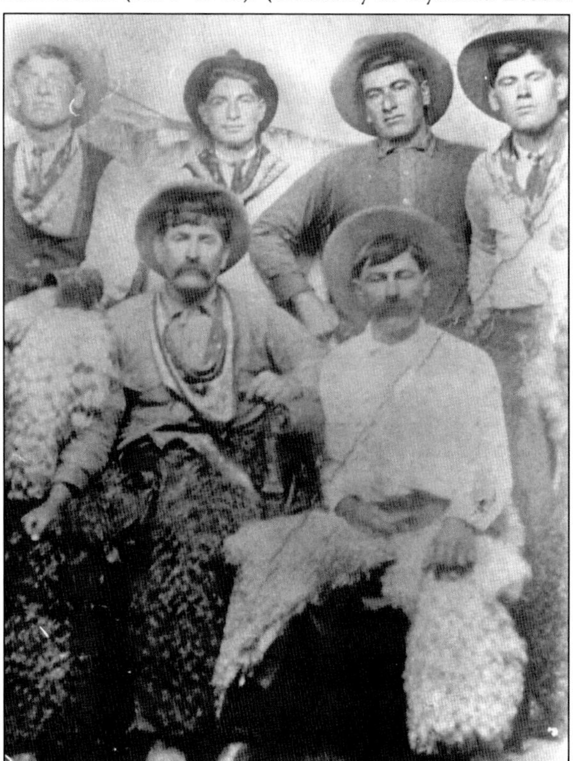

The Menchaca brothers wear angora goatskin chaps while working on their family ranch in the 1920s. The sons of Francisco and Catarina Menchaca are, from left to right, (first row) Manuel and Cristobal; (second row) Nicanor, Francisco, Antonio, and Celerino. (Courtesy of Juanita "Janie" Madla.)

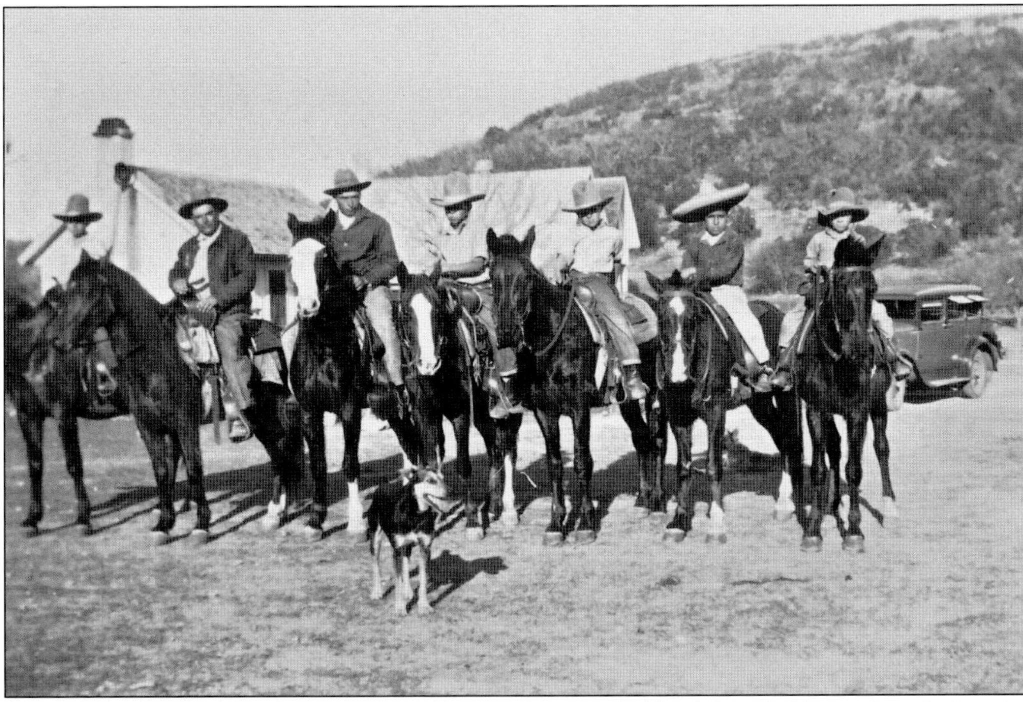

Only Jesse Madla (second from left) and his brother Frank (third from left) are identified in this 1930s photograph. The group poses before a ride on the 1,000-acre Madla Ranch. (Courtesy of Juanita "Janie" Madla.)

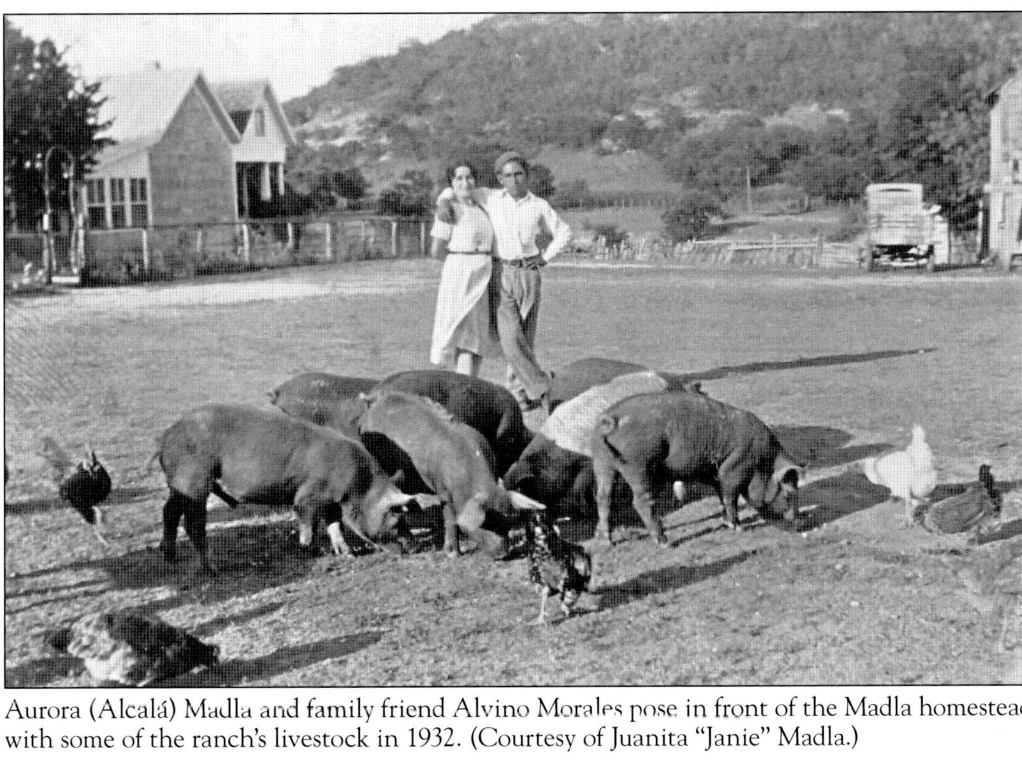

Aurora (Alcalá) Madla and family friend Alvino Morales pose in front of the Madla homestead with some of the ranch's livestock in 1932. (Courtesy of Juanita "Janie" Madla.)

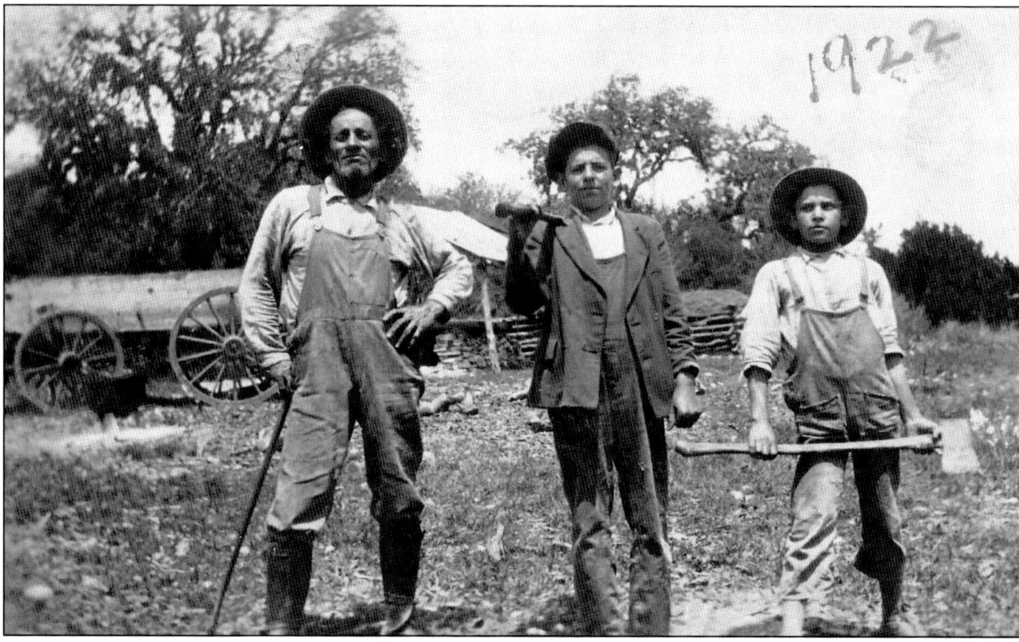

Máximo Martinez, shown in this 1922 photograph with sons Máximo Jr., and Rudy on their farm, grew corn, wheat, oats, potatoes, beans, and sugar cane. Martinez constructed a mill to make molasses, which he sold in San Antonio; he also raised horses, cattle, and hogs. Two of Martinez's older sons are shown below in horse-drawn plows. (Courtesy of Emma Leal.)

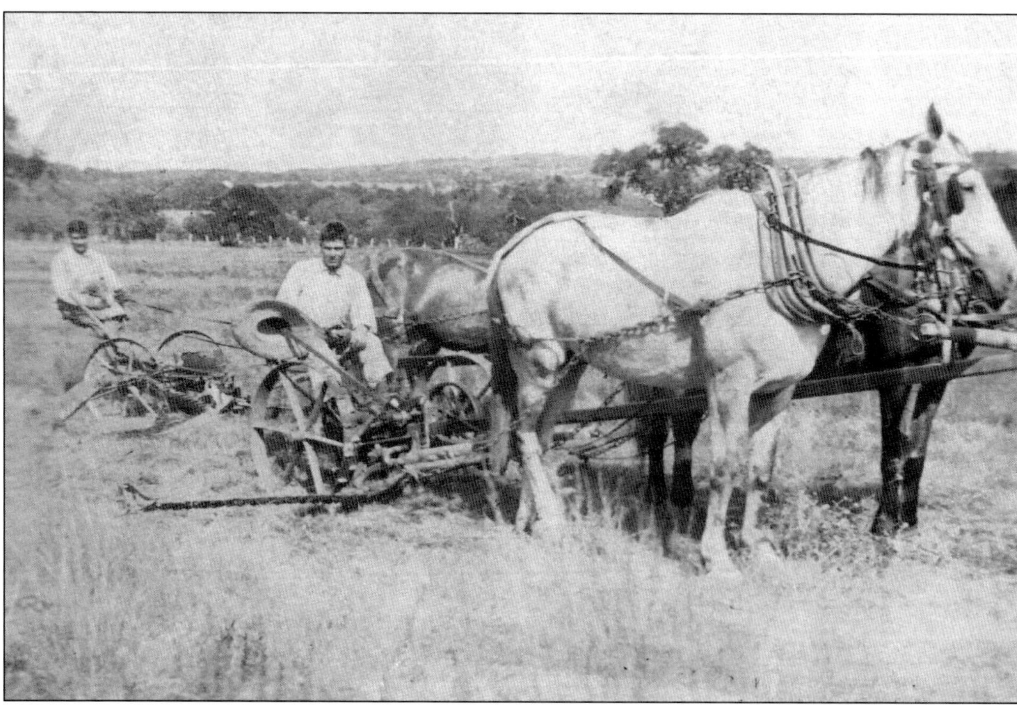

This 1920s photograph shows men in front of a well they had just finished digging at the William Braun homestead. (Courtesy of Fred W. Wendt.)

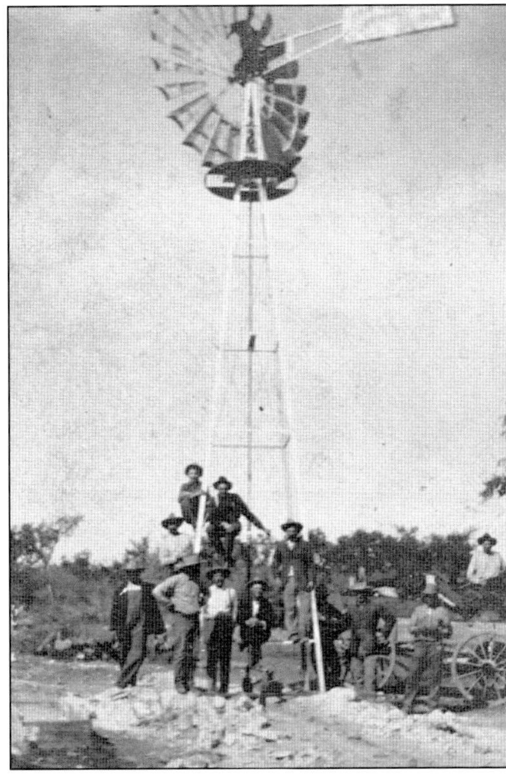

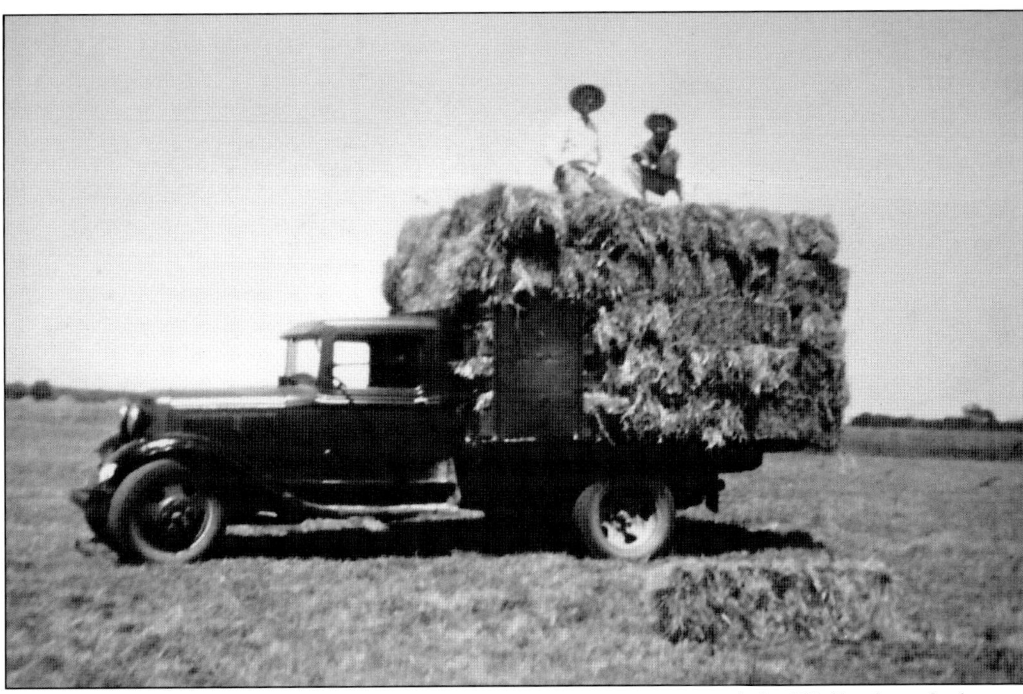

In 1986, the State of Texas Family Land Heritage Program recognized the Woller farm for having been owned and operated continuously by the same family for over 100 years. This 1946 photograph shows how hay was transported from the Woller farm. (Courtesy of Linda Bloom.)

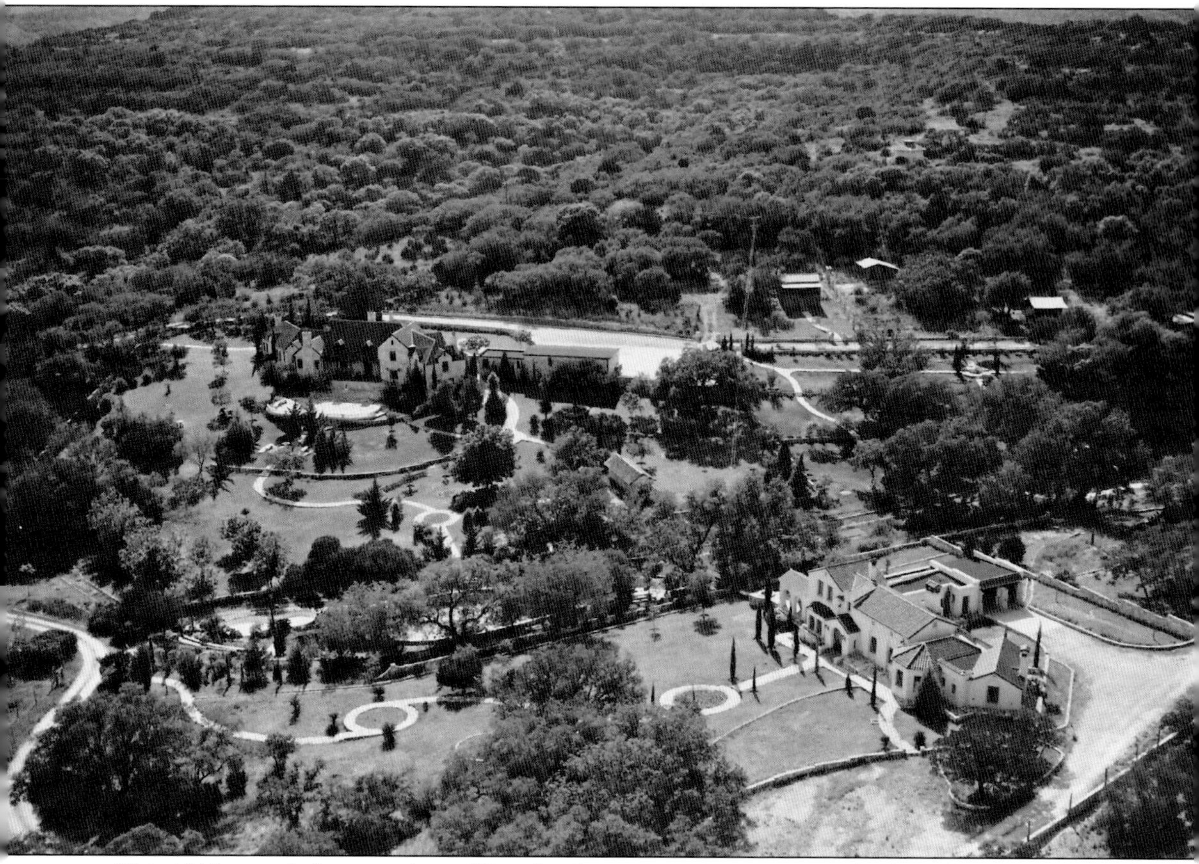

This 1940s aerial photograph is of Rancho Diana, a 1,208-acre estate built in the 1930s by Frank Huntress Sr., former publisher of the *San Antonio Express and News*. In 1951, John and Mazie Wagner purchased the property and raised cattle. The ranch, on the eastern border of the Francisco Menchaca property, employed some of Menchaca's descendants as ranch hands. After they moved to the ranch, the Wagners became active in the community, donating firefighting vehicles and other equipment to the Helotes Area Volunteer Fire Department. John Wagner passed away in 1974. In 2005, the city of San Antonio purchased 640 acres of the ranch, which had fallen into disrepair, for conservation. (Courtesy of Sandy Miles.)

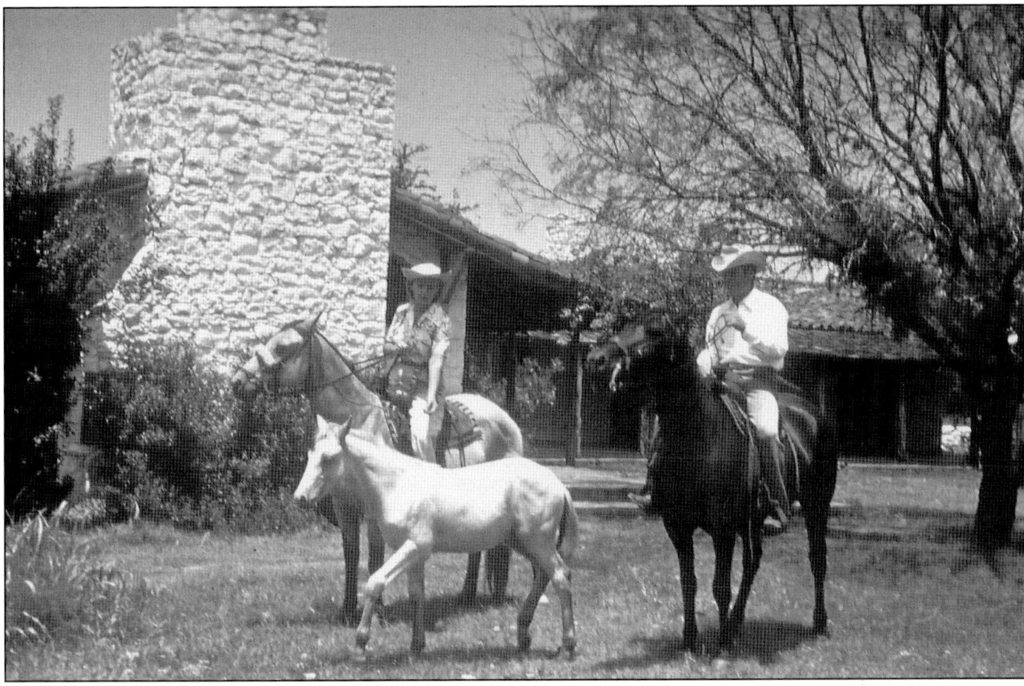

Built in 1937 as a getaway for developers Fernando and Kathryn Antonio, Casa Lejana was a 200-acre ranch in 1946, when Christy and Lola Mathewson, shown in this late-1940s photograph at the ranch, purchased the property along Helotes Creek and named it the CM Ranch. Lola and Christy (namesake son of the Baseball Hall-of-Famer) ran the property as a modest ranch and party house. In the photograph below, Lola pets one of her colts. The house has changed hands many times since Christy's death in 1951, operating as a public swimming pool, an exclusive dinner club and inn, and a restaurant. The buildings gradually fell into disrepair; the house complex on two acres off Dent Lane was restored in 2004 and is again a showplace. (Above and below, courtesy of Glen and Denise Vernon.)

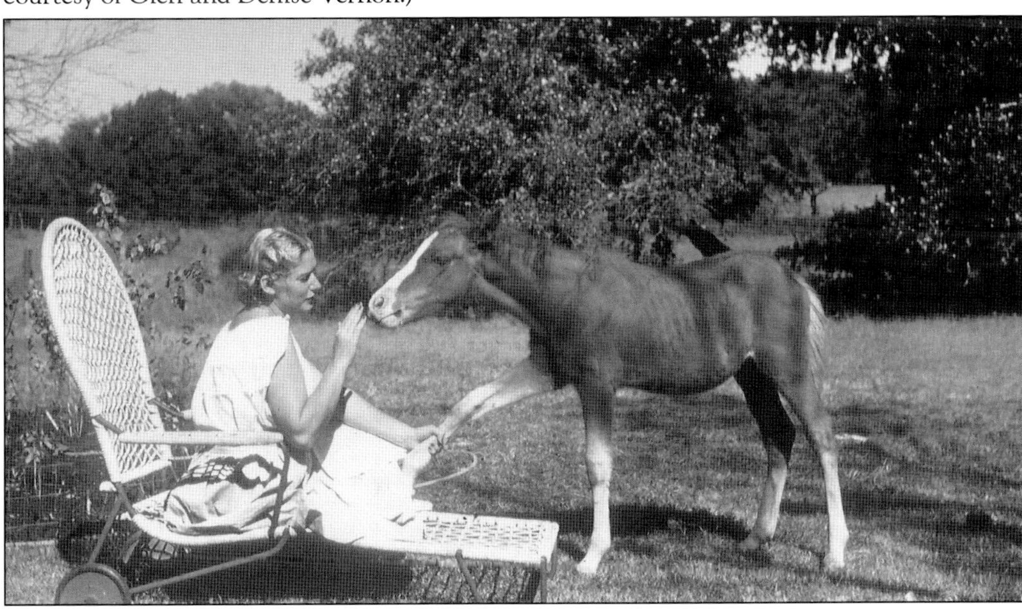

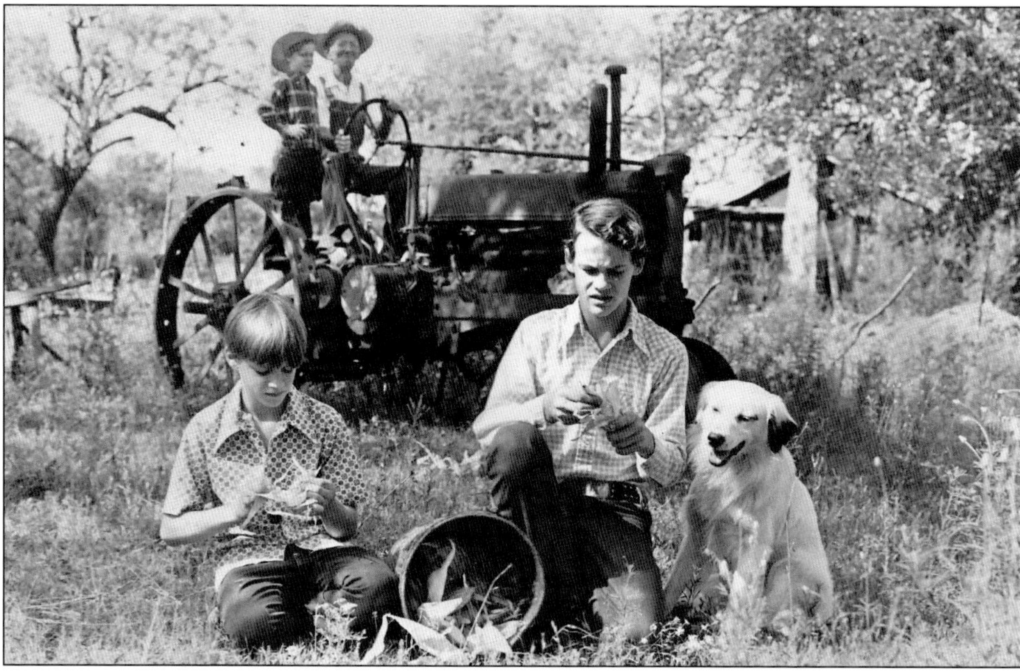

Newton A. Evans rides a tractor with his grandson while two older grandsons examine ears of corn to see if they are ripe in this June 1975 photograph. The Evans family farmed in Helotes beginning in 1928. They sold the majority of the land in the early 1970s, creating the Evans Valley subdivision off FM 1560. (Courtesy of HSH.)

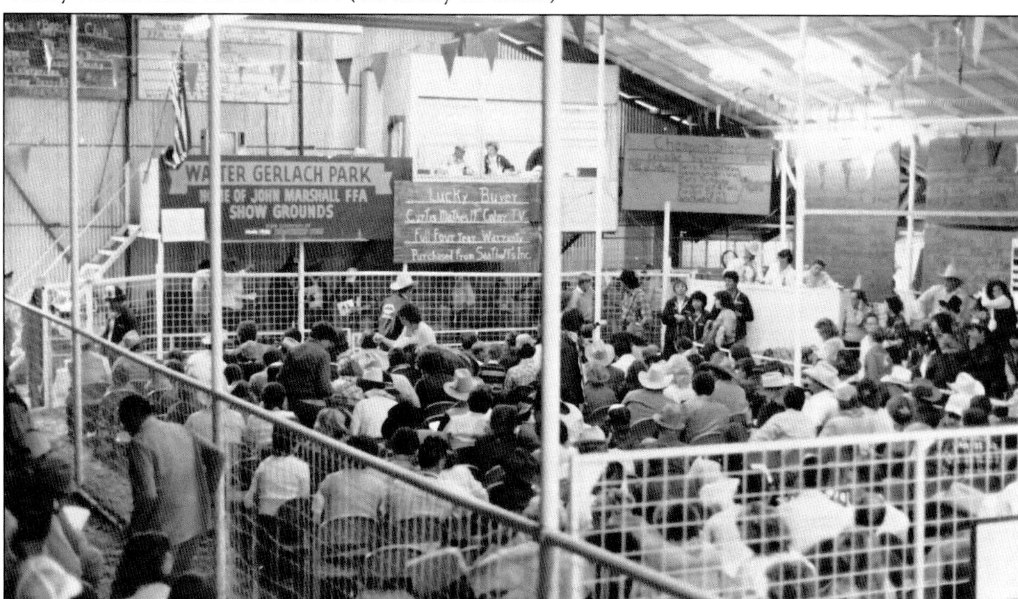

Helotes has long been associated with agriculture, kept alive through school FFA and 4-H programs. This photograph of the ninth annual Walter Gerlach Livestock Show and Sale, January 30, 1982, shows Helotes students—then attendees of John Marshall High School—at the auction. The Walter Gerlach Livestock Show, one of the largest scholarship programs in the country, has provided more than $8 million to students. (Courtesy of HSH.)

Six

Connecting Communities

Descendants of Spanish presidio soldiers, Canary Islanders who formed the first municipal government in San Antonio de Béjar, and Tejano soldiers for the Republic of Texas—these pioneers were granted land for their service and/or long tenure in Texas and were the earliest settlers in north Bexar County near Helotes. The early settlements were named for the pioneer families or for creeks that flowed through the land. The Zepeda settlement, founded on an 1847 land grant of 320 acres, was named for the family of José de Jesús Zepeda (1824–1905) and wife Juanita Rodriguez (1825–1887). Eight miles northwest of Helotes, the Zepeda settlement grew to almost 1,000 acres as the couple's children added their own land grants and purchases to the settlement. Their five children—Jesús, Victoriano, Fidencio, Adolfo, and Vicenta—were born in the stone house Zepeda built in 1848, which now stands on a two-acre lot owned by a descendant. Adjacent to the Zepeda settlement were the properties of Francisco Rivas and Manuel Hernandez, who settled in the area in the early 1850s. The San Geronimo settlement, named for the creek that flowed through the land, formed around the ghost town of Clifton, which in 1890 had a population of about 30 people. By the turn of the century, the town was mostly a scattered community of farms and ranches; one of the most prominent was the Schott Ranch. To the northeast, Leon Springs was founded in the early 1850s as a stagecoach stop and developed as a train depot after a railroad track was laid near the settlement. Nine miles to the south of Helotes, Leon Valley also started as a stagecoach stop on Bandera Road in the early 1860s, and became an incorporated town in 1952.

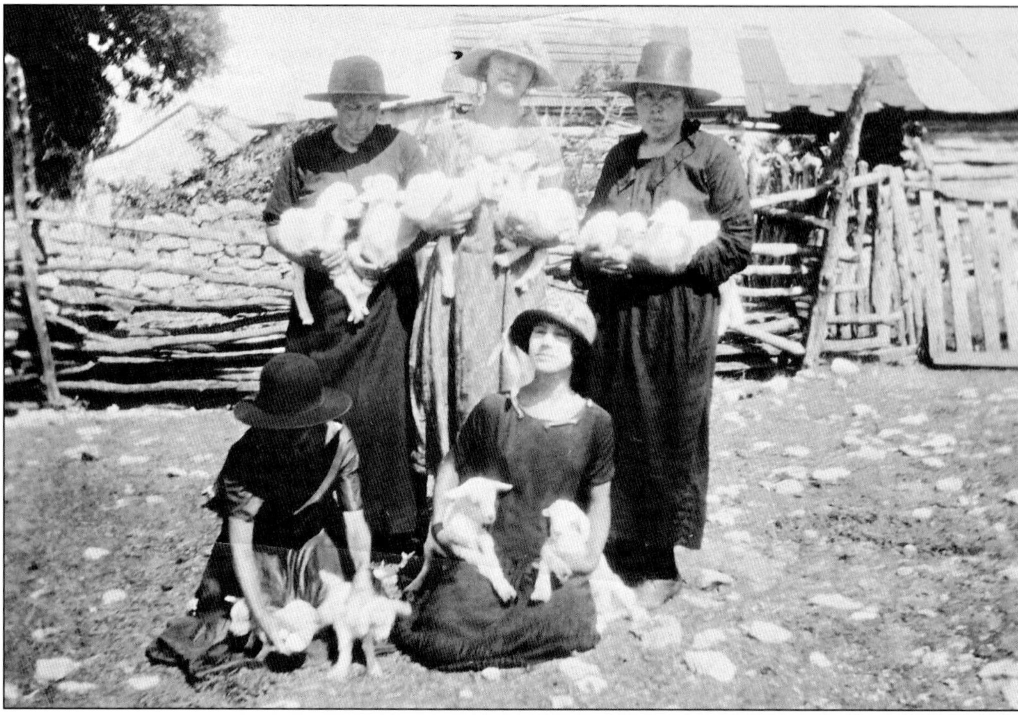

Adolfo Zepeda, son of pioneers José de Jesús and Juanita (Rodriguez) Zepeda, lived with wife Zenaida Perez and their four children in the Zepeda homestead, where he was born in 1856. The family raised sheep. This 1927 photograph shows their daughters and other relatives holding lambs. María de Jesus "Jesusita" Zepeda is standing on the left, and Zenaida is standing on the right. The other girls are unidentified. In the 1969 photograph below, Rosa (Caldera) Zepeda stands in front of the Zepeda homestead, built in 1848. (Above and below, courtesy of Mary Z. Reyes and Cynthia Z. Farmer.)

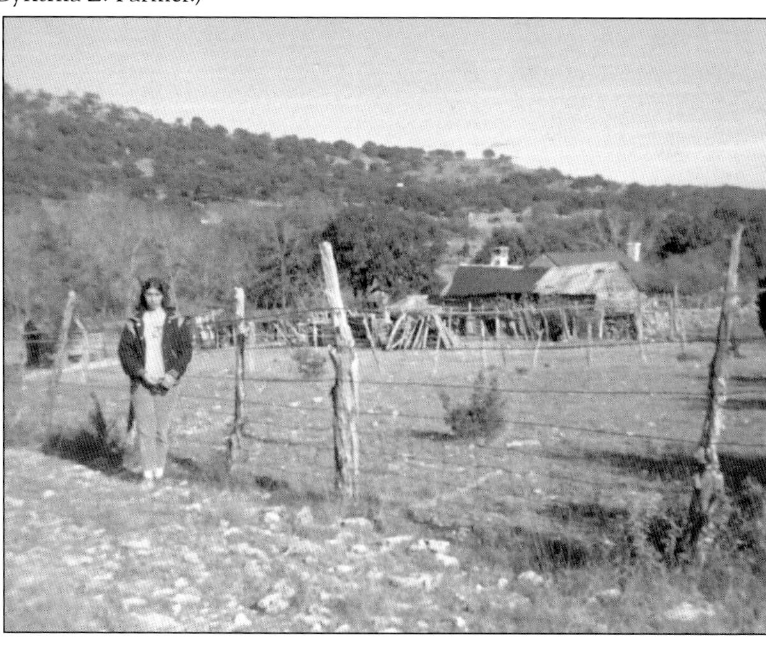

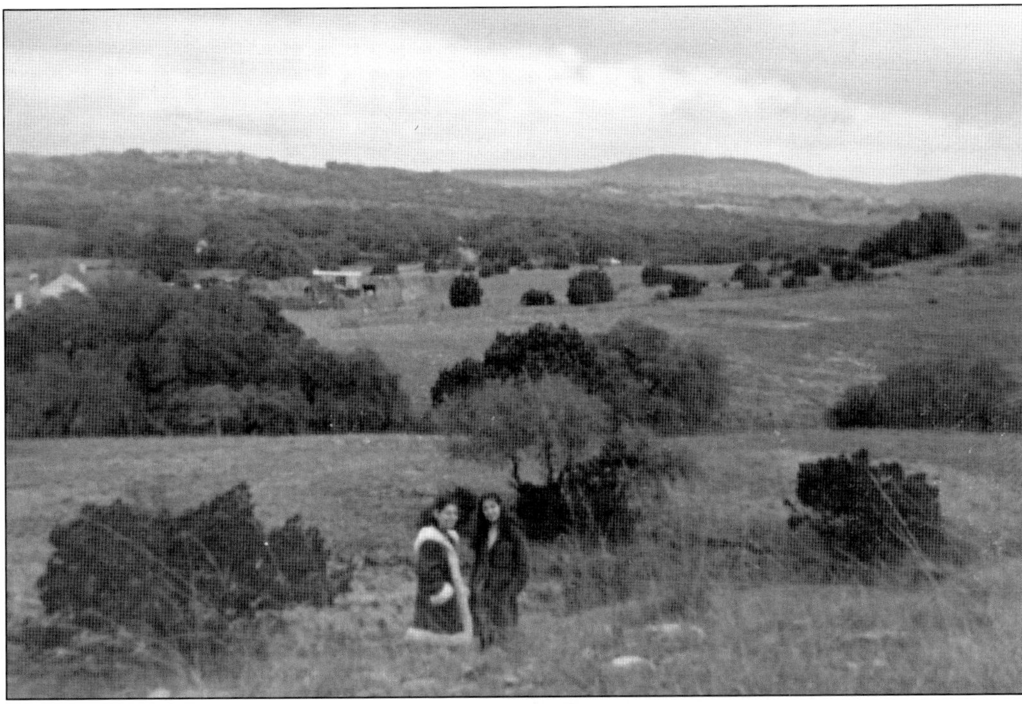

Mary Zepeda and Gerry Aldrete stand on a hill on the Zepeda property in 1969. The land is typical of the Texas hill country—oak-studded hills, rocky terrain, and flowing creeks—which lured the first Mexican and Spanish settlers to the area, even as Comanches still roamed the neighborhood. In the photograph on the right, neighbor Manuel Hernandez (1850–1927), a descendant of Canary Islanders, settled on 160 acres in the San Geronimo community some time after 1853. Named after his father, he also had a namesake son and three other children with wife Salomé Morales (1852–1893). He was often referred to as a doctor because of his knowledge of herbal remedies. (Above, courtesy of Mary Z. Reyes and Cynthia Z. Farmer; at right, courtesy of Ella Dunford.)

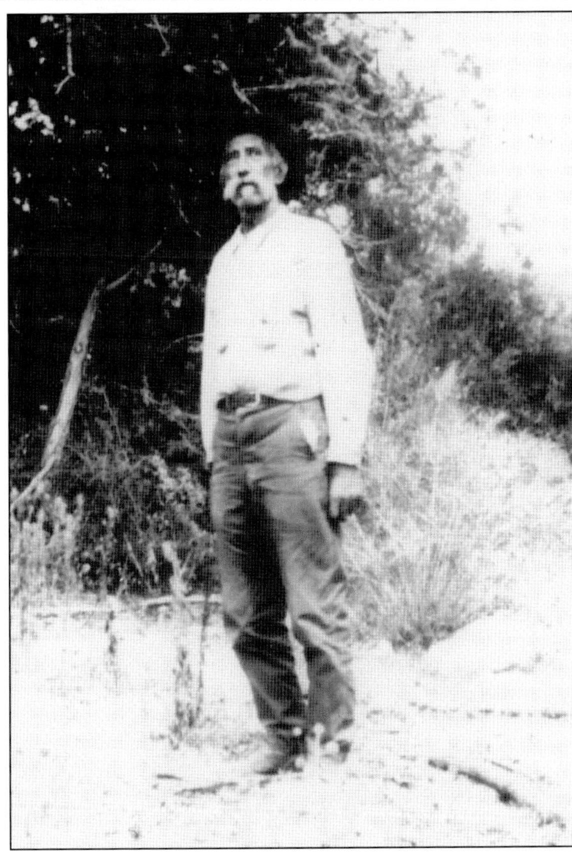

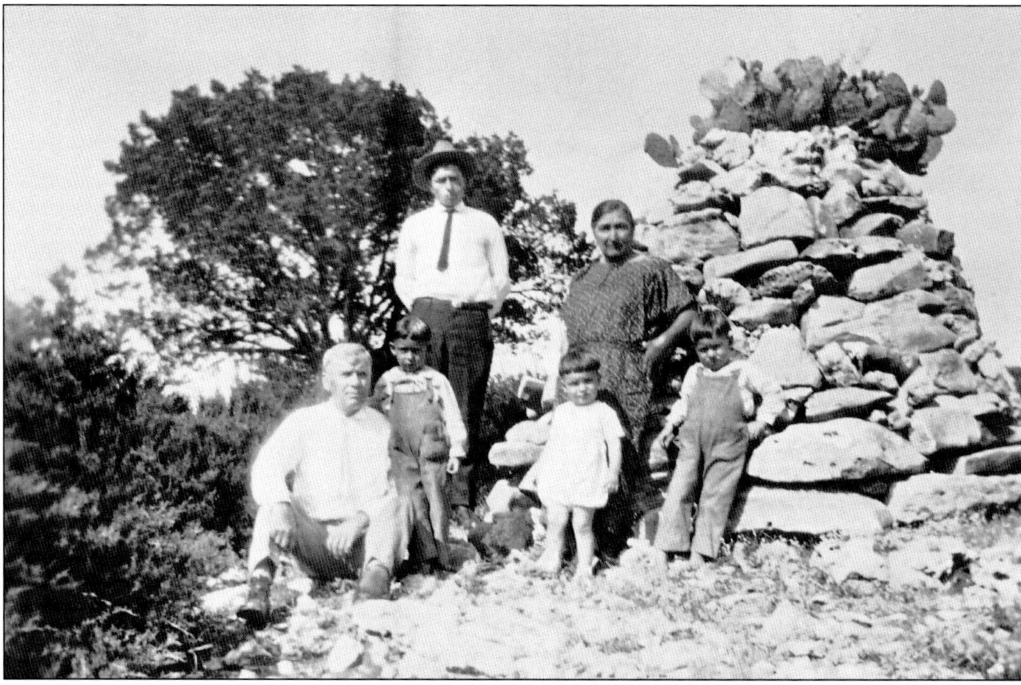

Scotsman David Logan (1871–1947) purchased 200 acres along San Geronimo Creek in 1912, where he built his homestead on top of a hill. On September 25, 1920, he married Mary Ann Madla. Seen from left to right in this 1926 photograph are (first row) David Logan and sons Frank, Alexander, and James; (second row) brother-in-law Frank Madla Jr. and mother-in-law Francisca Madla. (Courtesy of Juanita "Janie" Madla.)

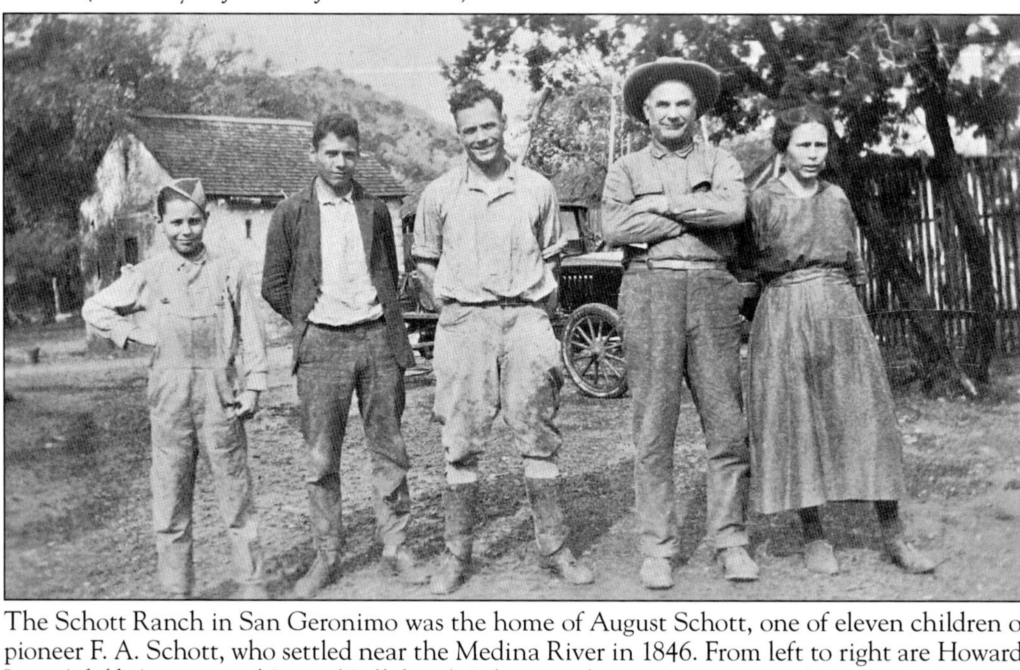

The Schott Ranch in San Geronimo was the home of August Schott, one of eleven children of pioneer F. A. Schott, who settled near the Medina River in 1846. From left to right are Howard, Leo, Adolf, August, and Lona (Callaham) Schott at their 1,500-acre ranch in the early 1920s. (Courtesy of Fred W. Wendt.)

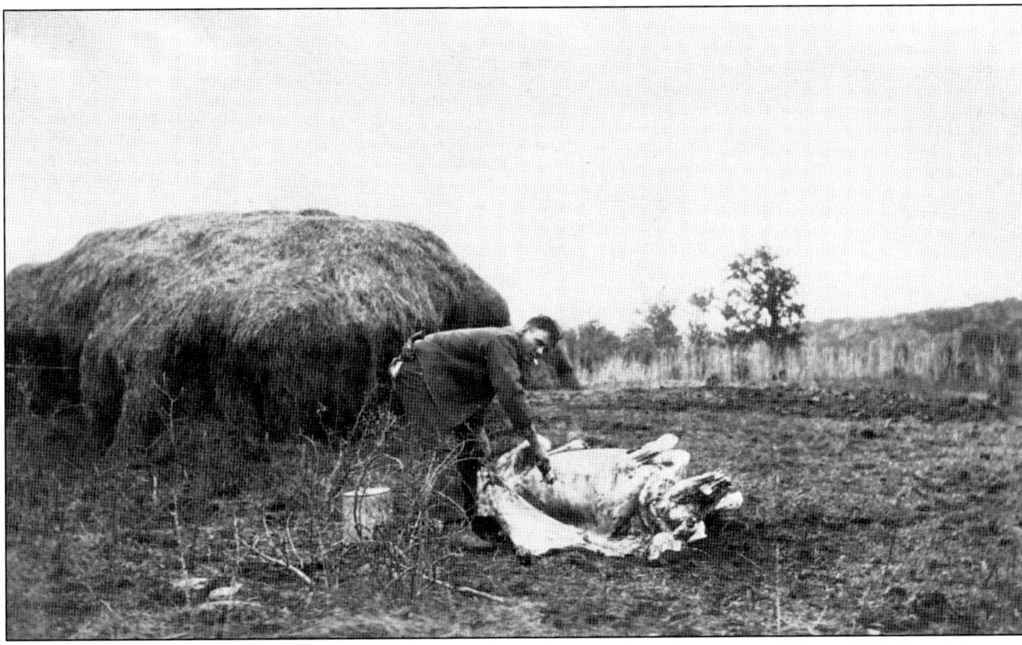
Adolf Schott skins a cow on the family ranch in the 1920s. (Courtesy of Fred W. Wendt.)

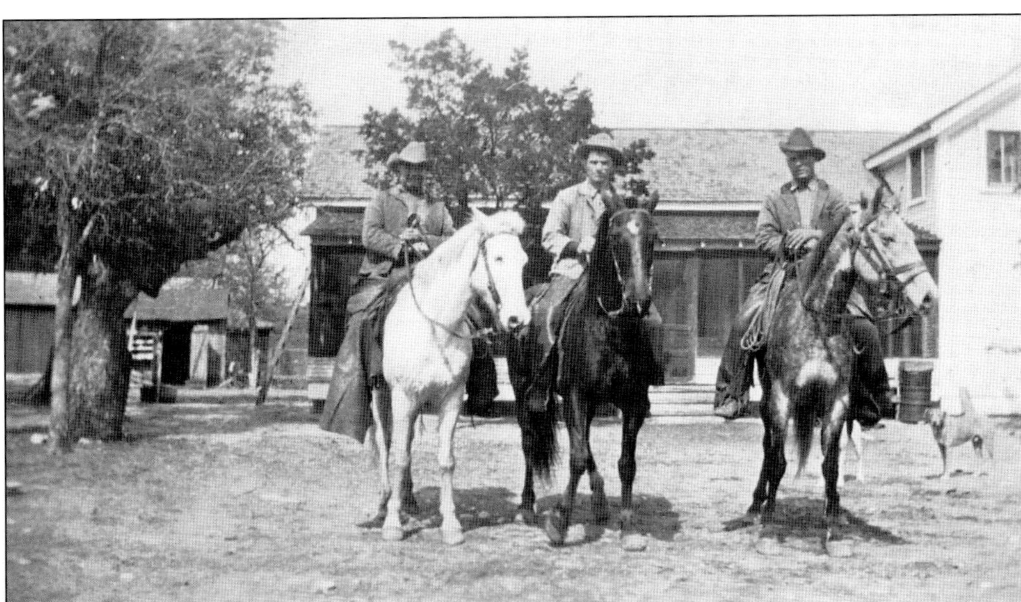
Horseback riding was a necessity in the early Helotes area ranches. From left to right are August Schott, Fred A. Wendt, and Adolf Schott at the Schott Ranch in the late 1920s. (Courtesy of Fred W. Wendt.)

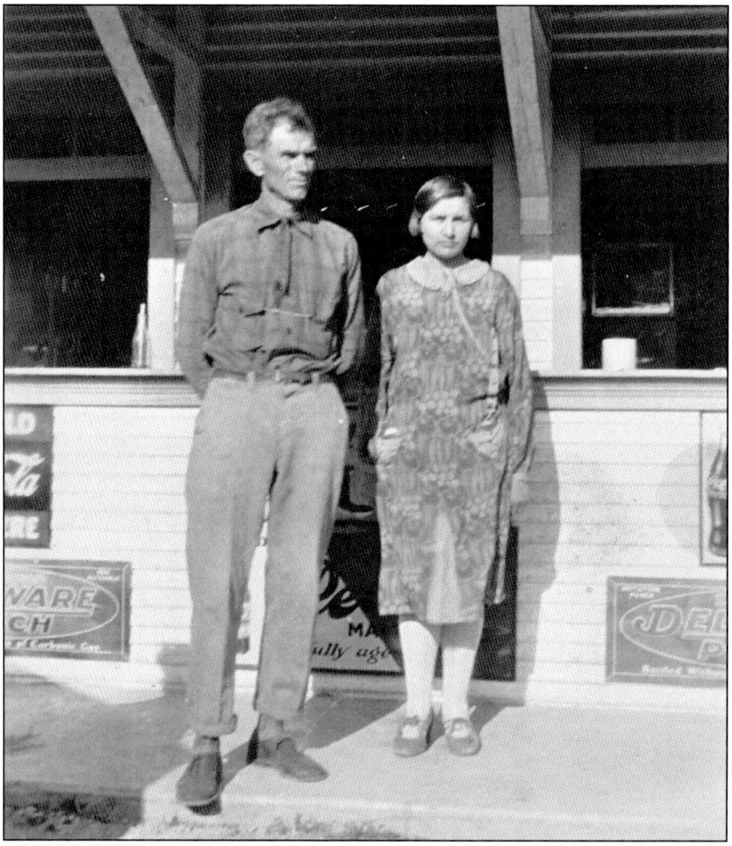

Fred A. Wendt with wife Thusnelda Braun, whom he married in 1927, stand in front of their general store on Bandera Road. Wendt, who was from Chicago, purchased a few acres from the Schott family and built the general store and gas station. The photograph below shows the property, which he called Rustic Park, a popular stop for weekenders on their way to Medina Lake. In front of the store is the Wendt's son, Fredrick William. (At left and below, courtesy of Fred W. Wendt.)

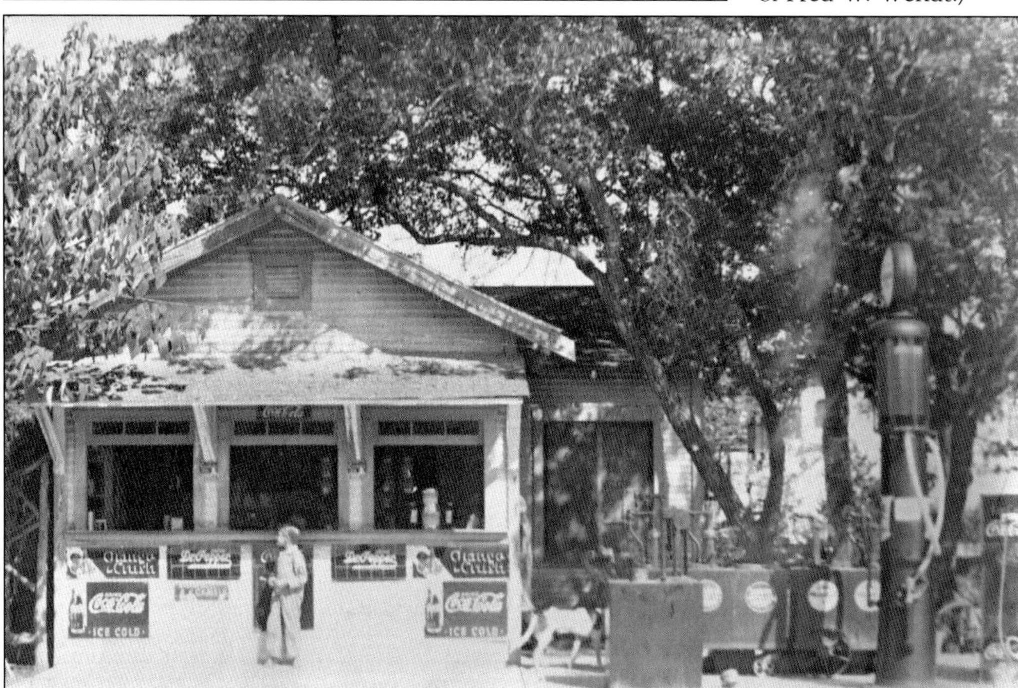

Wendt also built a dance hall atop his property, a popular destination in the 1930s that could only be reached by a bridge over San Geronimo Creek as seen in the photograph below. The dance hall was converted to a private residence by subsequent owners and is still standing today. (At right and below, courtesy of Fred W. Wendt.)

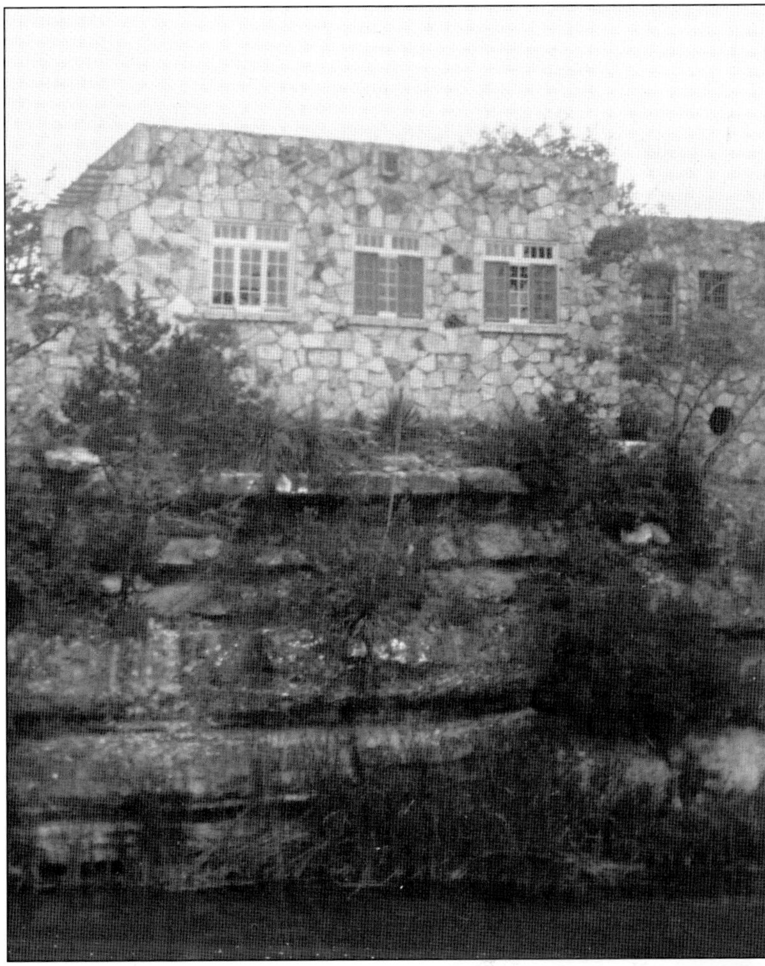

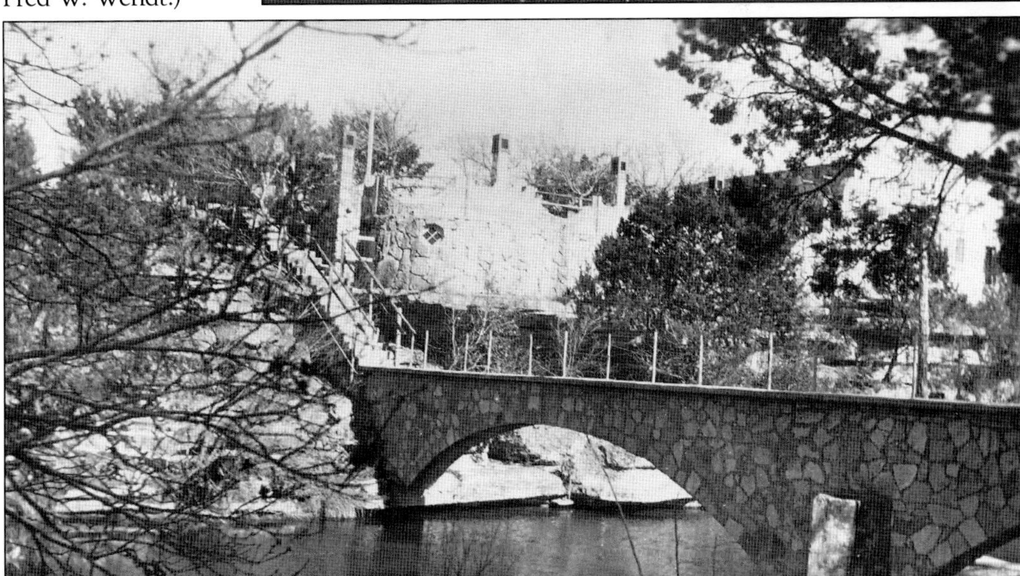

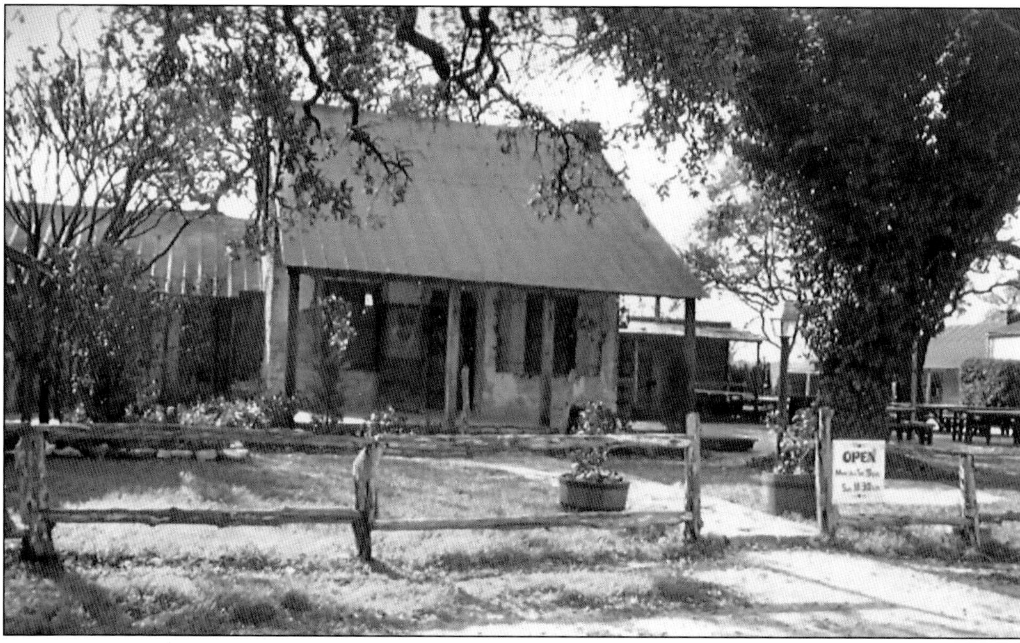

In 1852, Max Aue moved to Leon Springs, where he built the cabin shown in this photograph. At today's intersection of I-10 West and Boerne Stage Road, the Aue cabin served as a post office, stage stop, and general store. In the 1860s, Helotes residents picked up their mail in Leon Springs. (Courtesy of Marlene Richardson.)

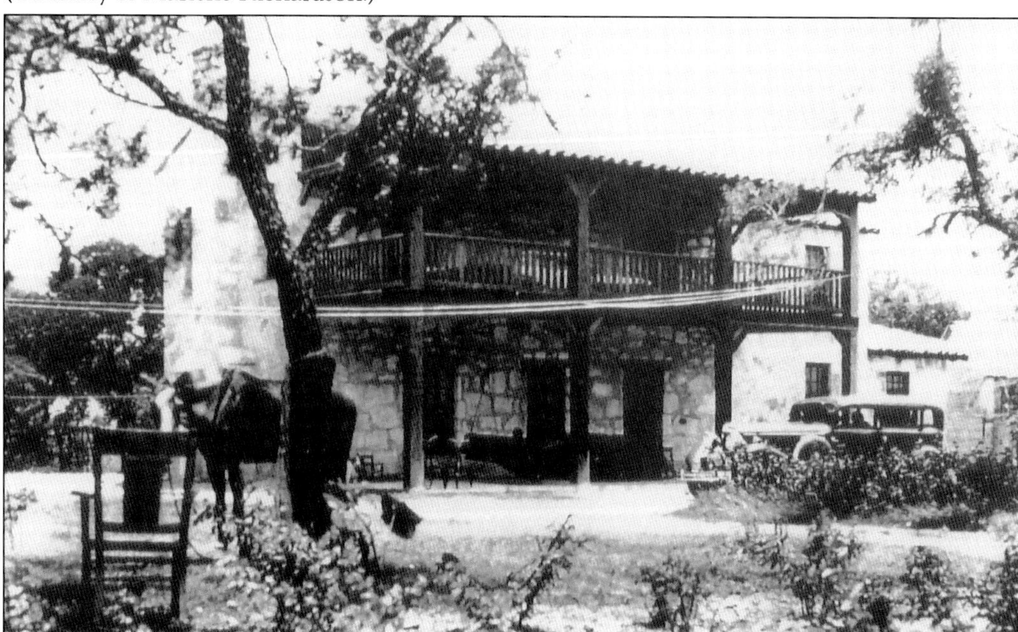

The Hucbner-Onion Homestead, built in 1862 by Joseph Huebner, also served as a stagecoach stop on Bandera Road, 9 miles south of Helotes. Judge John F. Onion purchased the property in Leon Valley in 1930, and his family lived there for 53 years. The Leon Valley Historical Society acquired the house in 2000. Seven years later, the homestead was awarded state and national historic recognition. (Courtesy of the Leon Valley Historical Society.)

Seven

John T. Floore Country Store

The sign above Floore Country Store reads, "Bar, Café, Dance, Meats, Groceries, Real Estate," an eclectic array of services and products that mirror the diversity of its founder. But John T. Floore's primary vision for his country store, which opened in 1946, was to make it *the* place for country-and-western singers and musicians to appear. Floore's respect for the music genre and his personal showmanship lured the best-known musicians to Helotes. Bob Wills, Ernest Tubb, Patsy Cline, Hank Williams, Elvis Presley, Willie Nelson, Ray Price, Bob Dylan, and Merle Haggard were just a few stars who graced the Floore Country Store stage in the early years. Floore liked to promote musicians whom he considered gifted. When Willie Nelson returned to Texas from Nashville, where music executives didn't appreciate his different style of singing, Floore gave him the venue of Floore Country Store to showcase his songs. Nelson became a regular at Floore and even penned a tribute to his friend, mentor, and business associate in his 1973 hit song, "Shotgun Willie." Floore's vision to bring top-rated musicians to his dance hall was realized over the next decades, putting Helotes on the world map of country music. The historic venue, which still features topnotch country-and-western bands, as well as up-and-coming artists, was recognized as a Texas Historic Landmark and was listed in the National Register of Historic Places in 2005. The Academy of Country Music selected John T. Floore Country Store as one of the five top nightclubs in the country in 2007.

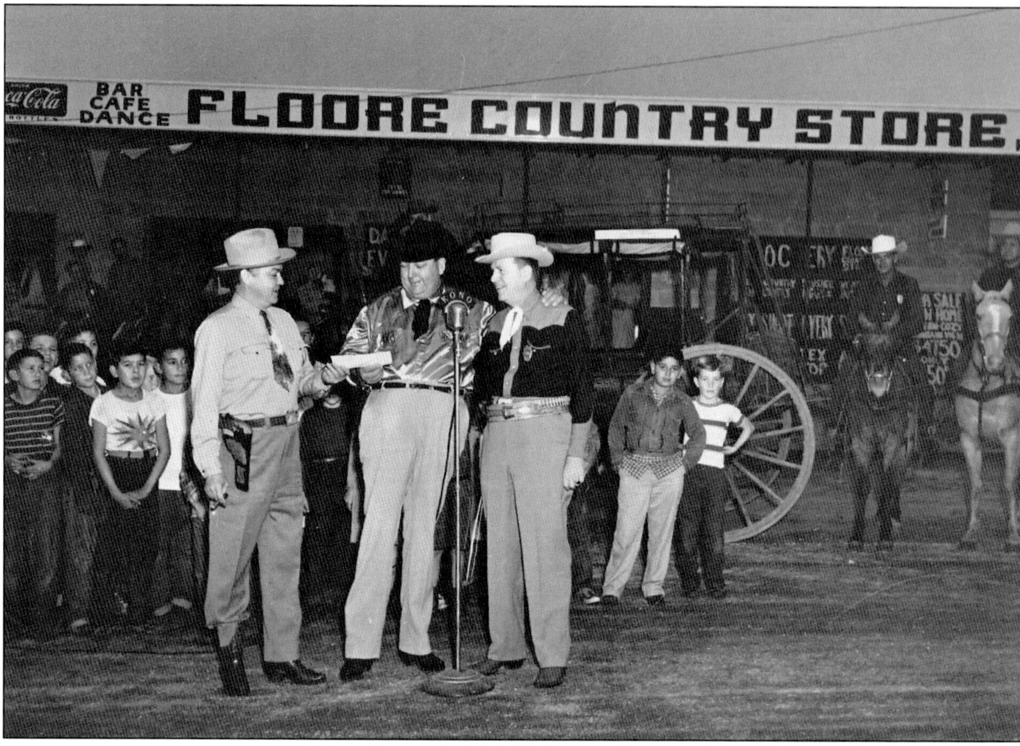

To celebrate the completion of the "biggest patio in the Southwest" at his dance hall, John T. Floore (1898–1975), in the black hat in the middle of this 1949 photograph, arranged a big event, including Helotes Elementary schoolchildren, local law enforcement, a radio personality, and a stagecoach to signify the town's historic roots. The photograph below shows the inside of the dance hall, known for its unique decoration of hanging signs, boots, hats, farm equipment, and other paraphernalia. (Above and below, courtesy of John T. Floore Country Store, JTFCS.)

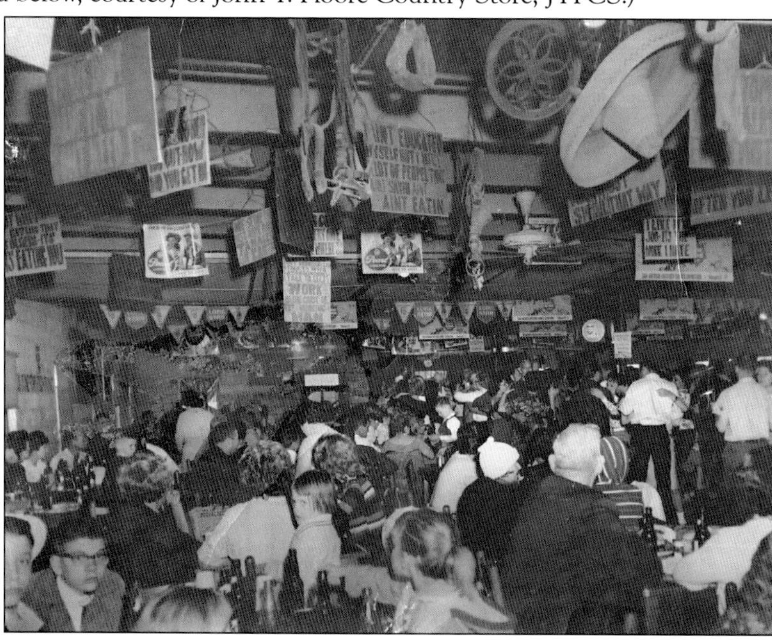

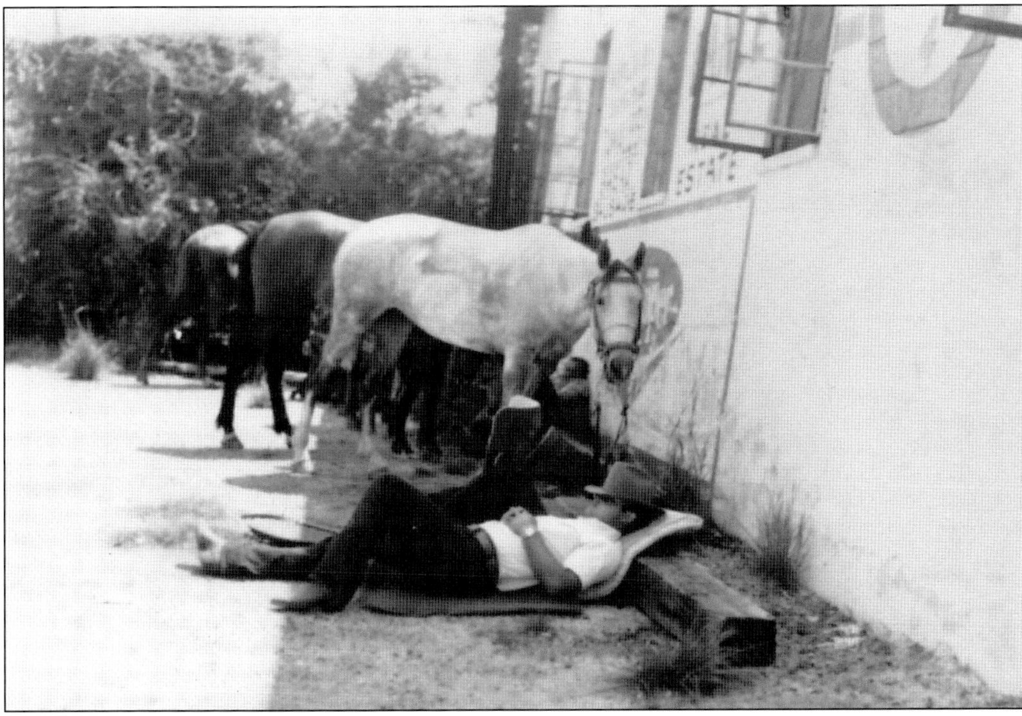

A cowboy rests with his horse outside Floore Country Store in this 1970s photograph. The dance hall was a popular stop on trail rides through town. John T. Floore wanted to make sure nobody missed it; his signs, as shown in this 1982 photograph, are an important part of the Floore brand. (Above and below, courtesy of HSH.)

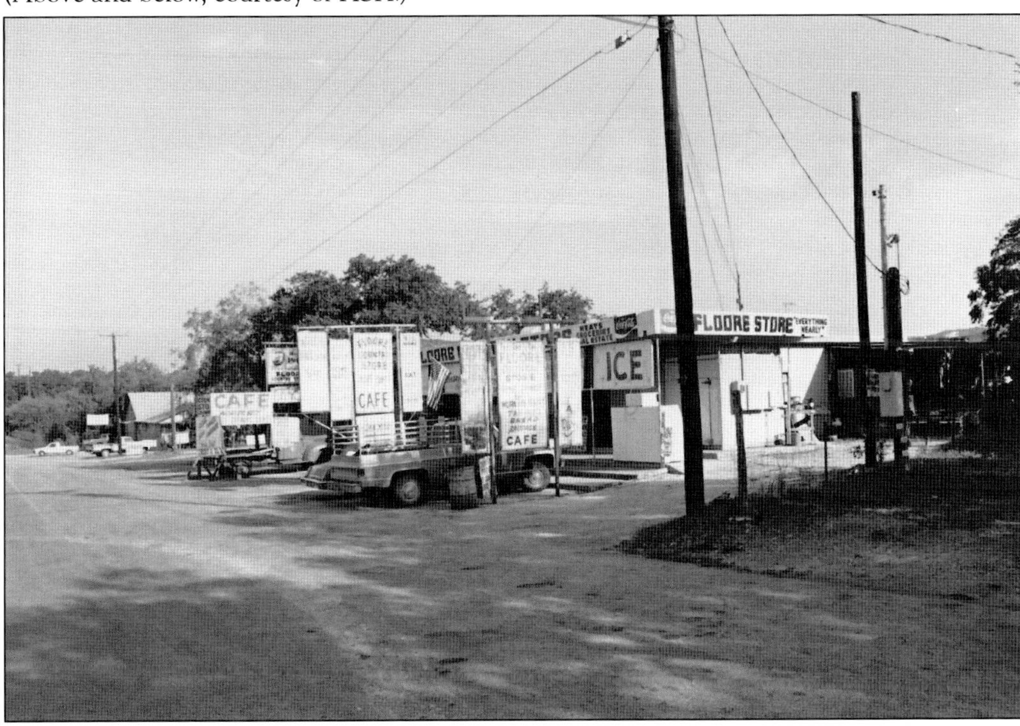

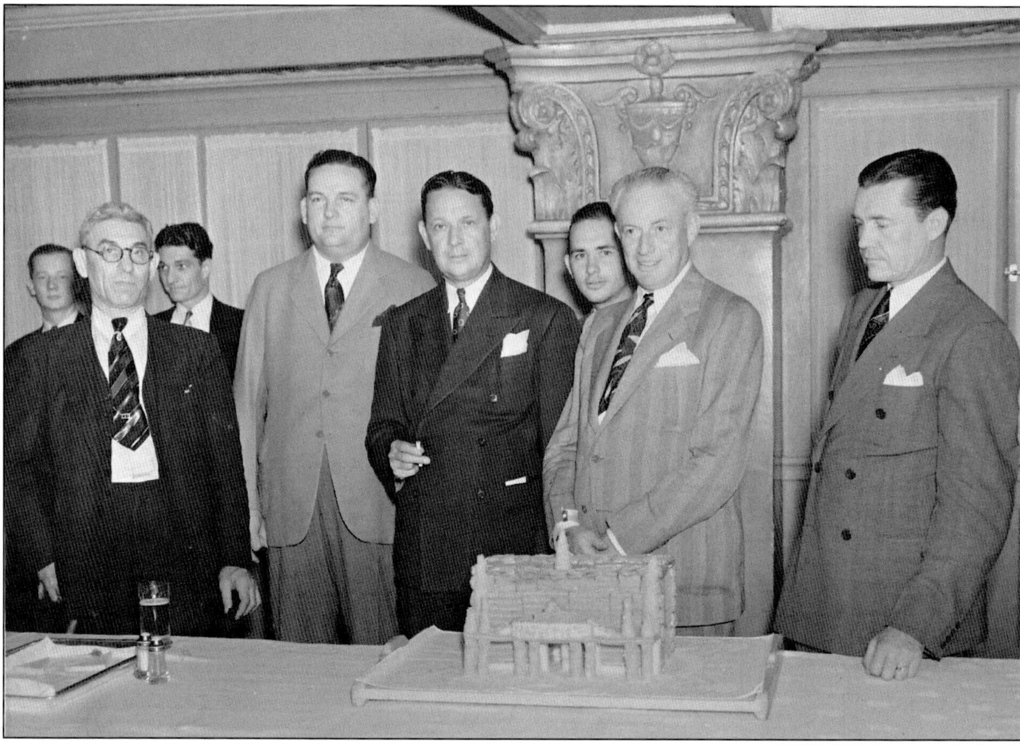

John T. Floore was born in Troup, Texas. He came to San Antonio in the 1930s and worked as a manager with Interstate Theaters. Eph Charninsky, co-owner of the theater chain, is on the far left of this photograph. Floore is standing next to him. The cake is a replica of the Majestic Theater, built in 1929. In the photograph below, Floore chats with Mexican comedian Cantinflas (Mario Moreno, 1911–1993), a popular performer in the 1940s and 1950s theater circuit who became known worldwide after he appeared in the 1956 film *Around the World in 80 Days* as a bumbling valet. (Above and below, courtesy of JTFCS.)

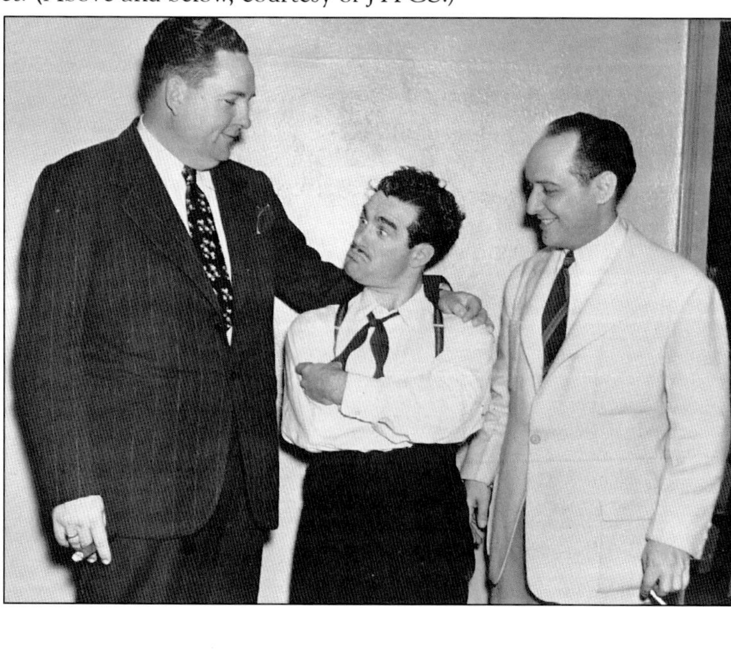

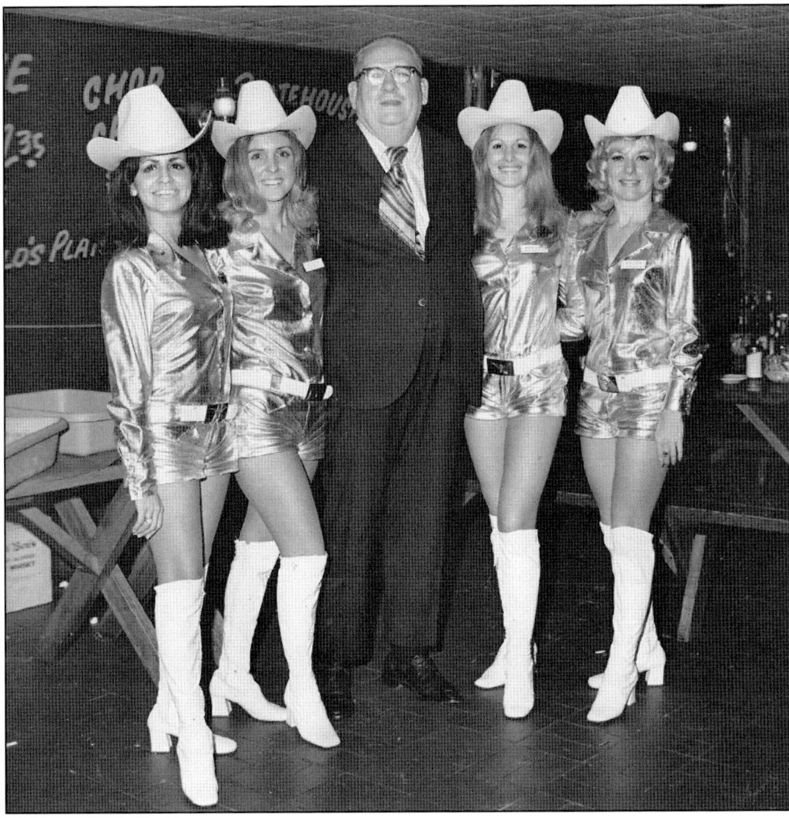

John T. Floore, whose leadership abilities conferred upon him the title "Honorary Mayor of Helotes" from his 1942 arrival in town, poses with waitresses at the Little Red Barn Steakhouse, which opened in San Antonio in 1963. (Courtesy of JTFCS.)

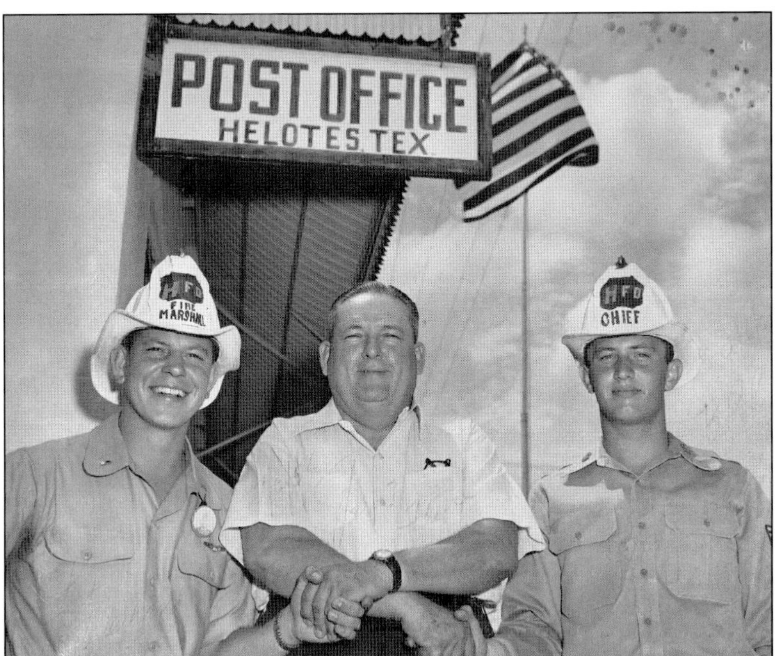

In this July 1956 photograph, Floore congratulated two Kelly Air Force Base servicemen after making them honorary fire marshals for saving Helotes residents thousands of dollars in fire damages. On the left, Lt. D. W. Weiland was piloting a plane when A1C B. R. Bindley, right, who worked at the Kelly control tower, asked him to investigate smoke in the Helotes hills. (Courtesy of JTFCS.)

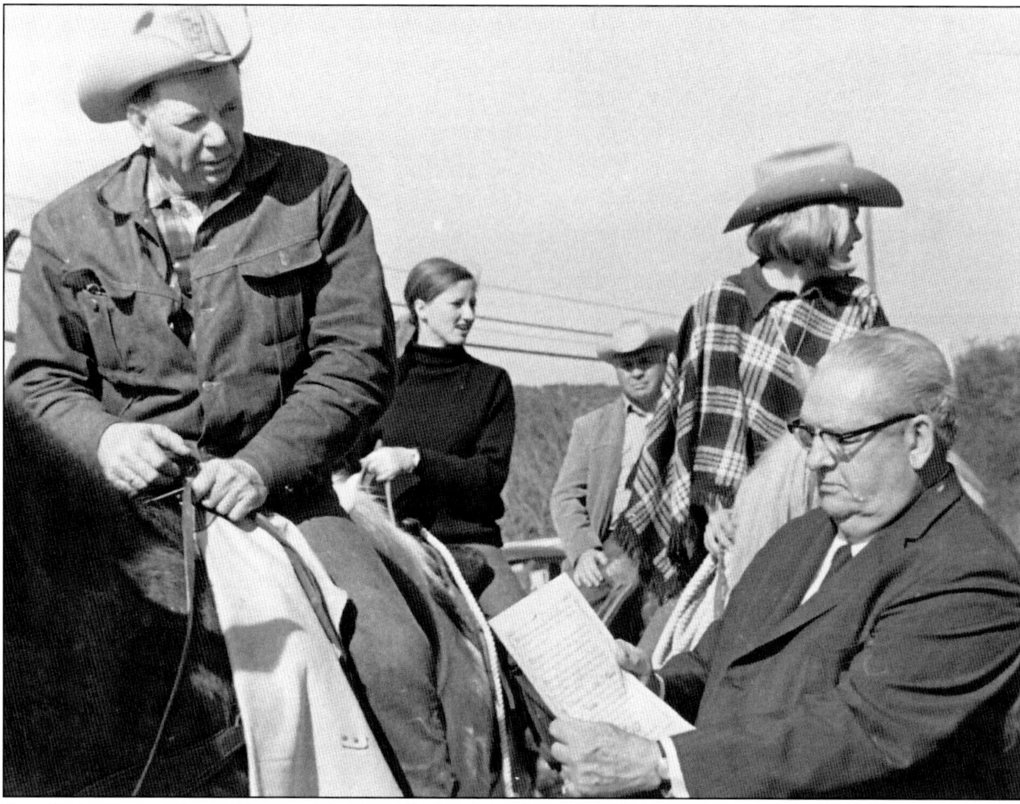

Frank Anderwald, trail boss of the Cowboy Capital Trail Ride, gave John T. Floore a commendation for his part as goodwill ambassador to the 1970 Stock Show and Rodeo in San Antonio. Floore greeted the trail riders in front of Floore Country Store, where several hundred gathered before heading to the livestock show. In the photograph below, John T. Floore welcomed Teresa Martinez, queen of the 1972 Cowboy Capital Trail Ride, along with trail boss Frank Anderwald, on their first stop at Floore Country Store before they continued on to the San Antonio Stock Show and Rodeo. From San Geronimo, Martinez was crowned there at Pete's Place during a dance and barbecue. (Above and below, courtesy of HSH.)

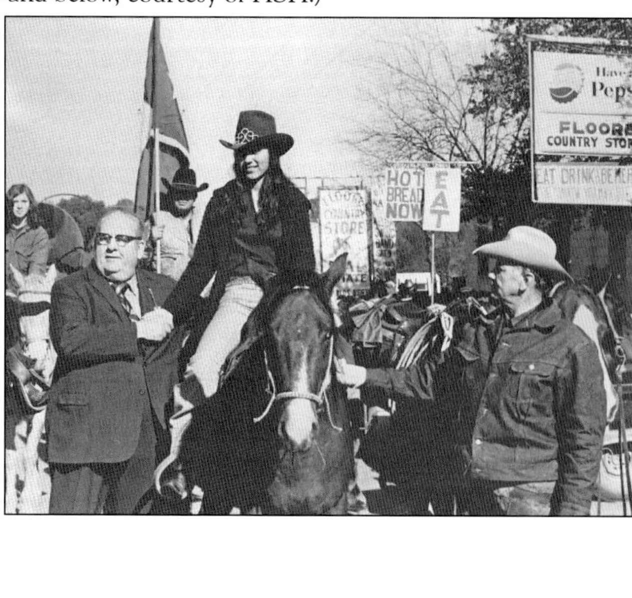

"Tex Allen" Ben Fischer, country-and-western harmonica virtuoso, recorded the "Helotes Polka," a tune that became a local hit in 1976. Known for the special mechanics of his harmonica, he often played at Floore Country Store with various bands, including his own—the South Texas Sound band. A resident of Grey Forest for many years, he also toured with Darrell McCall as one of his original Tennessee Volunteers. (Courtesy of HSH.)

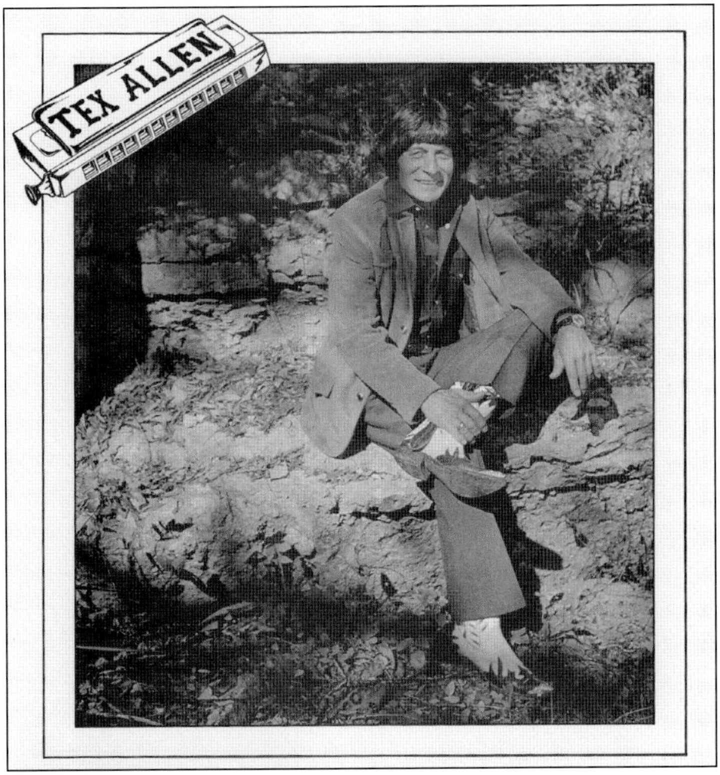

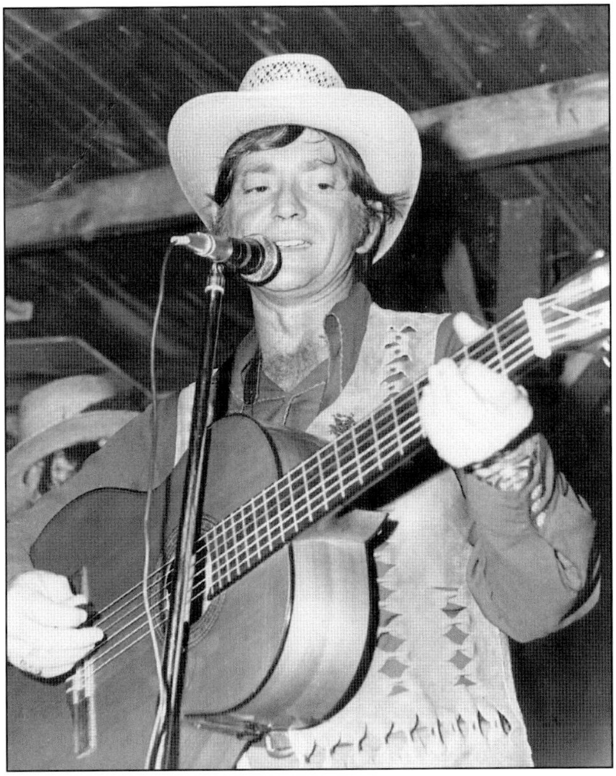

Singer/songwriter Willie Nelson sang at a benefit at Floore Country Store in May 1971 during the Cornyval Festival. John T. Floore and Nelson were partners in the original Willie Nelson Music Company. Floore introduced Nelson to Helotes in 1967. After that show with a scant 200 people in the audience, Nelson continued to perform at Floore regularly. By 1974, more than 2,000 people were showing up for his Floore's engagements. (Courtesy JTFCS.)

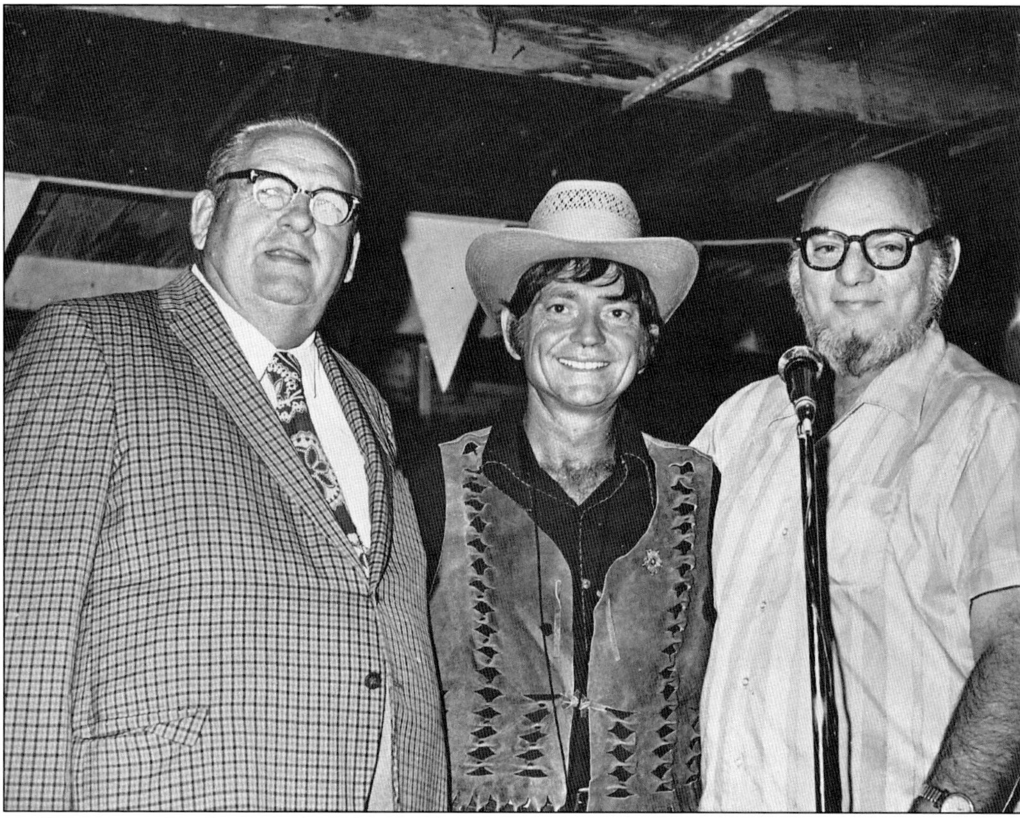

In this May 1971 photograph, John T. Floore, Willie Nelson, and an unidentified man were at a benefit concert at Floore Country Store. In the photograph below, Nelson, the 1971 Helotes Cornyval Parade Grand Marshal, rode in the parade with Floore, Helotes's honorary mayor. (Above and below, courtesy of JTFCS.)

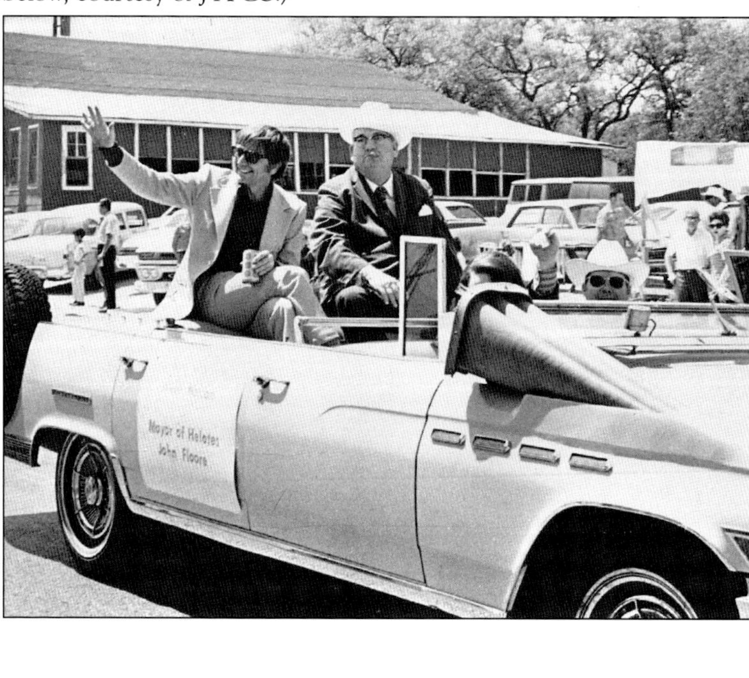

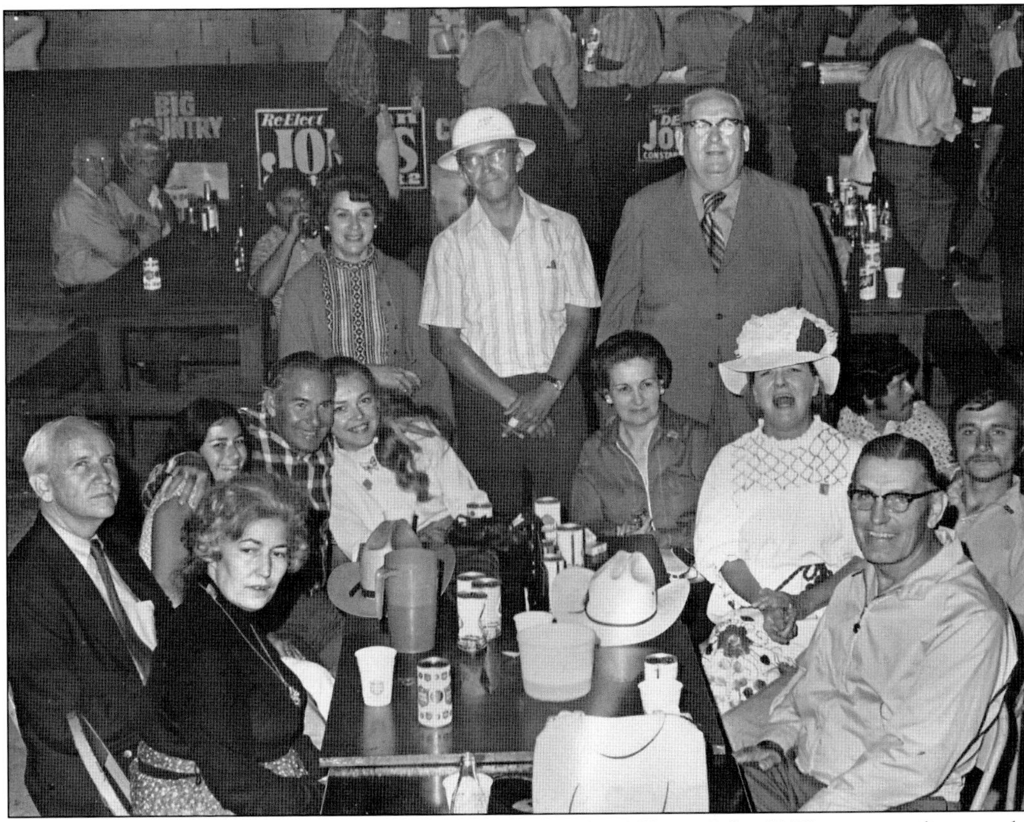

Enjoying themselves at Floore Country Store on May 17, 1972, are John T. Floore, standing on the right behind the table, and from the left side of the table, Lucy Perkins Brown, Charles Brown, and Carmen Madla. On the right side of the table, starting with the woman in the hat, are Dottie Bergstrom, Ralph Madla, and Leon Schueneman. All others are unidentified. (Courtesy of JTFCS.)

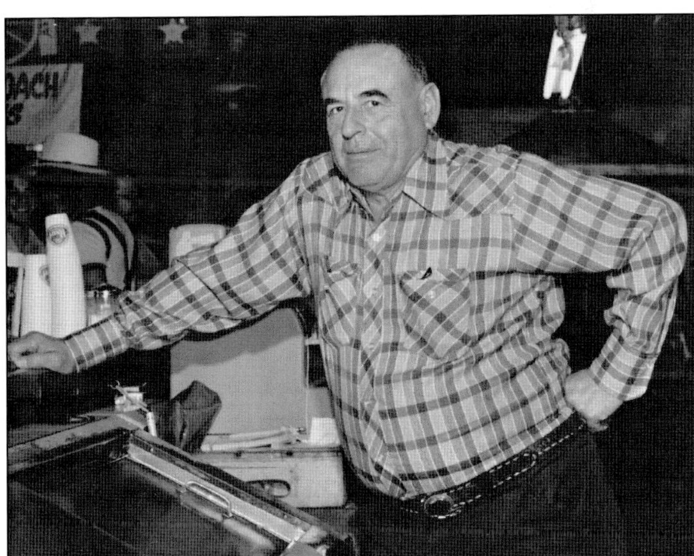

In October 1973, Floore, who had been suffering from ill health, sold Floore Country Store to Joe Algueseva (1920–2004), shown in this photograph, and wife Estella (Rosas) Algueseva. Both had worked for Floore for several years and wanted to continue Floore's legacy as an old-time country-western place. (Courtesy of JTFCS.)

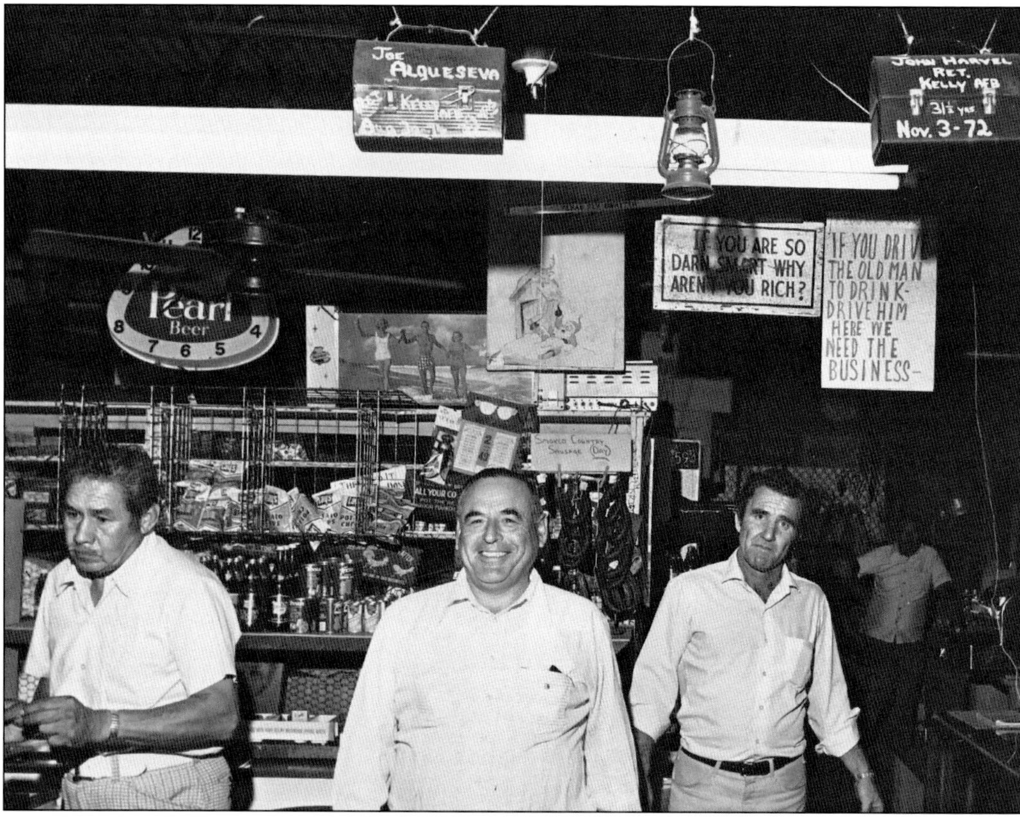

Cold beer and tamales have been regular staples at Floore Country Store from the start. Shown at the counter in this May 9, 1976, photograph are, left to right, cook Roy Zatarain, owner Joe Algueseva, and bartender Wayne Weed. (Courtesy of Estella R. Algueseva.)

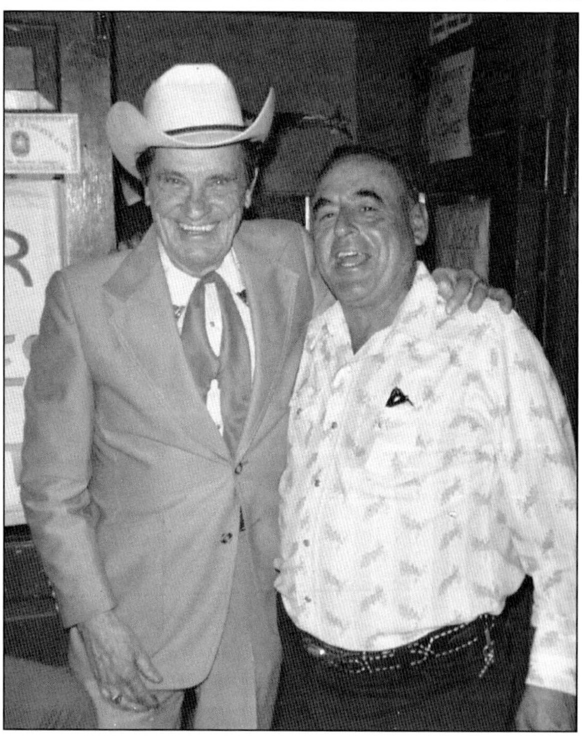

Ernest Tubb, the Texas Troubadour, shown in this late-1970s photograph with Joe Algueseva, was always a popular performer at Floore Country Store. (Courtesy of Estella R. Algueseva.)

Johnny Cash, with Joe Algueseva, filmed part of his TV special *Thaddeus Rose and Eddie* at Floore Country Store in December 1977. Algueseva had a small part in the film, playing himself. (Courtesy of Estella R. Algueseva.)

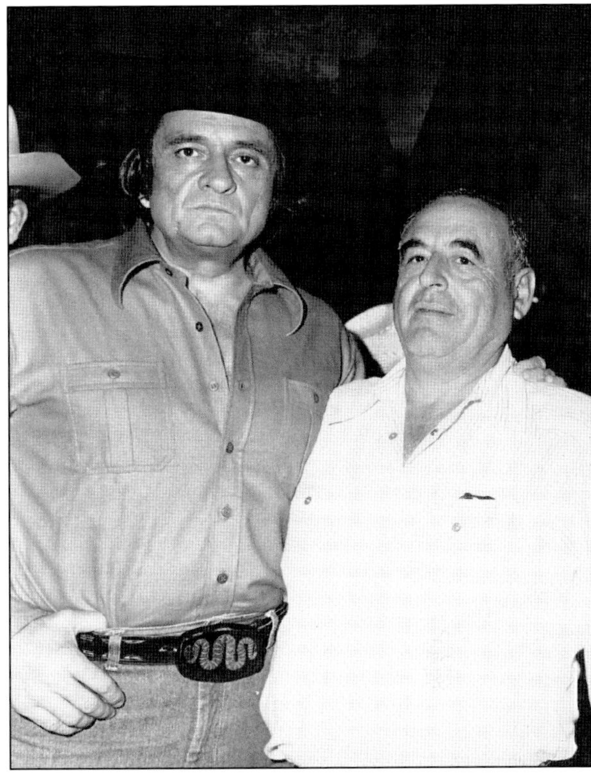

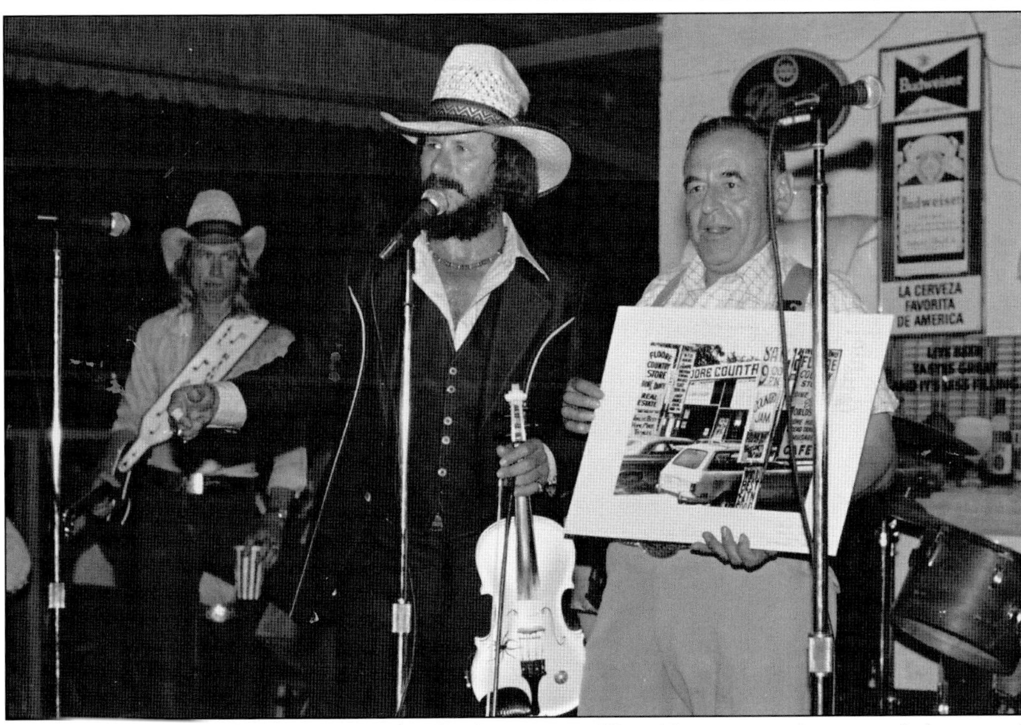

During a 1980 concert, Fiddlin' Frenchie Burke presented Joe Algueseva with a matted photograph of the outside of the dance hall. (Courtesy of Estella R. Algueseva.)

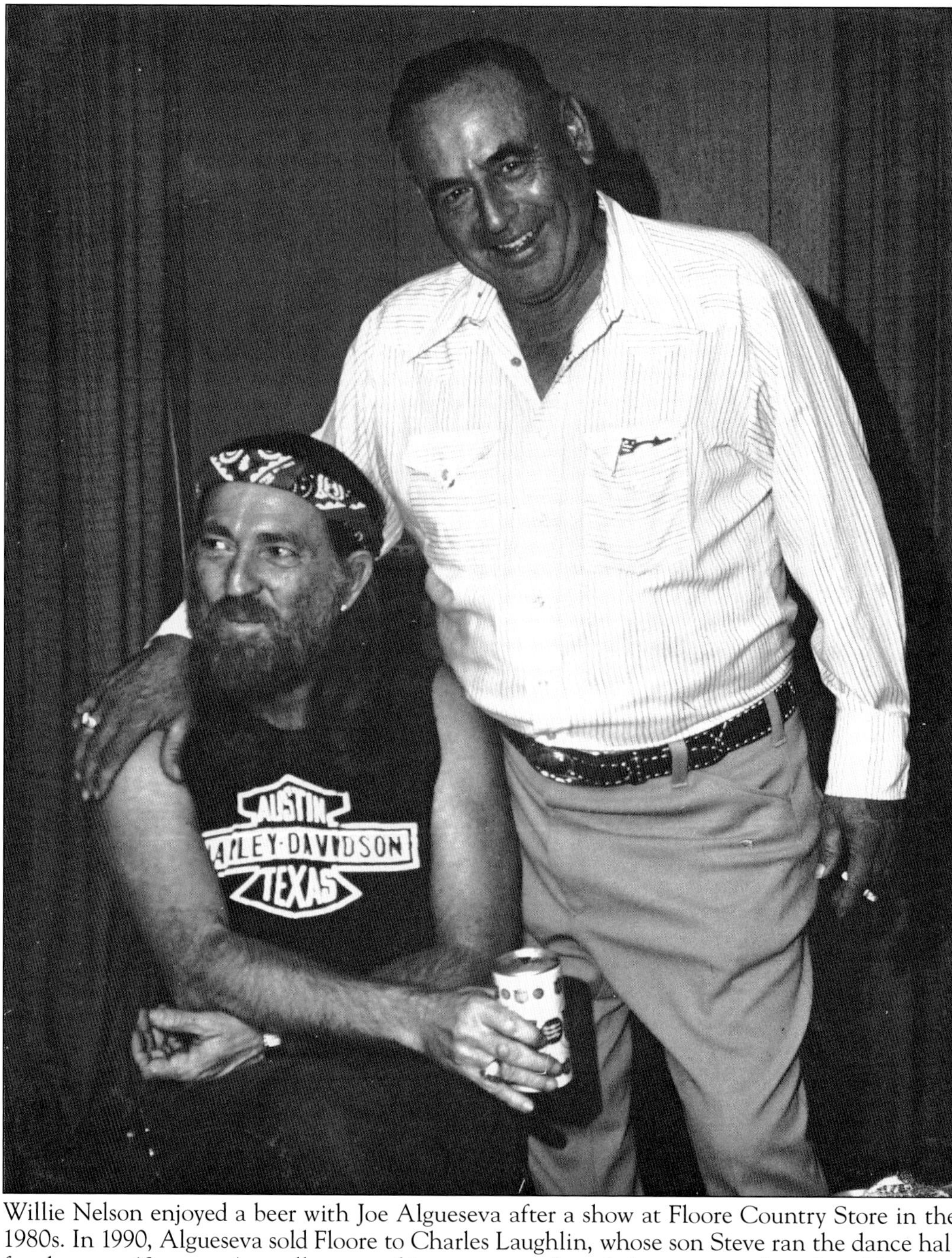

Willie Nelson enjoyed a beer with Joe Algueseva after a show at Floore Country Store in the 1980s. In 1990, Algueseva sold Floore to Charles Laughlin, whose son Steve ran the dance hall for the next 12 years. A small group of investors purchased the property from Laughlin, and like the dance hall's three previous owners, vowed to keep it a historic venue. In 2005, John T. Floore Country Store was honored with Texas Historic Landmark designation and a listing in the National Register of Historic Places. In 2010, a part of Old Bandera Road in front of Floore was renamed Willie Nelson Way in honor of Nelson's early ties to Helotes's historic dance hall. (Courtesy of Estella R. Algueseva.)

Eight

Cornyval, Spring Festival

Much of the lore of Helotes involves its early days as a post office and stagecoach route. For 93 years, Helotes postmasters relocated the post office to their residence or place of business. When a permanent post office was built, with completion marked for May 1966, the Lions Club, spurred on by financing from John T. Floore, spearheaded a community effort to celebrate the milestone. The dedication of the new post office on the first Saturday in May 1966 brought a few hundred people to downtown Helotes for refreshments and an art show. The festival, held again the next year with the addition of a parade and Miss Helotes Scholarship pageant, was so successful that in 1968 the Helotes Spring Festival Association was formed to sponsor an annual festival. In 1983, the association incorporated and changed its name to the Helotes Festival Association (HFA). The annual festival, called Cornyval, continued to be held the first weekend in May with proceeds donated to local nonprofit organizations. Over the years, Cornyval has grown into a four-day festival with food, music, dancing, rodeo events, arts and crafts booths, a carnival midway, and contests. In 1989, the HFA purchased a permanent site for the festival on Leslie Road, three-tenths of a mile from Bandera Road. The festival's growing popularity and increasing crowds—about 30,000 in past years—were major factors in obtaining the 44.2-acre site, which includes a covered pavilion and dance area, rodeo arena, and box seats, an office building, and permanent booths for ticket sales. Various organizations use the tree-studded festival grounds for fun events throughout the year. Cornyval is the highlight of them all.

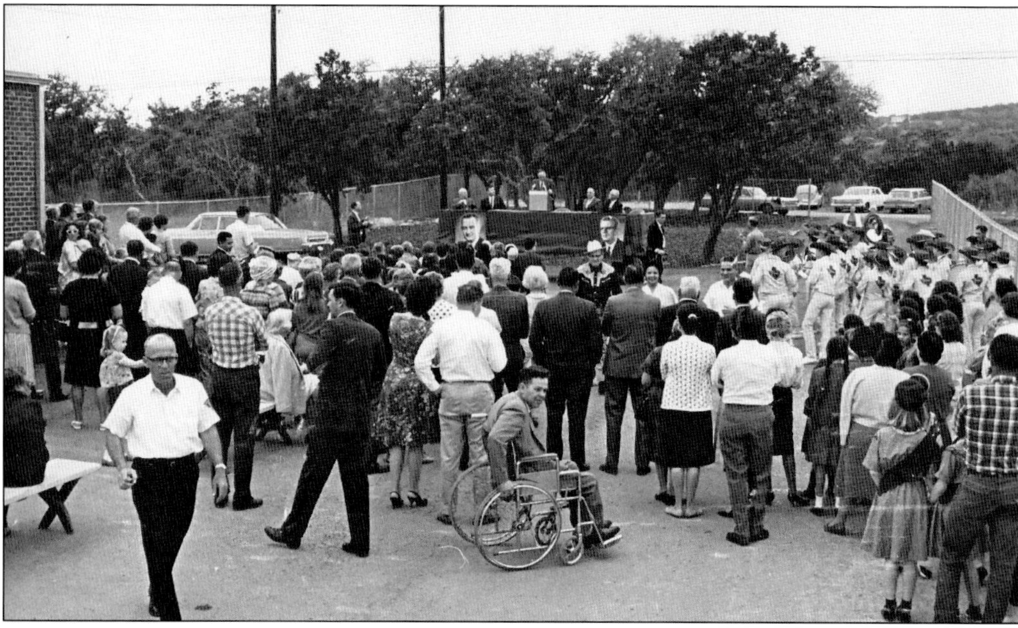

Helotes's Cornyval Festival started as a celebration for the dedication of the town's first permanent U.S. post office building in May 1966. Seen here at the head table from left to right are San Antonio postmaster Daniel J. Quill, Helotes postmaster Charles Davis, Helotes Lions Club representative Mike O'Hara (at the podium), U.S. Congressman Henry B. Gonzalez, and an unidentified man. (Courtesy of Sarah "Vi" Swift.)

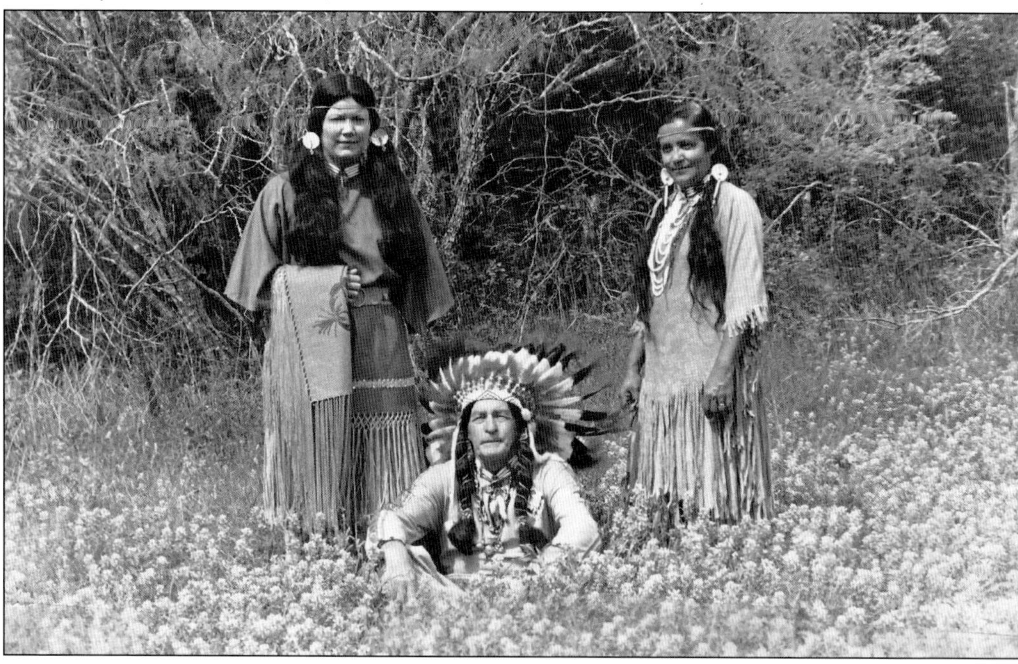

"Chief" Ray Garrison and "squaws" Lynn Menchaca and Margaret Beatty, seen here in a field of bluebonnets, declare that the corn is ripe and festival time has arrived. This reenactment on April 24, 1981, occurred a week before the 16th annual Cornyval, Helotes's spring festival. (Photograph by Leroy Galm; courtesy of HSH.)

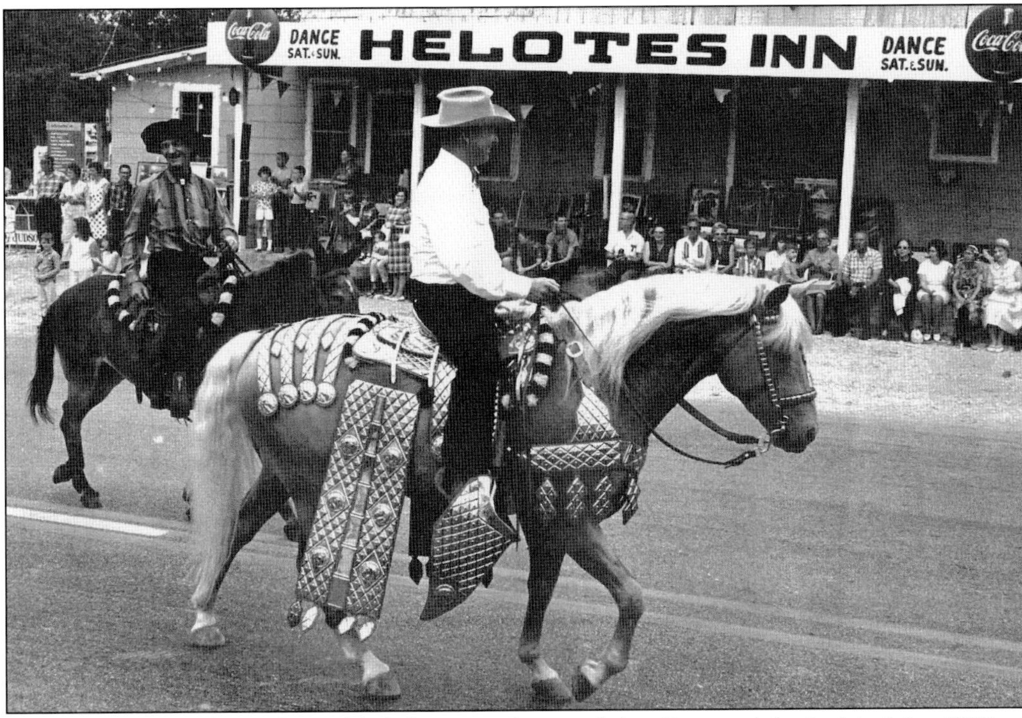

The first Cornyval parade—added the second year of the Cornyval festival in May 1967—is shown in progress in this photograph as two of the many horses pass in review before a well-known downtown landmark. Riding in the foreground is Fred Anderson, developer of Helotes Parks Estates, followed by Cowboy singer Charlie Moss, from McNeel Park in Grey Forest. (Photograph by Dade Rayfield; courtesy of HSH.)

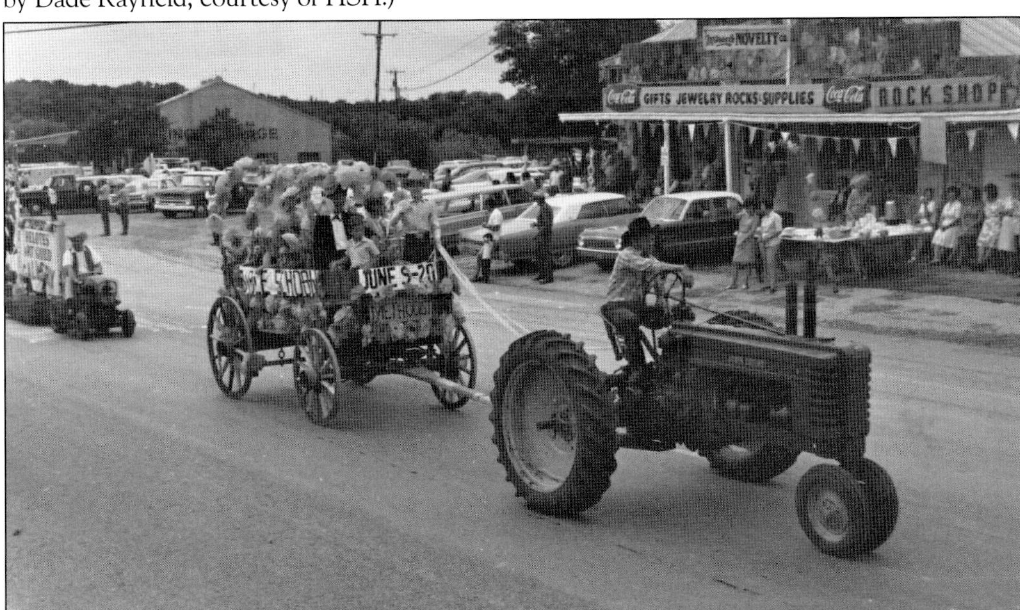

At the 1969 Cornyval Parade, the town's agricultural roots are highlighted by this parade entry. (Courtesy of HSH.)

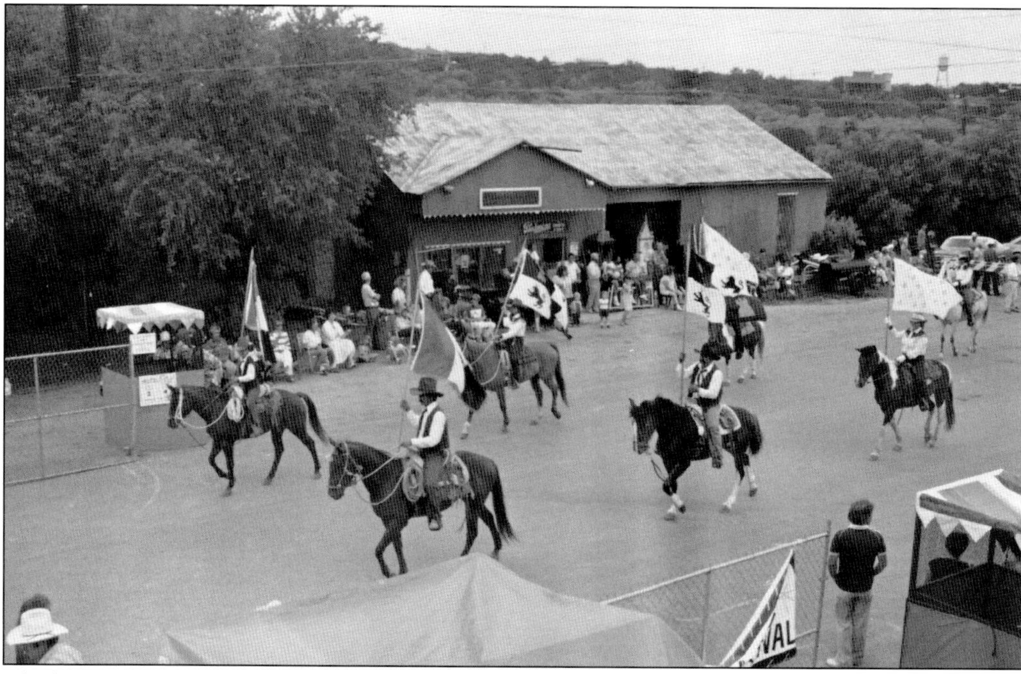

The last year the Cornvyal Festival was held in downtown Helotes was in 1988, the year this photograph was taken. The parade continued its trek through the Old Town Helotes District until a few years ago when it commenced at the edge of the district and traveled along Bandera Road for several miles, ending near the festival grounds. (Courtesy of the Helotes Festival Association, HFA.)

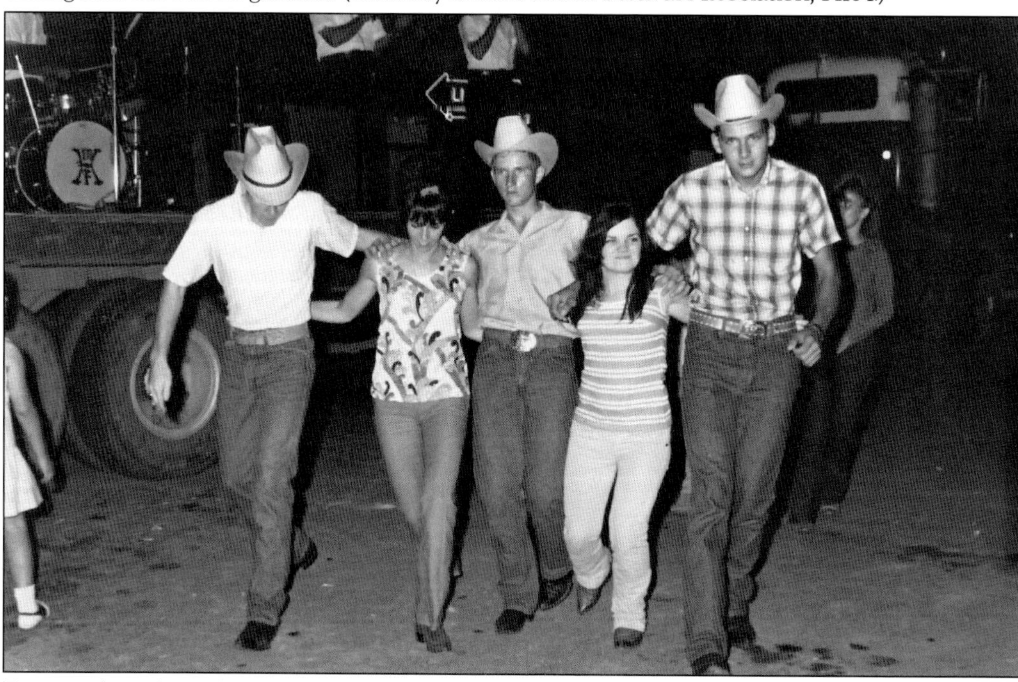

Dancing has always been a part of Cornvyal. In this May 1968 photograph taken in downtown Helotes, festival-goers appear to be dancing to the popular country tune, "Cotton-Eyed Joe." Only Leroy Galm Jr., on the far right, is identified in this photograph. (Courtesy of HSH.)

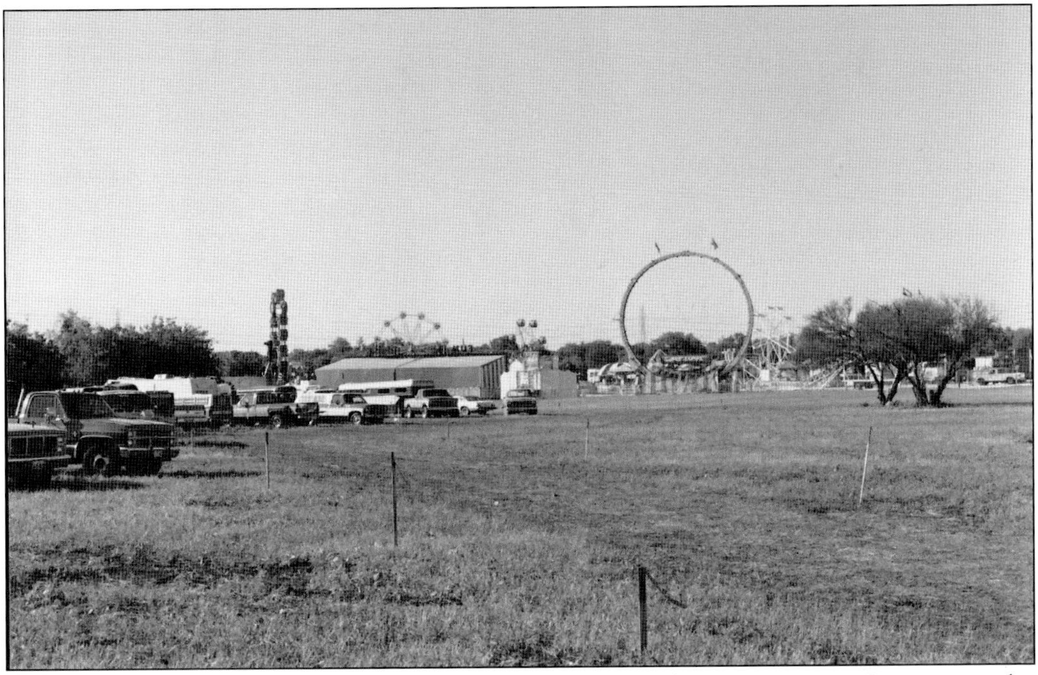

The carnival midway, which has been operated since 1986 by Alamo Attractions, Inc., is a popular attraction at Cornyval. This 1989 photograph shows the new Helotes Festival Association grounds with the carnival midway in the background. (Courtesy of HFA.)

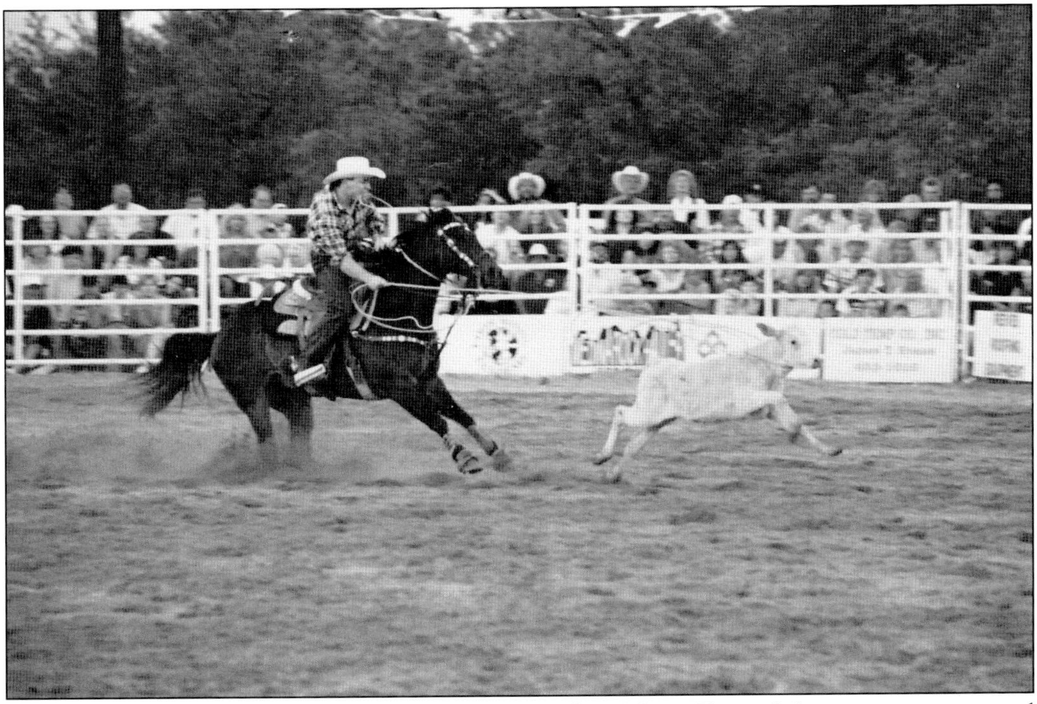

With festival grounds featuring a new rodeo arena, the Helotes Festival Association contracted with the Professional Rodeo Cowboys Association (PRCA) for performances at the Cornyval Festival. This photograph shows a PRCA cowboy roping a calf. (Courtesy of HFA.)

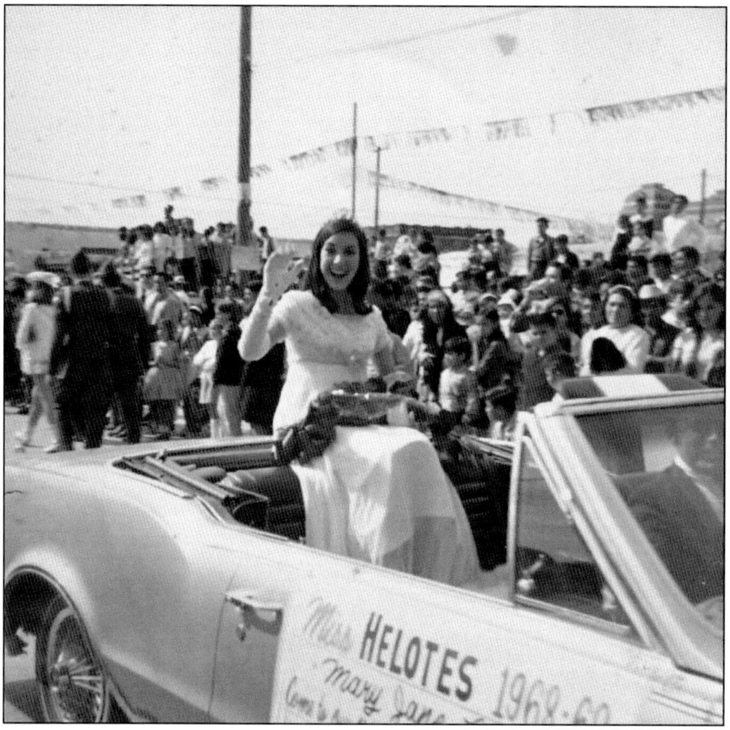

Mary Jane Logan, Miss Helotes 1968–1969, represented the town in the George Washington Parade in Laredo, Texas, February 25, 1969. The Miss Helotes Scholarship Pageant is an important part of Cornyval, and many local teens have participated over the years, raising money for local nonprofits. Each member of the court receives a cash award for college expenses and represents Helotes in out-of-town events throughout the year. (Courtesy of Mary Jane Blanco.)

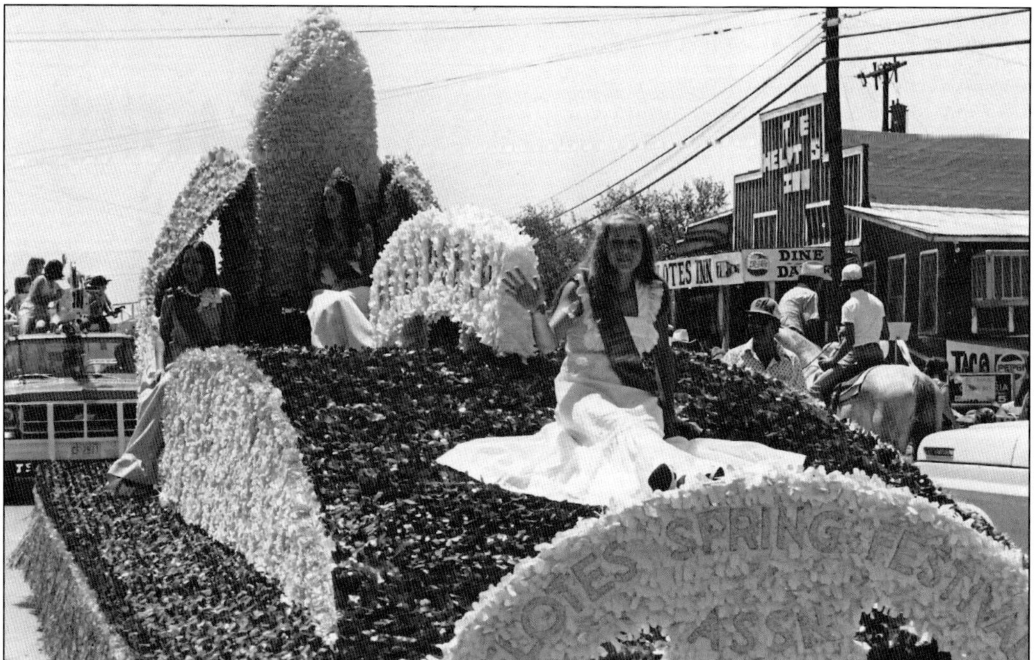

Miss Helotes 1974, Julie Walz, sits at the center of the float in front of the giant ear of corn at the annual Cornyval Parade. Next to her is duchess Lydia Algueseva. Princess JoAnn Tagliarino sits in the front of the float. Duchess Evette Sams is on the opposite side of the float out of camera range. (Courtesy of HSH.)

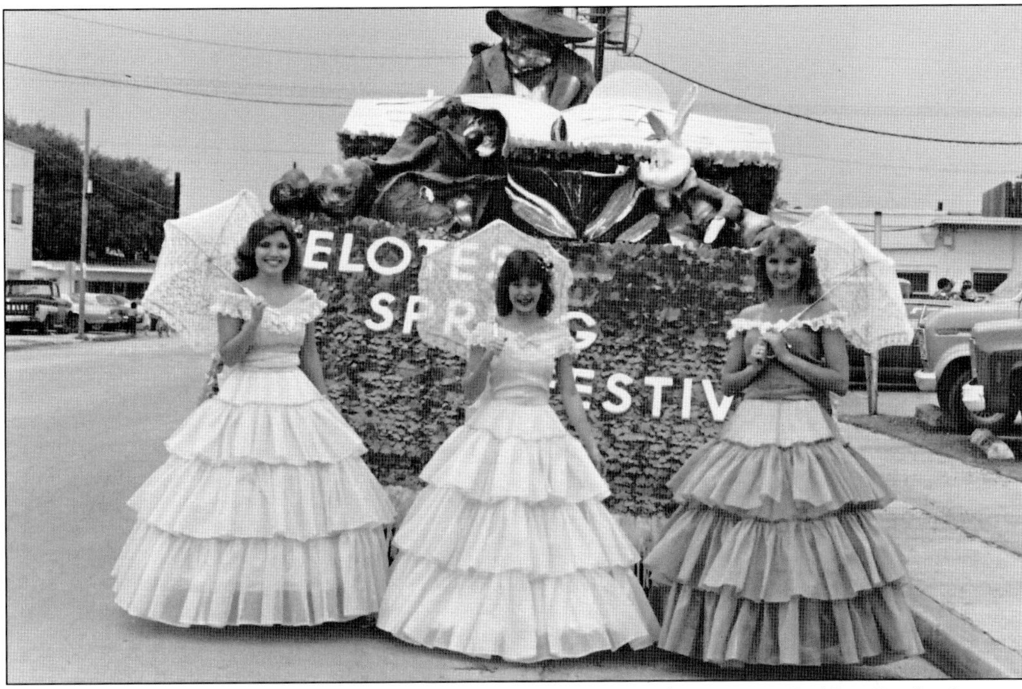

The members of the 1980 Miss Helotes Court are, from left to right, princess Robbin Storbeck, queen Angela Kay Moore, and duchess Elizabeth Lasher, who represented Helotes at the annual Battle of Flowers parade in downtown San Antonio. The theme of that year's parade was the Old South. Not shown are duchesses Elizabeth Anastas and Mary Lynn Toepperwein. (Courtesy of HFA.)

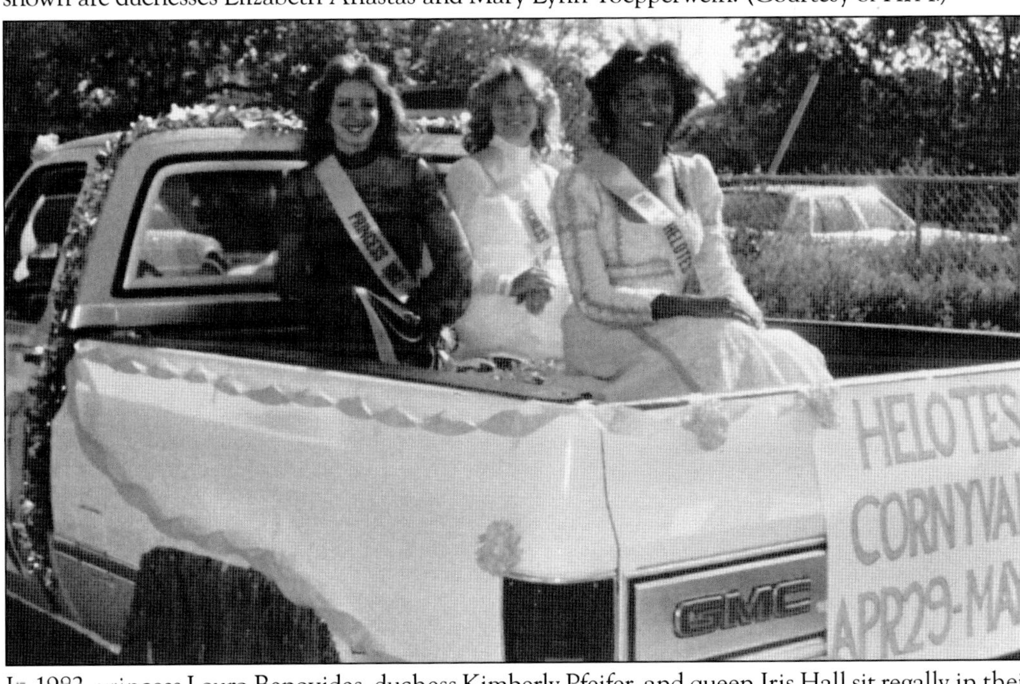

In 1982, princess Laura Benavides, duchess Kimberly Pfeifer, and queen Iris Hall sit regally in their truck-bed "throne," as they are ferried through the Cornyval Parade. Not shown are duchesses Mary Even and Anna Hitzfield. (Courtesy of HFA.)

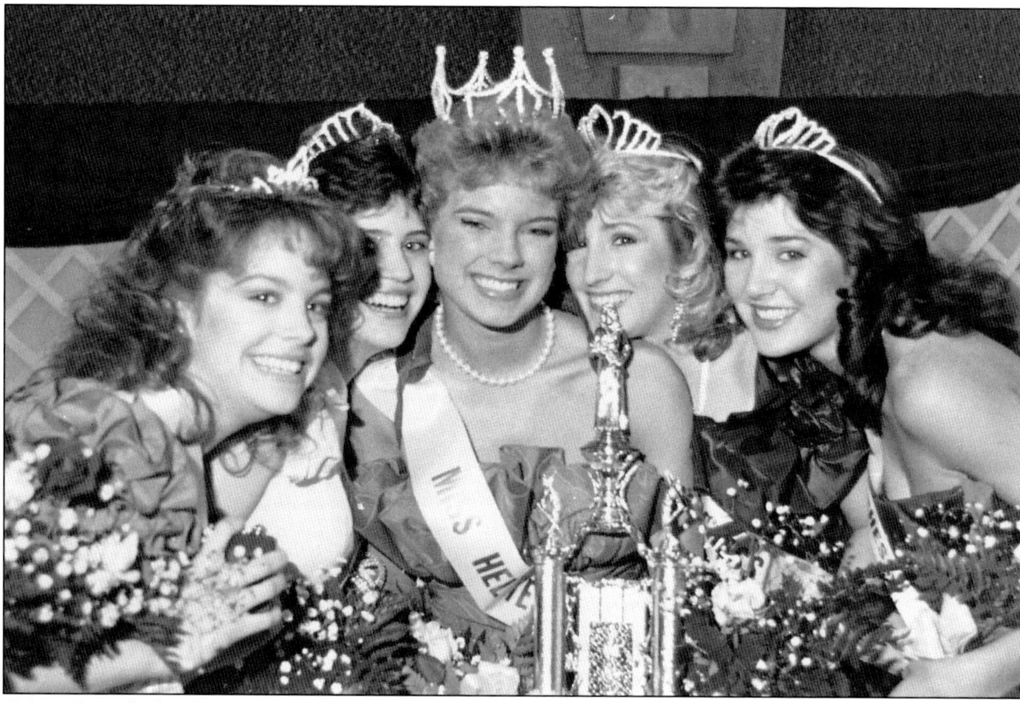

After the scholarship pageant on April 30, 1986, members of the new Miss Helotes Court posed for this photograph. From left to right are duchess Vanessa Jauer, duchess Peggy Flores, queen Syndi Kowalik, princess Sheila Brooks, and duchess Kelli Wade. (Courtesy of HFA.)

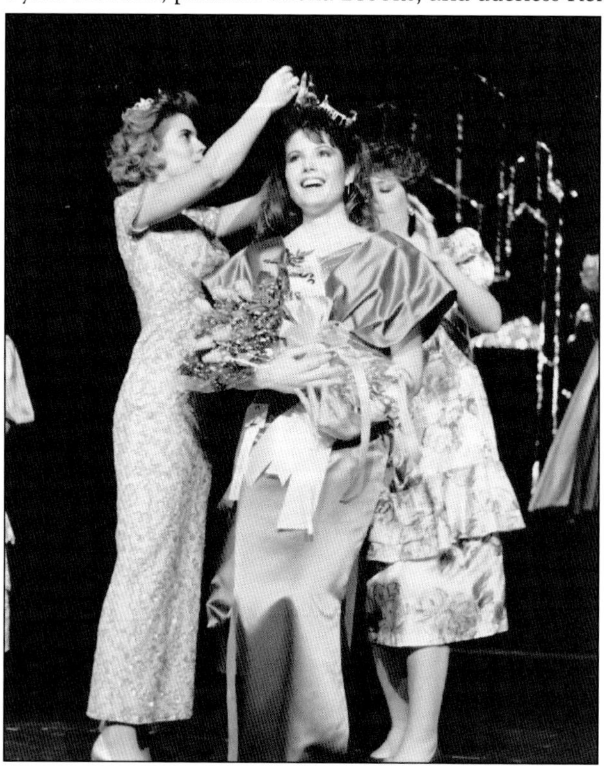

In 1990, Miss Helotes 1989, Samantha Rahmberg, crowns her successor, Linda Stowe. The annual pageant has provided thousands of dollars in scholarship money to motivated young women. (Courtesy of HFA.)

Nine

A City Is Born

"Helotes is a historical, identifiable community with its own traditions. . . . It has its own post office and zip code and always has been marked on Texas State Highway maps as a separate town," wrote the Helotes Merchants Association in 1978 to a state representative to enlist the legislature's help for Helotes's request for incorporation. As San Antonio continued to grow toward northwest Bexar County, annexing the University of Texas at San Antonio a few miles from Helotes, a group of residents formed as early as 1970 to discuss incorporating as a municipality to keep the town's historic identity and to enhance police protection. A petition for incorporation was circulated, and more than 80 percent of Helotes residents signed it. However, John T. Floore was against incorporation, afraid that the town might be taken over by "voting 18-year-old hippies." In addition, San Antonio city officials were not cooperative. After Floore passed away in 1975, Helotes residents renewed their efforts for incorporation. Negotiations with San Antonio began anew. On May 14, 1981, the San Antonio City Council in a 6-3 vote gave Helotes area residents permission to call an incorporation election. The area to be incorporated was 2.8 square miles, or 1,735 acres, with a population of a little more than 2,000. Retired U.S. Army Lt. Col. Thomas E. Beatty became the chairman of the Committee to Incorporate. On August 8, 1981, Helotes residents within the proposed incorporation boundaries went to the PARC building at Helotes Hills United Methodist Church to vote 426-68 in favor of incorporation. Helotes, long a distinct settlement in northwest Bexar County, became the City of Helotes.

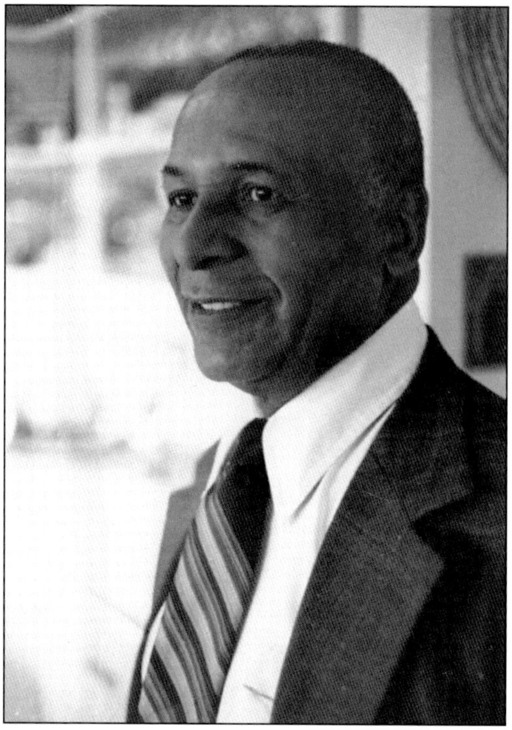

Thomas E. Beatty (1924–1996), a retired U.S. Army lieutenant colonel, was the first elected mayor of Helotes and Bexar County's first African American mayor, taking office in November 1981. Born in Boston, Massachusetts, Beatty moved his family to Helotes in the 1970s and became involved in the town's fight for incorporation. Although he served only one term, his strong leadership steered the fledgling town on a steady course. (Courtesy of HSH.)

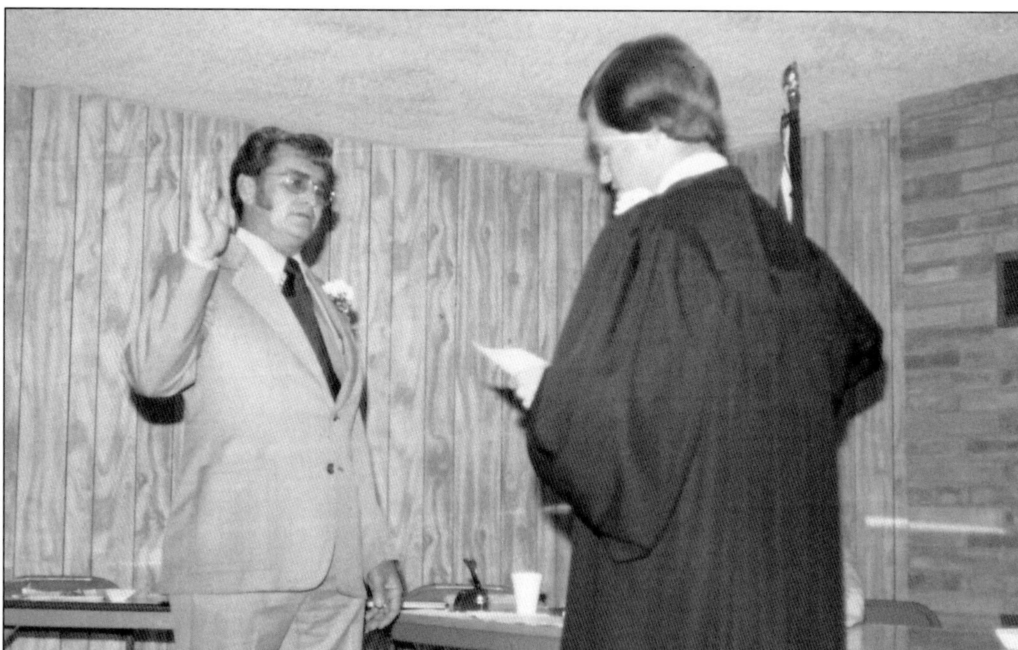

Judge David Berchelmann swore in Frank Thompson as Helotes's second mayor on April 15, 1983. Thompson, who was born in Poteet, Texas, moved to Helotes with wife Freda and their children in 1979. Thompson and city secretary Judy Reichardt worked out of the old Helotes Fire Department building, which doubled as a city office. Council meetings were held at the Methodist Church PARC Building. (Courtesy of Frank Thompson.)

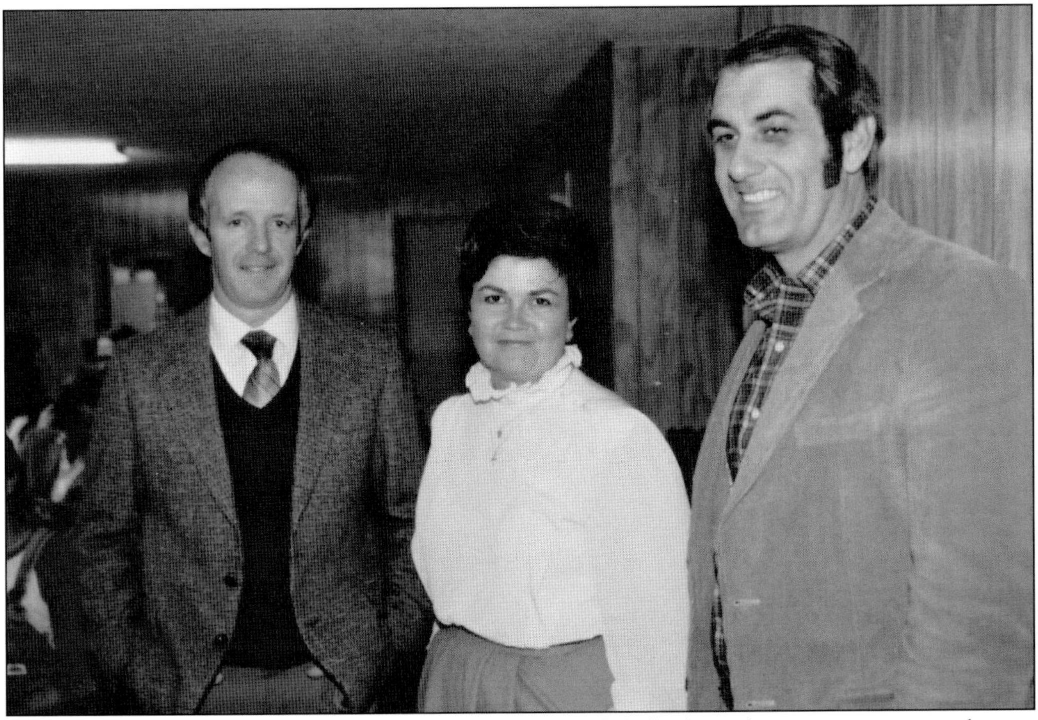

Councilmen Reudy Loeffler (left), and Leonard Hill, (right), flank newly sworn-in municipal court judge Barbara Galland in this February 1983 photograph. (Courtesy of Barbara Galland.)

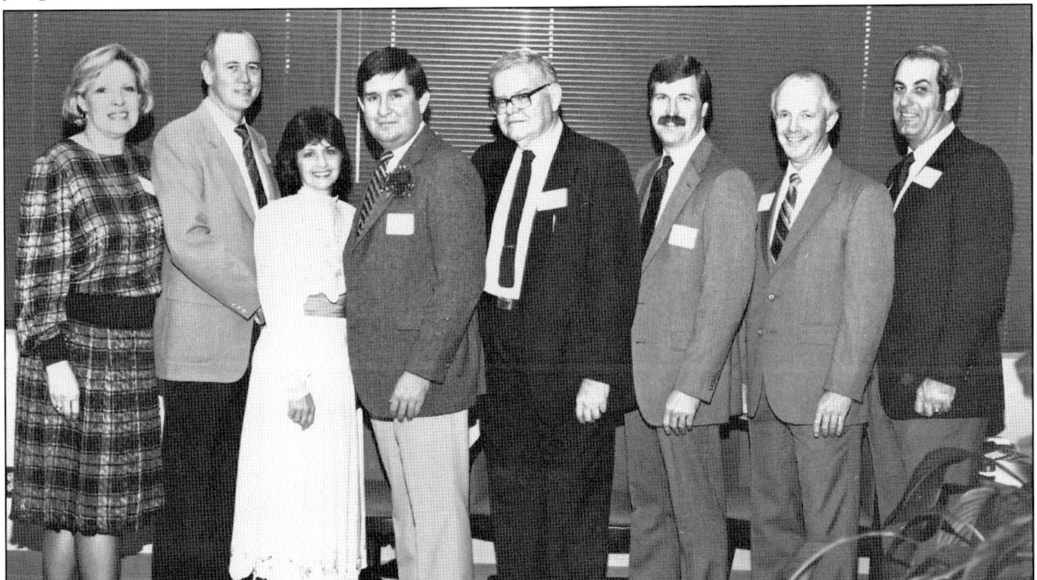

The Helotes City Council is seen here at a December 1987 reception for Bexar County District Court judge Emilio M. Garza. With their years of service indicated in parentheses, from left to right, the council members are Verna Thompson (1981–1993), Niels Jensen (1985–1992), mayor Vivian Hultz (1986–1993), Garza, city attorney Harvey Hardy, Gene Brigman (1985–1988), Ruedy Loeffler (1981–1991), and Leonard Hill (1981–1992). Mayor Hultz also served a term as a councilman from 1998 to 2000. (Courtesy of HSH.)

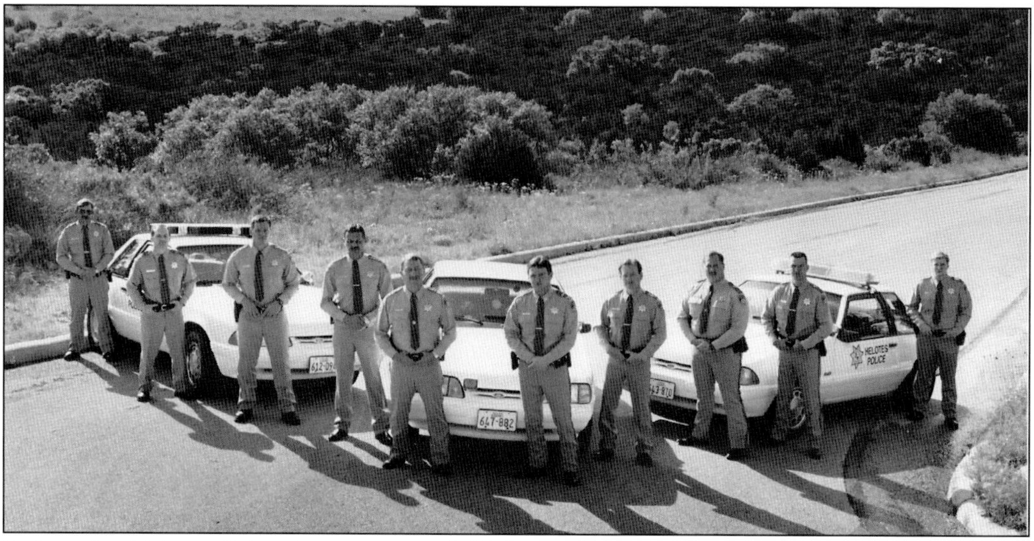

Before the Helotes Police Department (HPD) was formed when the city was incorporated, residents relied on the Bexar County Sheriff's Department for police protection, which proved insufficient. The HPD patrols a large rural area in addition to the city proper. The officers in this 1995 photograph are, from left to right, John Schepis, Chuck Fleckenstein, Chris Nordloh, Mort Ault, Chief William "Bill" Kleck, James Scoggins, Rob Hunley, Mike Crumrine, Tony Burgess, and Keith Spears. (Courtesy of Rob Hunley.)

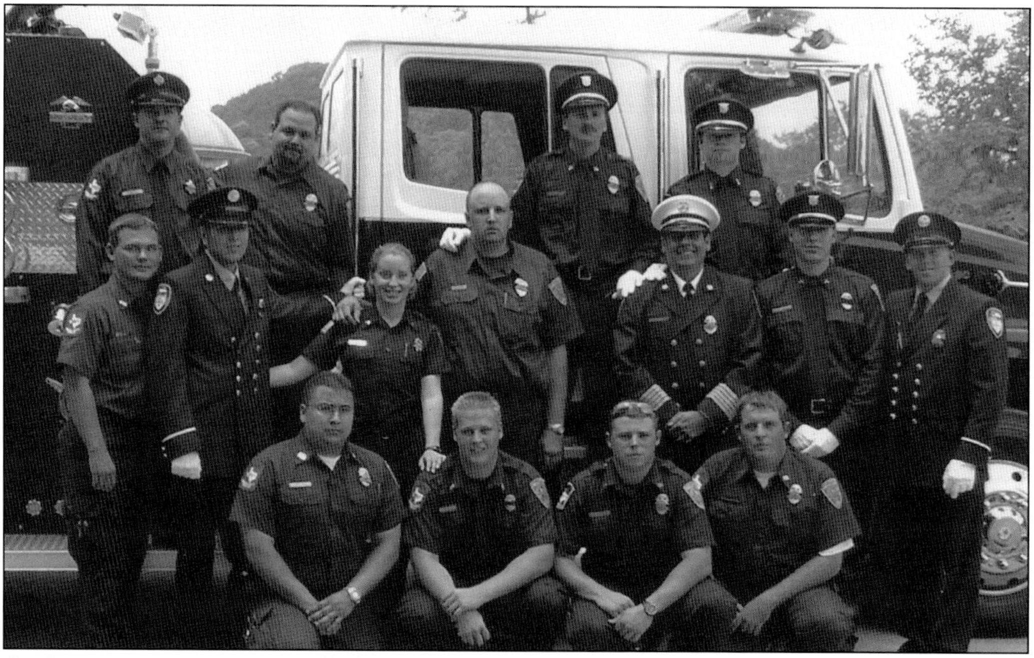

As the city grew, increasing calls for fire coverage prompted the Helotes City Council to establish the Helotes Municipal Fire Department, effective December 31, 2002. This 2004 photograph shows the fire department staff. From left to right, they are (first row) Jake Tristan, Donald "Wes" Richardson, Jason Bertie, and Travis Lorton; (second row) Walter Ball, Albert Castillo, Heather Larusso, Jeff Felty, Chief Walton Daugherty, Garett Daugherty, and Van Postell; (third row) Blake Smith, Soloman Nieves, Jack Quipp, and Keith Eldard. (Courtesy of Walton Daugherty.)

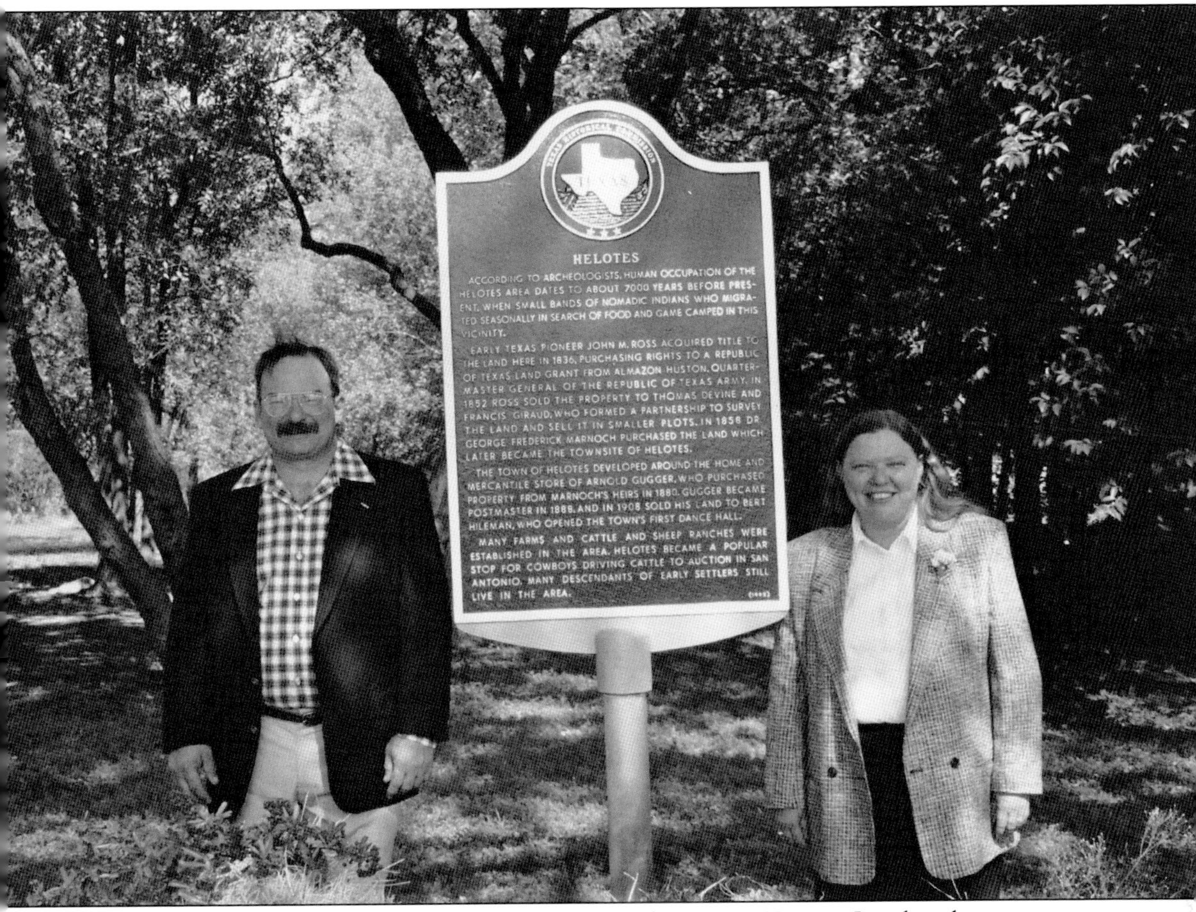

Hank and Kylene "Kyle" Cunningham flank Helotes's first Texas Historic Landmark monument, awarded in 1992 due to Kyle's efforts. After moving into the Gugger Homestead, which has been their home since the early 1980s, the Cunninghams became interested in the history of the area and were surprised that nothing had been published about Helotes, except for a few family stories in the town newspaper. Kyle's research resulted in a documented paper for a subject marker that she submitted to the Texas Historical Commission. Kyle's efforts revived interest in the historic legacy of the town, and since then, several more markers have been awarded to Helotes landmarks. (Courtesy of Hank and Kyle Cunningham.)

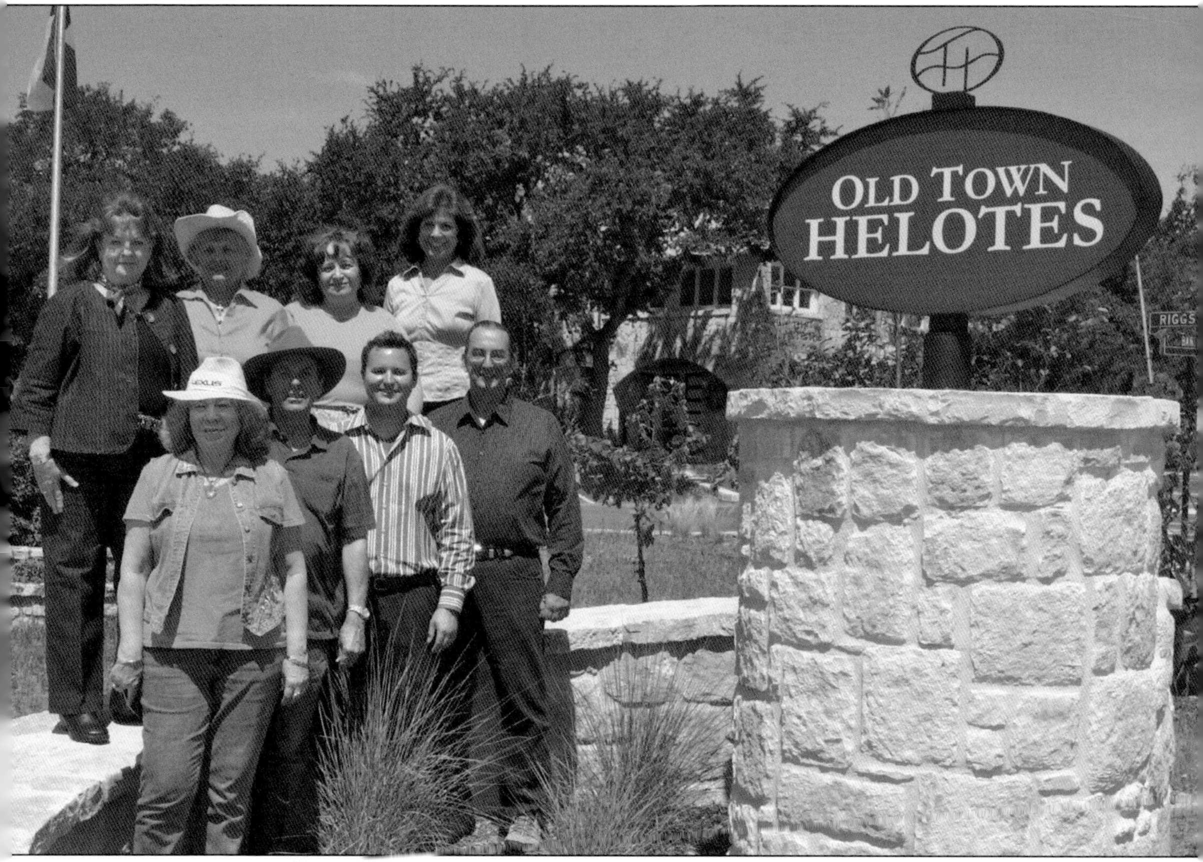

The 2009–2011 Historical Society of Helotes (HSH) board of directors are, from left to right, (first row) treasurer Lola Hill, assistant treasurer Walter Huegele, secretary Rick Schroder, and parliamentarian Charles D. Owen; (second row) club president Shirley Owen, vice president Gayle Green, corresponding secretary Diana Sarfin, and historian Cynthia Leal Massey. The Historical Society of Helotes is a nonprofit educational organization whose purpose is the discovery, preservation, and dissemination of knowledge about the history of Helotes, Texas, and the surrounding area. The HSH continues the legacy that started in 1966 with Lucy Perkins Brown and Wanda Terry. (Courtesy of Glenn Goolsby.)

INDEX

Algueseva, Joe, 109–112
Beatty, Thomas E., 122
Benke, Alexander, 18
Biering, Frederick August, 21
Boerner, William, 16
Brauchle, Henry T., 50
Braun Hall, 68
Braun, Mara Susanna, 20
Cadena, Máximo, 27
Clifton (Clifden) School, 56
El Chaparral, 46, 47
Ella's Barber Shop and Beauty Salon, 44
Floore, John T., 102–109
Gallagher Ranch, 84, 85
Galm, Clarence, 54, 80, 82
Government Canyon State Natural Area, 86
Grey Forest, 41, 71
Gugger Homestead, 33
Gugger, Anton, 14
Gugger, Arnold, 15, 32
Helotes Area Volunteer Fire Department, 81, 82
Helotes baseball and softball teams, 75
Helotes Brass Band, 67
Helotes City Council, 123
Helotes Echo, 78
Helotes Fire Department, 124
Helotes General Store, 33, 34
Helotes Police Department, 124
Helotes School, 51, 54, 57
Helotes Shooting Club, 66
Hernandez, Manuel, 95
Hileman, Wilbert S. "Bert," 35, 37
Historical Society of Helotes, 79, 126
Lee, Shelly Augustine, 19
Lions Club of Helotes, 76
Logan, David, 69, 96
Logan's Playground, 73
Los Reyes School, 55
Madla Ranch, 69, 72, 87
Madla, Frank, 23
Marnoch Homestead, 11
Marnoch, Gabriel Wilson, 12
Martinez, Máximo, 28, 88
Menchaca, Francisco, 22
Miss Helotes, 118–120
Morales, Lorenzo, 25
Mueller, Amalie (Stolz), 17
Nelson, Willie, 107, 108, 112
Our Lady of Guadalupe Catholic Church, 61–63
Rancho Diana, 90
Riggs, James, 39
Scenic Loop Playground, 71
Schott Ranch, 96, 97
Texas Historic Landmark, 11, 28, 33, 59, 71, 112, 125
Treviño, Pedro, 13
Villarreal's Ice House, 48
Woller, Frank, 29
Woller, Joseph, 30
Zepeda Homestead, 94
Zion Lutheran Church, 59, 60

Consistent with our mission to preserve history on a local level, this book was printed in South Carolina on American-made paper and manufactured entirely in the United States. Products carrying the accredited Forest Stewardship Council (FSC) label are printed on 100 percent FSC-certified paper.

MADE IN THE USA